HEADLIGHTS
AND
MARKERS

HEADLIGHTS AND MARKERS

An Anthology of Railroad Stories

EDITED BY

FRANK P. DONOVAN, Jr.

AND

ROBERT SELPH HENRY

NEW YORK

CREATIVE AGE PRESS, INC.

Fic
PS
509
R 3
D6

26816

 55

To

MABEL L. GILLESPIE

ACKNOWLEDGMENTS

THE EDITORS hereby make grateful acknowledgment to the following authors, publishers and authors' representatives for giving permission to reprint the material in this volume.

Charles Scribner's Sons for *The Yellow Mail Story* and *The Roadmaster's Story* from *Held for Orders* by Frank H. Spearman; for *A Ghost Train Illusion* from *The Express Messenger* by Cy Warman; and for *Run to Seed* by Thomas Nelson Page from *Stories of the Railway*.

Brandt & Brandt for *A Little Action* by Harold Titus; and for *Mrs. Union Station* by Doug Welsh, both from the *Saturday Evening Post*.

D. Appleton-Century for *The Birth of Hope* from *Epic Peters* by Octavus Roy Cohen.

Marquis James and The Bobbs-Merrill Company for *The Stolen Railroad Train* from *They Had Their Hour*.

Charles W. Tyler for *The Angel of Canyon Pass* from *Railroad Magazine*.

Jesse Stuart for *Huey, The Engineer* from *Esquire*.

William Wister Haines for *Remarks: None* from *Atlantic Monthly*.

A. W. Somerville for *Wide Open Throttle* and *Counterbalance* from the *Saturday Evening Post*.

Harry Bedwell for *Smart Boomer* and *Priority Special* from the *Saturday Evening Post*.

CONTENTS

INTRODUCTORY

RAILROADING IS A BUSINESS for many men, a hobby for others, an absorbing passion for some—all of whom find enjoyment in a well-told tale of the rails.

Many such stories have been published. Most of them, however, are now to be found only in the files of magazines, or in books that are out of print and almost equally hard for the casual reader to come by. This collection is offered, therefore, in the hope that it will bring in convenient form to the millions of railroaders, professional and amateur, some of the better stories of railroad life and operations.

The stories selected were originally published at various dates, beginning in the 1880's. Many phases of railroading are touched on. The background for some of the stories is completely fictional; others are related to actual railroads; at least one, the story of the capture, chase and recovery of the famous war engine *General,* is entirely factual. Many of the conditions and practices described in some of the stories have long since ceased to exist; some of them probably never existed just as they are described.

Some of the stories have as background the War between the States of the American Union in the 1860's. One, the latest of them, has as its background the movement in hospital trains of men wounded in the Second World War. How great has been the change in railroads and railroading in the period covered by this selection of stories is all but beyond realization.

In the time of the earliest stories, dispatching trains by telegraph was still something of a novelty, and automatic block signals were as yet undreamed of. In this one field of communications and signals there can be traced in the stories the evolution of the art of dispatching, the change from the telegrapher's key to the telephone and the loudspeaker, and the multiplication of communications circuits; the development and extension of the automatic block signals by means of which the moving train surrounds itself with the protection of signals set and changed without human intervention; the introduction of interlocking; and finally, the marvel of centralized train control, whereby the train itself automatically reports and records its movements and position to the man at the distant control board, where, by the pressure of a button, signals are set and switches thrown to order and control the movement of all trains in the district.

Equally great and significant have been the changes in the mechanical elements of railroading. The old American-type locomotive of the sixties—the engine that conquered a continent—has as its descendants an almost bewildering variety of locomotives, steam, electric and Diesel. With the gain in performance ability in the power which pulls the trains, there has gone a like improvement in the power to control and stop them with the stored-up pressure of air. Better power, either to start or to stop, has made possible the train as it is known in America—the most amazingly versatile and useful vehicle yet devised by man.

Under the train is the track, and track and the methods of laying it and keeping it up have undergone changes almost unimaginable. With all the changes, however, track remains fundamentally the same—a surface of raised parallel rails which, by smoothing the way, by supporting the load and above all by guiding the wheels of the cars, makes possible the train.

Physical changes are but part of the progressive transformation in railroading in the period of these stories. At the time of the early ones, each railroad was operated separately and without much regard to what was done on other lines. Now the 500 or so railroads of the United States, large and small, and the railroads of Canada and Mexico as well, are operated so nearly as a unit that any freight car of any railroad can, and does, run on the rails and in the trains of any other railroad. Back of this truly amazing example of effective industry-wide co-ordination there are long years of development of standard gauge of track, standard time, standard couplings, brakes and running parts of cars, standard methods of repair and of car hire and keeping trace of cars, and standard collection, accounting and apportionment of the revenues earned. There is co-ordination in services and schedules, conference with shippers as to rates and charges, and regulation by public authority of the whole business—all in all, a picture which would have been startling to the devil-may-care railroaders who figure in the earlier stories.

Railroad operation is a matter of many men doing hundreds of different sorts of work, and of many companies serving all sections of the continent in all seasons of the year. It calls for working together all along the line—teamwork of the highest order. That's the normal in railroad operation, but it is difficult, if not impossible, to make a story of the day-by-day meshing into a smooth-working whole of all these parts. Stories are to be found in what happens when something goes wrong, so railroad stories are, for the most part, stories of struggle. Many of them are stories of disaster narrowly averted, or perhaps not averted at all. Most of them do not deal with the ordinary, every-day work of railroading, but they do reveal, in flashes, something of how that work has been carried on in times past and, in some of the later stories, how it is done today.

The inauguration on railroads of the modern industrial safety movement, thirty-five years ago, and the spread of that gospel among railroad men ever since, together with the improvements in roadway, rolling stock, signals, communications and equipment of all sorts, have eliminated the situations which form the background of most of the stories of an older day. Nothing, however, has dimmed the determination of railroad men to get the job done, no matter what the obstacles—and that is the common thread which runs through these stories of the rails.

This determination was given its finest demonstration during the Second World War. After the long years of depression, when there was relatively little call for their services, railroads were suddenly called upon to shoulder not only the larger part of the increasing loads resulting from the war, but also much of the load which, as a result of war changes, other agencies of transport found themselves unable to handle. As a result, freight traffic more than doubled and passenger traffic more than quadrupled, while other war needs were such that materials and manpower for any substantial enlargement of railroad plant simply were not to be had.

The job was to be done with the materials at hand—and done it was. Something like nine-tenths of all the direct war traffic in the United States, freight and passenger, and nearly three-fourths of all traffic, was moved by rail. Of the total increase in traffic of all sorts, at least four-fifths was moved by rail—thus demonstrating once more the capacity and flexibility inherent in the railroad method of moving people and things in trains on tracks, and the adaptability and determination of the railroaders who, whether on the road or in the yards, in the shops or in the offices, work to keep the trains running.

At the front end of each train is the headlight, at the rear the markers. Indeed, in the language of the standard code of train rules of the Association of American Railroads, it takes markers, the flags or colored lanterns which appear on the rear car, to fulfill the definition of a train as "an engine or motor car, or more than one engine or motor car, coupled, with or without cars, displaying markers." Hence the title of this collection—*Headlights and Markers.*

ROBERT SELPH HENRY.

THE YELLOW
MAIL STORY

By Frank H. Spearman

Frank H. Spearman

FRANK HAMILTON SPEARMAN was the Old Master among railroad novelists and short-story writers. He wrote about people, recognizable human beings. His stories unfold easily, naturally, almost inevitably, with railroading not merely their background but in every way part of them. All his works on the industry— short stories, novels or articles—are accurate, "meaty" and reliable. And yet Spearman never worked for a railroad in his life.

He was born in Buffalo, New York, on September 6, 1859. At an early age he aspired to become a doctor, but ill health forced him into other fields. He became, in the order mentioned, a broker, traveling salesman, bank cashier and bank president. Spearman's literary career started at McCook, then and now a division point on the Burlington in western Nebraska, where as a banker he came in contact with railroad men. He would listen for hours to stories of the road and then, without taking a single note, go home and out of his phenomenal memory write down word for word what he had heard.

With the publication of *Held for Orders* in 1901, Spearman's standing as a railroad author was definitely established. This volume, a collection of short stories, is a classic in its field. His novel *Whispering Smith* probably set an all-time record in the sale of railroad fiction, while in the days before the "talkies," many of his stories were made into successful photoplays. In 1935 Spearman was awarded the Laetare Medal from Notre Dame University as the outstanding Catholic author of the year. He died in Los Angeles on December 29, 1937.

Some of Spearman's other works include *Carmen of the Rancho, Hell's Desert, The Daughter of a Magnate, Flambeau Jim* and *The Mountain Divide*—all novels. The first two, however, are not concerned with railroading. In addition, he wrote a book of railway short stories called *The Nerve of Foley* and a factual study entitled *The Strategy of Great Railroads*, which was used as a text book.

The Yellow Mail Story has its setting on the Union Pacific at the turn of the century. Fifty-six-inch drivers on a ten-wheeled engine seem small, to modern eyes, for such work as was to be done on the test run of the Transcontinental Mail, but the story is not so much about engines as it is about men organized to meet emergency, and about one man who seized the chance to win his most coveted desire.

A railroad is never finished. Railroads are built and rebuilt, and the second job, indeed, is sometimes more arduous than the first. *The Roadmaster's Story* is such an instance. As is true of so many of Spearman's stories, the selection is about the Union Pacific, a trunk line which was rebuilt from one end to the other under the Harriman regime—a program of rehabilitation which called for a hundred million dollars, a huge sum for the day and time, to be spent on track, bridges, shops, power, rolling stock, everything about the railroad. Back of all this reconstruction and carrying it forward were the engineers of whom Spearman wrote —such men as Brodie and Hailey among them.

THE YELLOW MAIL STORY

By Frank H. Spearman

THERE WASN'T ANOTHER ENGINEER on the division that dared talk to Doubleday the way Jimmie Bradshaw talked.

But Jimmie had a grievance, and every time he thought about it, it made him nervous.

Ninety-six years. It seemed a good while to wait; yet in the regular course of events on the Mountain Division there appeared no earlier prospect of Jimmie's getting a passenger run.

"Got your rights, ain't you?" said Doubleday, when Jimmie complained.

"I have and I haven't," grumbled Jimmie, winking hard; "there's younger men than I am on the fast runs."

"They got in on the strike; you've been told that a hundred times. We can't get up another strike just to fix you out on a fast run. Hang on to your freight. There's better men than you in Ireland up to their bilt in the bog, Jimmie."

"It's a pity they didn't leave you there, Doubleday."

"You'd have been a good while hunting for a freight run if they had."

Then Jimmie would get mad and shake his finger and talk fast: "Just the same, I'll have a fast run here when you're dead."

"Maybe; but I'll be alive a good while yet, my son," the master mechanic would laugh. Then Jimmie would walk off very warm, and when he got into the clear with himself, he

5

would wink furiously and say friction things about Doubleday that needn't now be printed, because it is different. However, the talk always ended that way, and Jimmie Bradshaw
knew it always would end that way.

The trouble was, no one on the division would take Jimmie seriously, and he felt that the ambition of his life would
never be fulfilled; that he would go plugging to gray hairs
and the grave on an old freight train; and that even when he
got to the right side of the Jordan there would still be something like half a century between him and a fast run. It was
funny to hear him complaining about it, for everything, even
his troubles, came funny to him, and in talking he had an
odd way of stuttering with his eyes, which were red. In fact,
Jimmie was nearly all red: hair, face, hands—they said his
teeth were sandy.

When the first rumors about the proposed Yellow Mail
reached the mountains Jimmie was running a new ten-
wheeler; breaking her in on a freight "for some fellow without a lick o' sense to use on a limited passenger run," as
Jimmie observed bitterly. The rumors about the mail came
at first like stray mallards, opening signs of winter, and as the
season advanced flew thicker and faster. Washington never
was very progressive in the matter of improving the transcontinental service, but once by mistake they put in a postmaster general down there who wouldn't take the old song.
When the bureau fellows that put their brains up in curl
papers told him it couldn't be done, he smiled softly and
sent for the managers of the crack lines across the continent,
without suspecting how it bore incidentally on Jimmie
Bradshaw's grievance against his master mechanic.

The postmaster general called the managers of the big
lines, and they had a dinner at Chamberlain's, and they told
him the same thing. "It has been tried," they said in the old,
tired way; "really it can't be done."

"California has been getting the worst of it for years on the

mail service," persisted the postmaster general moderately.
"But Californians ought to have the best of it. We don't
think anything about putting New York mail in Chicago in
twenty hours. It ought to be simple to cut half a day across
the continent and give San Francisco her mail a day earlier.
Where's the fall down?" he asked, like one refusing "no" for
an answer.

The general managers looked at our representative sympathetically, and coughed cigar smoke his way to hide him.

"West of the Missouri," murmured a Pennsylvania swell,
who pulled indifferently at a fifty-cent cigar. Everybody at
the table took a drink on the exposé, except the general manager who sat at that time for the Rocky Mountains.

The West End representative was unhappily accustomed
to facing the finger of scorn on such occasions. It has become
with our managers a tradition. There was never a conference
of transcontinental lines in which we were not scoffed at as a
weak link in the chain of everything: mail, passenger, specials, what not—the trouble was invariably laid at our door.

This time a new man was sitting for the line at the Chamberlain dinner; a youngish man with a face that set like
cement when the West End was trod on.

The postmaster general was inclined, from the reputation
we had, to look on our man as one looks at a dog without a
pedigree, or at a dray horse in a bunch of standard-breds.
But something in the mouth of the West End man gave him
pause; since the Rough Riders, it has been a bit different
with verdicts on things Western. The postmaster general
suppressed a rising sarcasm with a sip of Chartreuse, for the
dinner was ripening, and waited; nor did he mistake, the
West Ender was about to speak.

"Why west of the Missouri?" he asked, with a lift of the
face not altogether candid. The Pennsylvania man shrugged
his brows; to explain might have seemed indelicate.

"If it is put through, how much of it do you propose to

take yourself?" inquired our man, looking evenly at the Allegheny official.

"Sixty-five miles, including stops from the New York post-office to Canal Street," replied the Pennsylvania man, and his words flowed with irritating ease.

"What do you take?" continued the man with the jaw, turning to the Burlington representative, who was struggling, belated, with an artichoke.

"About seventy from Canal to Tenth and Mason. Say, seventy," repeated the "Q" manager, with the lordliness of a man who has miles to throw at almost anybody, and knows it.

"Then suppose we say sixty-five from Tenth and Mason to Ogden," suggested the West Ender. There was a well-bred stare the table round, a lifting of glasses to mask expressions that might give pain. Sixty-five miles an hour? Through the Rockies?

The postmaster general struck the table quick and heavily: he didn't want to let it get away. "Why, hang it, Mr. Bucks," he exclaimed with emphasis, "if you will say sixty, the business is done. We don't ask you to do the Rockies in the time these fellows take to cut the Alleghenies. Do sixty, and I will put mail in Frisco a day earlier every week in the year.

"Nothing on the West End to keep you from doing it," said General Manager Bucks. He had been put up then only about six months. "But—"

Everyone looked at the young manager. The Pennsylvania man looked with confidence, for he instantly suspected there must be a string to such a proposition, or that the new representative was "talking through his hat."

"But what?" asked the Cabinet member, uncomfortably apprehensive.

"We are not putting on a sixty-five-mile schedule just because we love our country, you understand, nor to heighten an already glorious reputation. Oh, no," smiled Bucks faintly, "we are doing it for 'the stuff.' You put up the money; we put up the speed. Not sixty miles; sixty-five—from the Missouri to the Sierras. No; no more wine. Yes, I will take a cigar."

The trade was on from that minute. Bucks said no more then; he was a good listener. But next day, when it came to talking money, he talked more money into the West End treasury for one year's running than was ever talked before on a mail contract for the best three years' work we ever did.

When they asked him how much time he wanted to get ready, and told him to take plenty, three months was stipulated. The contracts were drawn, and they were signed by our people without hesitation because they knew Bucks. But while the preparations were being made for the fast schedule, the government weakened on signing. Nothing ever got through a Washington department without hitch, and they said our road had so often failed on like propositions that they wanted a test. There was a deal of wrangling; then a test run was agreed on by all the roads concerned. If it proved successful, if the mail was put to the Golden Gate on the second of the schedule, public opinion and the interests in the Philippines, it was concluded, would justify the heavy premium asked for the service.

In this way the dickering and the figuring became, in a measure, public, and keyed up everybody interested to a high pitch. We said nothing for publication, but under Buck's energy sawed wood for three whole months. Indeed, three months goes as a day getting a system into shape for an extraordinary schedule. Success meant with us prestige; but failure meant obloquy for the road and for our division chief who had been so lately called to handle it.

The real strain, it was clear, would come on his old, the Mountain Division; and to carry out the point, rested on the Motive Power of the Mountain Division; hence, concretely, on Doubleday, master mechanic of the hill country.

In thirty days, Neighbor, superintendent of the Motive Power, called for reports from the division master mechanics on the preparations for the Yellow Mail run, and they reported progress. In sixty days he called again. The subordinates reported well except Doubleday. Doubleday said merely, "Not ready"; he was busy tinkering with his engines. There was a third call in eighty days, and on the eighty-fifth a peremptory call. Everybody said, "Ready," except Doubleday. When Neighbor remonstrated sharply he would say only that he would be ready in time. That was the most he would promise, though it was generally understood that if he failed to deliver the goods he would have to make way for somebody that could.

The Plains Division of the system was marked up for seventy miles an hour, and, if the truth were told, a little better; but, with all the help they could give us, it still left sixty for the mountains to take care of, and the Yellow Mail proposition was conceded to be the toughest affair the Motive Power at Medicine Bend had ever faced. However, forty-eight hours before the mail left the New York post-office, Doubleday wired to Neighbor, "Ready"; Neighbor to Bucks, "Ready"; and Bucks to Washington, "Ready"—and we were ready from end to end.

Then the orders began to shoot through the mountains. The best run was of especial importance, because the signing of the contract was believed to depend on the success of it. Once signed, accidents and delays might be explained; for the test run there must be no delays. Dispatchers were given the eleven, which meant Bucks; no lay-outs, no slows for the Yellow Mail. Roadmasters were notified: no track work in front of the Yellow Mail. Bridge gangs were warned, yard masters instructed, section bosses cautioned, track walkers spurred— the system was polished like a barkeeper's diamond, and swept like a parlor car for the test flight of the Yellow Mail.

Doubleday, working like a boiler washer, spent all day Thursday and all Thursday night in the roundhouse. He had personally gone over the engines that were to take the racket in the mountains. Ten-wheelers they were, the 1012 and the 1014, with fifty-six-inch drivers and cylinders big enough to sit up and eat breakfast in. Spick and span both of them, just long enough out of the shops to run smoothly to the work; and on Friday, Oliver Sollers, who, when he opened a throttle, blew miles over the tender like feathers, took the 1012, groomed like a Wilkes mare, down to Piedmont for the run up to the Bend.

Now Oliver Sollers was a runner in a thousand, and steady as a clock; but he had a fireman who couldn't stand prosperity—Steve Horigan, a cousin of Johnnie's. The glory was too great for Steve, and he spent Friday night in Gallagher's place celebrating, telling the boys what the 1012 would do to the Yellow Mail. Not a thing, Steve claimed after five drinks, but pull the stamps clean off the letters the minute they struck the foot-hills. But when Steve showed up at 5:00 A.M. to superintend the movement, he was seasick. The minute Sollers set eyes on him he objected to taking him out. Mr. Sollers was not looking for any unnecessary chances on one of Bucks' personal matters, and for the general manager the Yellow Mail test had become exceedingly personal. Practically everybody East and West had said it would fail; Bucks said no.

Neighbor himself was on the Piedmont platform that morning, watching things. The McCloud dispatchers had promised the train to our division on time, and her smoke was due with the rise of the sun. The big superintendent of Motive Power, watching anxiously for her arrival, and planning anxiously for her outgoing, glared at the bunged fireman in front of him, and, when Sollers protested, Neighbor turned on the swollen Steve with sorely bitter words. Steve swore mightily he was fit and could do the trick—but what's the word of a railroad man who drinks? Neighbor spoke wicked words, and while they poured on the guilty Steve's crop there was a shout down the platform. In the east the sun was breaking over the sandhills, and below it a haze of black thickened the horizon. It was McTerza with the 808 and the Yellow Mail. Neighbor looked at his watch: she was, if anything, a minute to the good, and before the car tinks could hustle across the yard, a streak of gold cut the sea of purple alfalfa in the lower valley, and the narrows began to smoke with the dust of the race for the platforms.

When McTerza blocked the big drivers at the west end of the depot, every eye was on the new equipment. Three standard railway mail cars, done in varnished buttercup, strung out behind the sizzling engine, and they looked pretty as cowslips. While Neighbor vaguely meditated on their beauty and on his boozing fireman, Jimmie Bradshaw, just in after a night run down from the Bend, walked across the yard. He had seen Steve Horigan making a "sneak" for the bath-house, and from the yard gossip Jimmie guessed the rest.

"What are you looking for, Neighbor?" asked Jimmie Bradshaw.

"A man to fire for Sollers—up. Do you want it?"

Neighbor threw it at him cross and carelessly, not having any idea Jimmie was looking for trouble. But Jimmie surprised him; Jimmie did want it.

"Sure, I want it. Put me on. Tired? No. I'm fresh as rain-water. Put me on, Neighbor; I'll never get fast any other way. Doubleday wouldn't give me a fast run in a hundred years.

"Neighbor," cried Jimmie, greatly wrought, "put me on, and I'll plant sunflowers on your grave."

There wasn't much time to look around; the 1012 was being coupled on to the mail for the hardest run on the line.

"Get in there, you blamed idiot," roared Neighbor presently at Jimmie. "Get in and fire her; and if you don't give Sollers two hundred and ten pounds every inch of the way I'll set you back wiping."

Jimmie winked furiously at the proposition while it was being hurled at him, but he lost no time climbing in. The 1012 was drumming then at her gauge with better than two hundred pounds. Adam Shafer, conductor for the run, ran backward and forward a minute examining the air. At the final word from his brakeman he lifted two fingers at Sollers; Oliver opened a notch, and Jimmie Bradshaw stuck his head out of the gangway. Slowly, but with swiftly rising speed, the yellow string began to move out through the long lines of freight cars that blocked the spurs; and those who watched that morning from the Piedmont platform thought a smoother equipment than Bucks' mail train never drew out of the mountain yards.

Jimmie Bradshaw jumped at the work in front of him. He had never lifted a pick in as swell a cab. The hind end of the 1012 was big as a private car; Jimmie had never seen so much play for a shovel in his life, and he knew the trick of his business better than most men even in West End cabs, the trick of holding the high pressure every minute, of feeling the drafts before they left the throttle; and as Oliver let the engine out very, very fast, Jimmie Bradshaw sprinkled the grate bars craftily and blinked at the shivering pointer, as much as to say, "It's you and me now for the Yellow Mail, and nobody else on earth."

There was a long reach of smooth track in front of the foothills. It was there the big start had to be made, and in two minutes the bark of the big machine had deepened to a chest tone full as thunder. It was all fun for an hour, for two hours. It was that long before the ambitious fireman realized what the new speed meant: the sickening slew, the lurch on lurch so fast the engine never righted, the shortened breath along the tangent, the giddy roll to the elevation and the sudden shock of the curve, the roar of the flight on the car, and, above and over it all, the booming purr of the maddened steel. The canoe in the heart of the rapid, the bridge of a liner at sea, the gun in the heat of the fight, take something of this—the cab of the mail takes it all.

When they struck the foothills Sollers and Jimmie Bradshaw looked at their watches and looked at each other like men who had turned their backs on every mountain record. There was a stop for water—speed drinks so hard—an oil round, an anxious touch on the journals; then the Yellow Mail drew reeling into the hills. Oliver eased her just a bit for the heavier curves, but for all that the train writhed frantically as it cut the segments, and the men thought, in spite of themselves, of the mountain curves ahead. The worst of the run lay ahead of the pilot, because the art in mountain running is not alone or so much in getting up hill; it is in getting down hill. But by the way the Yellow Mail got that day up hill and down, it seemed as if Steve Horigan's dream would be realized, and the 1012 actually would pull the stamps off the letters. Before they knew it they were through the gateway, out into the desert country, up along the crested buttes, and then, sudden as eternity, the wheel-base of the 1012 struck a tight curve, a pentdown rail sprang out like a knitting-needle, and the Yellow Mail shot staggering off track into a gray borrow-pit.

There was a crunching of truck and frame, a crashing splinter of varnished cars, a scream from the wounded engine, a cloud of gray ash in the burning sun, and a ruin of human effort in the ditch. In the twinkle of an eye the mail train lay spilled on the alkali; for a minute it looked desperate bad for the general manager's test.

It was hardly more than a minute; then like ants out of a trampled hill men began crawling from the yellow wreck. There was more—there was groaning and worse, yet little for so frightful a shock. And first on his feet, with no more than scratches, and quickest back under the cab after his engineer, was Jimmie Bradshaw, the fireman.

Sollers, barely conscious, lay wedged between the tank and

the footboard. Jimmie, all by himself, eased him away from the boiler. The conductor stood with a broken arm directing his brakeman how to chop a crew out of the head mail car, and the hind crews were getting out unaided. There was a quick calling back and forth, and the cry, "Nobody killed!" But the engineer and the conductor were put out of action. There was, in fact, only one West End man unhurt—Jimmie Bradshaw.

The first wreck of the fast mail—there have been worse since—took place just east of Crockett's siding. A westbound freight lay at that moment on the passing track waiting for the mail. Jimmie Bradshaw, the minute he righted himself, cast up the possibilities of the situation. Before the freight crew had reached the wreck Jimmie was hustling ahead to tell them what he wanted. The freight conductor demurred; and when they discussed it with the freight engineer, Kingsley, he objected. "My engine won't never stand it; it'll pound her to scrap," he argued. "I reckon the safest thing to do is to get orders."

"Get orders!" stormed Jimmie Bradshaw, pointing at the wreck. "Get orders! Are you running an engine on this line and don't know the orders for those mail bags? The orders is to move 'em! That's orders enough. Move 'em! Uncouple three of those empty box-cars and hustle 'em back. By the Great United States!—any man that interferes with moving this mail will get his time, that's what he'll get. That's Doubleday, and don't you forget it. The thing is to move the mail, not to stand here chewing about it!"

"Bucks wants the stuff hustled," put in the freight conductor, weakening before Jimmie's eloquence, "everybody knows that."

"Uncouple there!" cried Jimmie, climbing into the mogul cab. "I'll pull the bags, Kingsley; you needn't take any chances. Come back there, every mother's son of you, and help on the transfer."

He carried his points with a gale. He was conductor and engineer and general manager all in one. He backed the boxes to the curve below the spill, and set every man at work piling the mail from the wrecked train to the freight cars. The wounded cared for the wounded, and the dead might have buried the dead; Jimmie moved the mail. Only one thing turned his hair gray; the transfer was so slow, it threatened to defeat his plan. As he stood fermenting, a stray party of Sioux bucks on a vagrant hunt rose out of the desert passes, and halted to survey the confusion. It was Jimmie Bradshaw's opportunity. He had the blanket men in council in a trice. They talked for one minute; in two, he had them regularly sworn in and carrying second-class. The registered stuff was zealously guarded by those of the mail clerks who could still hobble—and who, head for head, leg for leg, and arm for arm, can stand the wrecking that a mail clerk can stand? The mail crews took the registered matter; the freight crews and Jimmie, dripping sweat and anxiety, handled the letter-bags; but second- and third-class were temporarily hustled for the Great White Father by his irreverent children of the Rockies.

Before the disabled men could credit their senses the business was done, they made as comfortable as possible, and, with the promise of speedy aid back to the injured, the Yellow Mail, somewhat disfigured, was heading again westward in the box-cars. This time Jimmie Bradshaw for once in his life had the coveted fast run, and till he sighted Fort Rucker he never for a minute let up.

Meantime, at Medicine Bend, there was a desperate crowd around the dispatcher. It was an hour and twenty minutes after Ponca station reported the Yellow Mail out, before Fort Rucker, eighteen miles west, reported the box-cars and Jimmie Bradshaw in, and followed with a wreck report from the Crockett siding. When that end of it began to tumble into the Wickiup office Doubleday's face turned hard; fate was against him, the contract gone glimmering, and he didn't feel at all sure his own head and the roadmaster's wouldn't follow it. Then the Rucker operator began again to talk about Jimmie Bradshaw, and "Who's Bradshaw?" asked somebody; and Rucker went on excitedly with the story of the mogul and of three box-cars, and of a war party of Sioux squatting on the brake-wheels; it came so mixed that Medicine Bend thought everybody at Rucker Station had gone mad.

While they fumed, Jimmie Bradshaw was speeding the mail through the mountains. He had Kingsley's fireman, big as an ox and full of his own enthusiasm. In no time they were flying across the flats of the Spider Water, threading the curves of the Peace River, and hitting the rails of the Painted Desert, with the mogul sprinting like a Texas steer, and the box-cars leaping like yearlings at the joints. It was no case of scientific running, no case of favoring the roadbed, of easing the strain on the equipment; it was simply a case of galloping to a Broadway fire with a Silsby rotary on a 4-11 call. Up hill and down, curve and tangent, it was all one. There was speed made on the plains with that mail, and there was speed made in the foothills with the fancy equipment, but never the speed that Jimmie Bradshaw made when he ran the mail through the gorges in three box-cars; and frightened operators and paralyzed station agents all the way up the line watched the fearful and wonderful train, with Bradshaw's red head sticking out of the cab window, shiver the switches.

Medicine Bend couldn't get the straight of it over the wires. There was an electric storm in the mountains, and the wires went bad in the midst of the confusion. They knew there was a wreck, and understood there was mail in the ditch, and, with Doubleday frantic, the dispatchers were trying to get the track to run a train down to Crockett's. But Jimmie Bradshaw had asked at Rucker for rights to the Bend, and in an unguarded moment they had been given;

after that it was all off. Nobody could get action on Jimmie Bradshaw. He took the rights, and stayed not for stake nor stopped not for stone. In thirty minutes the operating department were wild to kill him, but he was making such time it was concluded better to humor the lunatic than to hold him up anywhere for a parley. When this was decided Jimmie and his war party were already reported past Bad Axe, fifteen miles below the Bend, with every truck on the box-cars smoking.

The Bad Axe run to the Bend was never done in less than fourteen minutes until Bradshaw that day brought up the mail. Between those two points the line is modeled on the curves of a ram's horn, but Jimmie with the mogul found every twist on the right of way in eleven minutes; that particular record is good yet. Indeed, before Doubleday, then in a frenzied condition, got his cohorts fairly on the platform to look for Jimmie, the hollow scream of the big freight engine echoed through the mountains. Shouts from below brought the operators to the upper windows; down the Bend they saw a monster locomotive flying from a trailing horn of smoke. As the stubby string of freight cars slewed quartering into the lower yard, the startled officials saw them from the Wickiup windows wrapped in a stream of flame. Every journal was afire, and the blaze from the boxes, rolling into the steam from the stack, curled hotly around a bevy of Sioux Indians, who clung sternly to the footboards and brake-wheels on top of the box-cars. It was a ride for the red men that is told around the council fires yet. But they do not always add in their traditions that they were hanging on, not only for life, but likewise for a butt of plug tobacco promised for their timely aid at Crockett siding.

By the time Jimmie slowed up his astounding equipment the fire brigade was on the run from the roundhouse. The Sioux warriors climbed hastily down the fire escapes, a force of bruised and bare-headed mail clerks shoved back the box-car doors, the car tinks tackled the conflagration, and Jimmie Bradshaw, dropping from the cab with the swing of a man who has done a trick, waited at the gangway for the questions to come at him. For a minute they came hot.

"What the blazes do you mean by bringing in an engine in that condition?" choked Doubleday, pointing to the blown machine.

"I thought you wanted the mail?" winked Jimmie.

"How the devil are we to get the mail with you blocking the track two hours?" demanded Callahan, insanely.

"Why, the mail's here, in these box-cars," answered Jimmie Bradshaw, pointing to his bobtail train. "Now don't look daffy like that; every sack is right here. I thought the best way to get the mail here was to bring it. Hm? We're forty minutes late, ain't we?"

Doubleday waited to hear no more. Orders flew like curlews from the superintendent and the master mechanic. They saw there was a life for it yet. Before the fire brigade had done with the trucks a string of new mail cars was backed down beside the train. The relieving mail crews waiting at the Bend took hold like cats at a pudding, and a dozen extra men helped them sling the pouches. The 1014, blowing porpoisewise, was backed up just as Benedict Morgan's train pulled down for Crockett's siding, and the Yellow Mail, rehabilitated, rejuvenated, and exultant, started up the gorge for Bear Dance, only fifty-three minutes late, with Hawksworth in the cab.

"And if you can't make that up, Frank, you're no good on earth," sputtered Doubleday at the engineer he had put in for that especial endeavor. And Frank Hawksworth did make it up, and the Yellow Mail went on and off the West End on the test, and into the Sierras for the coast, ON TIME.

"There's a butt of plug tobacco and transportation to Crockett's coming to these bucks, Mr. Doubleday," wheezed Jimmie Bradshaw uncertainly, for with the wearing off of the strain came the idea to Jimmie that he might have to pay for it himself. "I promised them that," he added, "for helping with the transfer. If it hadn't been for the blankets we wouldn't have got off for another hour. They chew Tomahawk, rough and ready preferred, Mr. Doubleday. Hm?"

Doubleday was looking off into the yard.

"You've been on a freight run some time, Jimmie," said he tentatively.

The Indian detachment was crowding in pretty close on the red-headed engineer. He blushed. "If you'll take care of my tobacco contract, Doubleday, we'll call the other matter square. I'm not looking for a fast run as much as I was."

"If we get the mail contract," resumed Doubleday reflectively, "and it won't be your fault if we don't—hm?—we may need you on one of the runs. Looks to me as if you ought to have one."

Jimmie shook his head. "I don't want one, don't mind me; just fix these gentlemen out with some tobacco before they scalp me, will you?"

The Indians got their leaf, and Bucks got his contract, and Jimmie Bradshaw got the pick of the runs on the Yellow Mail, and ever since he's been kicking to get back on a freight. But they don't call him Bradshaw any more. No man in the mountains can pace him on a run. And when the head brave of the hunting party received the butt of tobacco on behalf of his company, he looked at Doubleday with dignity, pointed to the sandy engineer, and spoke freckled words in the Sioux.

That's the way it came about. Bradshaw holds the belt for the run from Bad Axe to Medicine Bend; but he never goes any more by the name of Bradshaw. West of McCloud, everywhere up and down the mountains, they give him the name the Sioux gave him that day—Jimmie the Wind.

THE ROADMASTER'S
STORY

By Frank H. Spearman

THE ROADMASTER'S STORY

By Frank H. Spearman

NOT OFFICIALLY; I don't pretend to say that. You might travel the West End from fresh water to salt—and we dip into both—without ever locating the Spider Water by map or by name.

But if you should happen anywhere on the West End to sit among a gang of bridge carpenters; or get to confidence with a bridge foreman; or find the springy side of a roadmaster's heart; then, you might hear all you wanted about the Spider Water—maybe more. Anyway, full plenty, as Hailey used to say.

The Sioux named it; and whatever may be thought of their interpretation of Scriptural views on landgrabbing, no man with sense ever attempted to improve on their names for things, whether birds, or braves, or winds, or waters—they know.

Our General Managers hadn't always sense—this may seem odd, but on the system it would excite no comment—and one of them countenanced a shameful change in the name of the Spider Water. Some polytechnical idiot at a safe distance dubbed it the Big Sandy; and the Big Sandy it is to this day on map and in folder—but not in the lingo of trackmen or the heart of the Sioux. Don't say Big Sandy to trackmen and hand out a cigar. It will not go. Say Spider Water without any cigar and you will get a word and a stool, and if you ask it, fine cut.

The Spider Water—although ours is the pioneer line—

was there when we first bridged it. It is probably as old as sundown, and nothing like as pretty. The banks—it has none to speak of. Its stones—they are whiskered. Its bed—full of sand-burrs. Everything about the villain stream has a dilapidate, broken-down air: the very mud of the Spider Water is rusty.

So our people bridged it; and the trouble began. A number of matters bothered our pioneer managements—Indians, outlaws, cabinet officers, congressional committees, and Wall Street magnates—but at one time or another our folks managed all of them. The only thing they couldn't at any time satisfactorily manage was the Spider Water. Bridge after bridge they threw across it—and into it. Year after year the Spider Water toyed with our civil engineers and our material department. One man at Omaha given to asthma and statistics estimated, between spells, that the Spider Water had cost us more money than all the water courses together from the Missouri to the Sierras.

Then came to the West End a masterful man, a Scotchman, pawky and hard. Brodie was his name, an Edinburgh man with no end of degrees and master of every one. Brodie came to be superintendent of bridges on the Western Division, and to boss every water course on the plains and in the mountains. But the Spider Water took a fall even out of Brodie. It swept out a Howe truss bridge for Brodie before he got his bag unpacked, and thereafter Brodie, who was reputed not to care a stringer for anybody, did not conceal a distinct respect for the Spider.

Brodie went at it right. He tried, not to make friends with the Spider, for nobody could do that, but to get acquainted with it. For this he went to its oldest neighbors, the Sioux. Brodie spent weeks and weeks up the Spider Water hunting, summers; and with the Sioux he talked Spider Water and drank fire-water. That was Brodie's shame—the fire-water. But he was pawky, and he chinned unceasingly the braves and the medicine men about the uncommonly queer water that took the bridges so fast. The river that month in and month out couldn't squeeze up water enough to baptize a pollywog and then, of a sudden, and for a few days, would rage like the Missouri, restore to the desert its own and living image, and leave our bewildered rails hung up either side in the wind.

Brodie talked cloudbursts up country; for the floods came, times, under clear skies—and the Sioux sulked in silence. He suggested an unsuspected inlet from some mountain stream which maybe, times, sent its storm water over a low divide into the Spider—and the redmen shrugged their faces. As a last resort and in desperation he hinted at the devil; and the skeptics took a quick brace with as much as to say, now you are talking; and muttered very bad medicine.

Then they gave him the Indian stuff about the Spider Water; took him away up where once a party of Pawnees had camped in the dust of the river bed to surprise the Sioux; and told Brodie how the Spider, more sudden than buck, fleeter than pony, had come down in the night and surprised the Pawnees—and so well that the next morning there wasn't enough material left for a scalp dance.

They took Brodie out in the ratty bed himself, and when he said, heap dry, and said, no water, they laughed, Indianwise, and pointed to the sand. Scooping little wells with their hands they showed him the rising and the filling; the instant water where before was no water. And dropping into the wells feathers of the grouse, they showed Brodie how the current carried them always across the well—every time, and always, Brodie noticed—southeast. Then Brodie made Hailey dig many holes, and the Spider welled into them, and he threw in bits of notebooks and tobacco wrappers, but always they travelled southeast—always the same; and a bigger fool than Brodie could see that the water was all there, only underground. But when did it rise? asked Brodie. When the

Chinook spoke, said the Sioux. And why? persisted Brodie.
Because the Spider woke, said the Sioux. And Brodie went
out of the camp of the Sioux wondering.

And he planned a new bridge which should stand the
Chinook and the Spider and the de'il himself, said Brodie,
medicine or no medicine. And full seven year it lasted; then
the fire-water spoke for the wicked Scotchman—and he himself went out into the night.

And after he died, miserable wreck of a man—and of a
very great man—the Spider woke and took his pawky bridge
and tied up the main line for two weeks and set us crazy,
for we were already losing our grip on the California fast
freight business. But at that time Hailey was superintendent
of bridges on the West End.

I

His father was a section foreman. When Hailey was a kid
—a mere kid—he got into Brodie's office doing errands; but
whenever he saw a draughtsman at work he was no good for
errands. At such times he went all into a mental tangle that
could be neither thrashed nor kicked out of him, though
both were conscientiously tried by old man Hailey and
Superintendent Brodie; and Brodie, since he could do nothing else with him, finally kicked him into learning to read—
and to cipher, Brodie called it. Then, by and by, Hailey got
an old table and part of a cake of India ink himself, and himself became a draughtsman, and soon, with some cursing
from Brodie and a "Luk a' that now!" from his paralyzed
daddy, became chief draughtsman in Brodie's office. Hailey
was no college man—Hailey was a Brodie man. Single mind
on single mind—concentration absolute. Mathematics, drawing, bridges, brains—that was Hailey. But no classics except
Brodie, who himself was a classic. All that Brodie knew,

Hailey had from him; and where Brodie was weak, Hailey was strong—master of himself. When Brodie shamed the image he was made in, Hailey hid the shame best he could —though never touched or made it his own—and Brodie, who hated even himself, showed still a light in the wreck by molding Hailey to his work. For, one day, said Brodie in his heart, this boy shall be master of these bridges. When I am rot, he will be here what I ought to have been—this Irish boy—and they will say he was Brodie's man. And better than any of these dough-heads they send me out, better than any of their Eastern graduates he shall be, if he was made engineer by a drunkard. And Hailey was better, far, far better than the graduates, better than Brodie—and to Hailey came the time to wrestle the Spider.

Stronger than any man before or since he was for that work. All Brodie knew, all the Indians knew, all that a life's experience, eating, living, watching, sleeping with the big river had taught him, that Hailey knew. And when Brodie's bridge went out, Hailey was ready with his new bridge for the Spider Water which should be better than Brodie's, just as he was better than Brodie. It was to be such a bridge as Brodie's bridge with the fire-water left out. And the plans for a Howe truss, two-pier, two-abutment, three-span, pneumatic-caisson bridge to span the Big Sandy River were submitted to headquarters.

But the cost! The directors jumped their table when they saw the figures. We were being milked at that time—to put it bluntly, being sucked, worse than lemons—by a Wall Street clique that robbed our good road, shaved our salaries, impoverished our equipment, and cut our maintenance to the quick. They talked economy and studied piracy. In the matter of appropriations, for themselves they were free-booters; for us, they were thrifty as men of Hamelin town. When Hailey demanded a thousand guilders for his Spider Water bridge, they laughed and said, "Come, take fifty." He

couldn't do anything else; and he built a fifty-guilder bridge
to bar the Spider's crawl. It lasted really better than the
average bridge, and since Hailey never could get a thousand
guilders at once, he kept drawing fifty at a time and throwing
them annually at the Spider.

But the dream of his life—this we all knew, and the Sioux
would have said the Spider knew—was to build a final bridge
over the Spider Water: a bridge to throttle it for all time.

It was the one subject on which you could get a rise out
of Hailey any time, day or night—the two-pier, two-abutment, three-span, pneumatic-caisson Spider bridge. He would
talk Spider bridge to a Chinaman. His bridge foreman, Ed
Peeto, a staving big one-eyed French Canadian, actually had
but two ideas in life: one was Hailey; the other the Spider
bridge. When the management changed again—when the
pirates were sent out on the plank so many good men had
walked at their command—and a great and public-spirited
man took control of the system, Ed Peeto kicked his little
water spaniel in a frenzy of delight. "Now, Sport, old boy,"
he exclaimed riotously, "we'll get the bridge!"

So there were many long conferences at division headquarters between Bucks, superintendent, and Callahan, assistant, and Hailey, superintendent of bridges; and after,
Hailey went once more to general headquarters lugging all
his estimates revised and all his plans refigured. All his expense estimates outside the Spider bridge and one other
point were slight, because Hailey could skin along with less
money than anybody ever in charge of the bridge work. He
did it by keeping everything up; not a sleeper, not a spike—
nothing got away from him.

The new president, as befitted a very big man, was no end
of a swell, and received Hailey with a considerate dignity
unknown on our End. He listened carefully to the superintendent's statement of the necessities at the Big Sandy River.
The amount looked large; but the argument, supported by a

mass of statistics, was convincing. Three bridges in ten years, and the California fast freight business lost twice. Hailey's budget called, too, for a new bridge at the Peace River—and a good one. Give him these, he said in effect, and he would guarantee the worst stretch on the system for a lifetime against tie-up disasters. Hailey stayed over to await the decision; but he was always in a hurry, and he haunted the general offices until the president told him he could have the money. To Hailey this meant, particularly, the bridge of his dreams. The wire flashed the word to the West End: everybody at the Wickiup was glad, but Ed Peeto burned red fire and his little dog Sport ate rattlesnakes.

The old shack of a depot building that served as division headquarters at Medicine Bend we called the Wickiup. Everybody in it was crowded for room, and Hailey, whose share was what was left, had hard work to keep out of the wastebasket. But right away now it was different. Two extra offices were assigned to Hailey, and he took his place with those who sported windows and cuspidors—in a word, had departments in the service. Old Denis Hailey went very near crazy. He resigned as section boss and took a place at smaller wages in the bridge carpenter's gang so he could work on the boy's bridge, and Ed Peeto, savage with responsibility, strutted around the Wickiup like a Cyclops.

For a wonder the bridge material came in fast—the Spider stuff first—and early in the summer Hailey, very quiet, and Peeto, very profane, with all and several, their traps and slaves and belongings, moved into construction headquarters at the Spider, and the first airlock ever sunk west of the Missouri closed over the heads of tall Hailey and big Ed Peeto. Like a swarm of ants the bridge-workers cast the refuse up out of the Spider bed. The blow-pipes never slept: night and day the sand streamed from below, and Hailey's caissons, like armed cruisers, sunk foot by foot toward the rock; by the middle of September the masonry was crowd-

ing high-water mark, and the following Saturday Hailey and
Peeto ran back to Medicine Bend to rest up a bit and get
acquainted with their families. Peeto was so deaf he couldn't
hear himself swear, and Hailey looked ragged and thin, like
the old depot, but immensely happy.

Sunday morning counted a little even then in the mountains. It was at least a day to get your feet on the tables up
in Bucks' office and smoke Callahan's Cavendish—which was
enough to make a man bless Callahan if he did forget his
Maker. Sunday mornings Bucks would get out the dainty,
pearl-handled Wostenholm that Lillienfeld, the big San
Francisco spirit-shipper, left annually for him at the Bend,
and open the R. R. B. mail and read the news aloud for the
benefit of Callahan and Hailey and such hangers-on as Peeto
and an occasional stray dispatcher.

"Hello," exclaimed Bucks, chucking a nine-inch official
manila under the table, "here's a General Order—Number
Fourteen—"

The boys drew their briers like one. Bucks read out a lot
of stuff that didn't touch our End, and then he reached this
paragraph:

" 'The Mountain and the Inter-mountain divisions are
hereby consolidated under the name of the Mountain Division with J. F. Bucks as Superintendent, headquarters at
Medicine Bend. C. T. Callahan is appointed Assistant Superintendent of the new division.' "

"Good boy!" roared Ed Peeto, straining his ears.

"Well, well, well," said Hailey, opening his eyes, "here's
promotions right and left."

" 'H. P. Agnew is appointed Superintendent of bridges of
the new division with headquarters at Omaha, vice P. C.
Hailey,' " Bucks read on, with some little surprise growing
into a shock. Then he read fast, looking for some further
mention of Hailey. Hailey promoted, transferred, assigned—
but there was no further mention of Hailey in G. O. Number

Fourteen. Bucks threw down the order in a silence. Ed Peeto broke out first.

"Who's H. P. Canoe?"

"Agnew."

"Who the hell is he?" roared Ed. Nobody answered: nobody knew. Bucks attempted to talk; Callahan lit his lighted pipe; but Ed Peeto stared at Hailey like a drunken man.

"Did you hear that?" he snorted at his superior.

Hailey nodded.

"You're out!" stormed Peeto.

Hailey nodded. The bridge foreman took his pipe from his mouth and dashed it into the stove. He got up and stamped across to the window and was like to have sworn the glass out before Hailey spoke.

"I'm glad we're up to high water at the Spider, Bucks," said he at last. "When they get in the Peace River work, the division will run itself for a year."

"Hailey," Bucks spoke slowly, "I don't need to tell you what I think of it, do I? It's a damned shame. But it's what I've said for a year—nobody ever knows what Omaha will do next."

Hailey rose to his feet.

"Where you going, Phil?" asked Bucks.

"Going back to the Spider on Number Two."

"Not going back this morning—why don't you wait for Four, tonight?" suggested Bucks.

"Ed," Hailey raised his voice at the foreman, "will you get those stay-bolts and chuck them into the baggage-car for me on Number Two? I'm going over to the house for a minute." He forgot to answer Bucks; they knew what it meant. He was bracing himself to tell the folks before he left them. Preparing to explain why he wouldn't have the Sunday at home with the children. Preparing to tell the wife—and the old man—that he was out. Out of the railroad system he had given his life to help build up and make what it was. Out

of the position he had climbed to by studying like a hermit
and working like a hobo. Out—without criticism, or allega-
tion, or reason—simply, like a dog, out.

Nobody at the Wickiup wanted to hear the telling over at
the cottage; nobody wanted to imagine the scene. As Number
Two's mellow chime whistle rolled down the gorge, they saw
Hailey coming out of his house, his wife looking after him,
and two little girls tugging at his arms as he hurried along;
old Denis behind, head down, carrying the boy's shabby
valise, trying to understand why the blow had fallen.

That was what Callahan up with Bucks at the window was
trying to figure—what it meant.

"The man that looks to Omaha for rhyme or reason will
beggar his wits, Callahan," said Bucks slowly, as he watched
Ed Peeto swing the stay-bolts up into the car so they would
crack the baggageman across the shins, and then try to get
him into a fight about it. "They never had a man—and I bar
none, no, not Brodie—that could handle the mountain-water
like Hailey; they never will have a man—and they dump him
out like a pipe of tobacco. How does it happen we are cursed
with such a crew of blooming idiots? Other roads aren't."

Callahan made no answer. "I know why they did it," Bucks
went on, "but I couldn't tell Hailey."

"Why?"

"I think I know why. Last time I was down, the president
brought his name up and asked a lot of questions about
where he was educated and so on. Somebody had plugged
him, I could see that in two minutes. I gave him the facts—
told him that Brodie had given him his education as an engineer. The minute he found out he wasn't regularly graduated, he froze up. Very polite, but he froze up. See? Experience, actual acquirements," Bucks extended his hand from
his vest pocket in an odd wavy motion till it was lost at arm's
length, "nothing—nothing—nothing."

As he concluded, Hailey was climbing behind his father

into the smoker; Number Two pulled down the yard and out; one thing Hailey meant to make sure of—that they shouldn't beat him out of the finish of the Spider bridge as he had planned it; one monument Hailey meant to have— one he has.

The new superintendent of bridges took hold promptly; we knew he had been wired for long before his appointment was announced. He was a good enough fellow, I guess, but we all hated him. Bucks did the civil, though, and took Agnew down to the Spider in a special to inspect the new work and introduce him to the man whose bread and opportunity he was taking. "I've been wanting to meet you, Mr. Hailey," said Agnew pleasantly after they had shaken hands. Hailey looked at Agnew silently as he spoke; Bucks looked steadfastly at the grasshopper derrick.

"I've been expecting you'd be along pretty soon," replied Hailey presently. "There's considerable to look over here. After that we'll go back to Peace River canyon. We're just getting things started there: then we'll run up to the Bend and I'll turn the office over."

"No hurry about that. You've got a good deal of a bridge here, Mr. Hailey?"

"You'll need a good deal of a bridge here."

"I didn't expect to find you so far along out here in the mountains. Where did you get that pneumatic process?"

It touched Hailey, the pleasant, easy way Agnew took him. The courtesy of the East against the blunt of the West. There wasn't a mean drop anywhere in Hailey's blood, and he made no trouble whatever for his successor.

After he let go on the West End, Hailey talked as if he would look up something farther east. He spoke about it to Bucks, but Bucks told him frankly he would find difficulty without a regular degree in getting a satisfactory connection. Hailey himself realized that; moreover, he seemed reluctant to quit the mountains. He acted around the cottage and the

Wickiup like a man who has lost something and who looks for it abstractedly—as one might feel in his pockets for a fish-pole or a burglar. But there were lusty little Haileys over at the cottage to be looked after, and Bucks, losing a roadmaster about that time, asked Hailey (after chewing it a long time with Callahan) to take the place himself and stay on the staff. He even went home with Hailey and argued it.

"I know it doesn't seem just right," Bucks put it, "but, Hailey, you must remember this thing at Omaha isn't going to last. They can't run a road like this with Harvard graduates and Boston typewriters. There'll be an entire new deal down there some fine day. Stay here with me, and I'll say this, Hailey, if I go, ever, you go with me."

And Hailey, sitting with his head between his hands, listening to his wife and to Bucks, said one day, "Enough," and the first of the month reported for duty as roadmaster.

Agnew, meantime, had stopped all construction work not too far along to discontinue. The bridge at the Spider fortunately was beyond his mandate; it was finished to a rivet as Hailey had planned it. Three spans, two piers, and a pair of abutments—solid as the Tetons. But the Peace River canyon work was caught in the air. Hailey's caissons gave way to piles which pulled the cost down from one hundred to seventy-five thousand dollars, and incidentally it was breathed that the day for extravagant expenditures on the West End was past—and Bucks dipped a bit deeper than usual into Callahan's box of cross-cut, and rammed the splintered leaf into his brier a bit harder and said no word.

"But if we lose just one more bridge it's good-by and gone to the California fast freight business," muttered Callahan. "It's taken two years to get it back as it is. Did you tell the president that?" he growled at Bucks, smoking. Bucks put out his little wave.

"I told him everything. I told him we couldn't stand another tie-up. I showed them all the records. One bridge at Peace River, three at the Spider in ten years."

"What did they say?"

"Said they had entire confidence in Agnew's judgment: very eminent authority and that sort—new blood was making itself felt in every department; that, of course, was fired at me; but they heard all I intended to say, just the same. I asked the blooming board whether they wanted my resignation and"—Bucks paused to laugh silently—"the president invited me up to the Millard to dine with him. Hello, Phil Hailey!" he exclaimed as the new roadmaster walked in the door. "Happy New Year. How's your culverts, old boy? Ed Peeto said yesterday the piles were going in down at Peace River."

"Just as good as concrete as long as they stay in," smiled Hailey, "and they do cost a heap less. This is great bridge weather—and for that matter great track weather."

We had no winter that year till spring; and no spring till summer; and it was a spring of snow and a summer of water. Down below, the plains were lost in the snow after Easter, even—the snow that brought the Blackwood disaster with three engines and a rotary to the bad, not to speak of old man Sankey, a host in himself. After that the snow let up; it was then no longer a matter of keeping the line clear; it was a matter of lashing the track to the right of way to keep it from swimming clear. Hailey had his hands full; he caught it all the while and worse than anybody, but he worked like two men, for in a pinch that was his way. Bucks, irritable from repeated blows of fortune, leaned on the wiry roadmaster as he did on Callahan or Neighbor. Hailey knew Bucks looked to him for the track, and he strained every nerve making ready for the time the mountain snows should go out.

There was nobody easy on the West End: and least of all

Hailey, for that spring, ahead of the suns, ahead of the thaws, ahead of the waters, came a going out that unsettled the oldest calculator in the Wickiup. Brodie's old friends began coming out of the upper country, out of the Spider valley. Over the Eagle pass and through the Peace canyon the Sioux came in parties and camps and tribes—out and down and into the open country. And Bucks stayed them and talked with them. Talked the Great White Father and the Ghost Dance and the Bad Agent. But the Sioux grunted and did not talk; they traveled. Then Bucks spoke of good hunting, far, far south; if they were uneasy Bucks was willing they should travel far, for it looked like a rising. Some kind of rising it must have been to take the Indians out of winter quarters at such a time. After Bucks, Hailey tried, and the braves listened, for they knew Hailey, and when he accused them of fixing for fight they shook their heads, denied, and turned their faces to the mountains. They stretched their arms straight out under their blankets like stringers and put out their palms, downward, and muttered to Hailey.

"Plenty snow."

"I reckon they're lying," said Bucks, listening. "There's some deviltry up. They're not the kind to clear out for snow."

Hailey made no comment—only looked thoughtfully at the ponies shambling along, the squaws trudging, the braves loitering to ask after the fire-water chief who slept under a cairn of stones off the right of way above the yard. Bucks didn't believe it. He could fancy rats deserting a sinking ship, because he had read of such things—but Indians clearing out for snow!

"Not for snow, nor for water," muttered Bucks, "unless it's fire-water." And once more the redman was misunderstood.

Now the Spider wakes regularly twice; at all other times irregularly. Once in April—that is the foothills water; once in June—that is the mountain water. And the June rise is like this ⌒. But the April rise is like this ⌄⌄.

Now came an April without any rise; that April nothing rose—except the snow. "We shall get it all together," suggested Bucks one night.

"Or will it get us altogether?" asked Hailey.

"Either way," said Callahan, "it will be mostly at once."

May opened bleaker than April; even the trackmen walked with set faces; the dirtiest half-breed on the line knew now what the mountains held. At last, while we looked and wondered, came a very late Chinook; July in May; then the water.

2

Section gangs were doubled and track-walkers put on. By-passes were opened, bridge crews strengthened, everything buckled for grief. Gullies began to race, culverts to choke, creeks to tumble, rivers to madden. From the Muddy to the Summit the water courses swelled and boiled—all but the Spider; the big river slept. Through May and into June the Spider slept; but Hailey was there at the Wickiup, always, and with one eye running over all the line, one eye turned always to the Spider where two men and two, night and day, watched the lazy surface water trickle over and through the vagabond bed between Hailey's monumental piers. Never an hour did the operating department lose to the track. East and west of us railroads everywhere clamored in despair. The flood reached from the Rockies to the Alleghenies. Our trains never missed a trip; our schedules were unbroken; our people laughed; we got the business, dead loads of it; our treasury flowed over; and Hailey watched; and the Spider slept.

Big Ed Peeto, still foreman of the bridges, hung on Hailey's steps and tried with his staring, swearing eye to make it all out; to guess what Hailey expected to happen, for it was plain he was thinking. Whether smoking or speaking, whether

waking or sleeping, he was thinking. And as May turned soft
and hot into June, with every ditch bellying and the mountains still buried, it put us all thinking.

On the thirtieth there was trouble beyond Wild Hat, and
all our extra men, put out there under Hailey, were fighting
to hold the Rat Valley levels where they hug the river on the
west slope. It wasn't really Hailey's track. Bucks sent him
over there because he sent Hailey wherever the Emperor sent
Ney. Sunday while Hailey was at Wild Hat it began raining.
Sunday it rained. Monday it rained all through the mountains; Tuesday it was raining from Omaha to Eagle pass, with
the thermometer climbing for breath and the barometer flat
as an adder—and the Spider woke.

Woke with the April water and the June water and the
rain water all at once. Trackmen at the bridge Tuesday night
flagged Number One and reported the river wild, and sheet
ice running. A wire from Bucks brought Hailey out of the
west and into the east; and brought him to reckon for the
last time with his ancient enemy.

He was against it Wednesday morning with dynamite. All
the day, the night and the next day the sullen roar of the
giant powder shook the ice-jams. Two days more he spent
there watching, with only an occasional thunderbolt to heave
and scatter the Spider water into sudden, shivery columns of
spray; then he wired, "ice out," and set back dragged and
silent for home and for sleep—ten hours out of two hundred,
maybe, was all he reckoned to the good when he struck a
pillow again. Saturday night he slept and Sunday all day and
Sunday night. Monday about noon Bucks sent up to ask, but
Hailey was asleep; they asked back by the lad whether they
should wake him; Bucks sent word, "No."

Tuesday morning the tall roadmaster came down fresh as
sunshine and all day he worked with Bucks and the dispatchers watching the line. The Spider raced like the Missouri,
and the men at the bridge sent in panic messages every night

and morning, but Hailey lit his pipe with their alarms. "That bridge will go when the mountains go," was all he said.

Tuesday was his wedding date, old Denis told Peeto: it was Hailey's wooden wedding, and when he found everybody knew they were going to have a little spread over at the cottage, Hailey invited the boys up for the evening. Just a little celebration, Hailey said, and everybody he spoke wrung his hand and slapped his iron shoulders till Hailey echoed good cheer through and through. Callahan was going over; Bucks had promised to look in, and Ed Peeto and the boys had a little surprise for Hailey, had it in the dark of the baggage-room in the Wickiup, a big Morris chair. No one would ever guess how it landed at Medicine Bend, but it was easy. Ed Peeto had pulled it badly demoralized out of a freight wreck at the Sugar Buttes and done it over in company screws and varnish to surprise Hailey. The anniversary made it just right, very hot stuff, Ed Peeto said, and the company had undoubtedly paid a claim voucher for it—or would.

It was nine o'clock, night, and every star blinking when Hailey looked in again at the office for the track-walkers' reports and the Railway weather bulletins. Bucks, Callahan and Peeto sat about Duffy, who in his shirt-sleeves threw the stuff out off the sounder as it trickled in, dot and dash, dot and dash, over the wires. The west wire was good, but east everything below Peace River was down. We had to get the eastern reports around by Omaha and the south—a good thousand miles of loop—but bad news travels even around a Robin Hood loop.

And Wild Hat came first from the west with a stationary river and the Loup creek falling—clear—good night. And Ed Peeto struck the table heavily and swore it was well in the west. Then from the east came Prairie Portage, all the way around, with a northwest rain, a rising river, and anchor ice pounding the piers badly, track in fair shape and—and—

The wire went wrong. As Duffy knit his eyes and tugged

and cussed a little, the wind outside took up the message and whirled a bucket of rain against the windows. But the wires wouldn't right and stuff that no man could get tumbled in like a dictionary upside down. And Bucks and Callahan and Hailey and Peeto smoked, silent, and listened to the deepening drum of the rain on the roof.

Then Duffy wrestled mightily yet once more, and the long way came word of trouble in the Omaha yards with the river at twenty-two feet and cutting; rising at Bismarck one foot an hour.

"Hell to pay on the Missouri, of course," growled the foreman, staring single-eyed at the inoffensive bulletin. "Well, she don't run our way; let her boil, damn her."

"Keep still," exclaimed Duffy, leaning heavily on the key. "Here's something—from—the Spider."

Only the hum of the rain and the nervous break of the sounder cut the smoke that curled from the pipes. Duffy snatched a pen and ran it across a clip, and Bucks, leaning over, read aloud from his shoulder:

"Omaha.

"J. F. Bucks.—Trainmen from Number Seventy-five stalled west of Rapid City—track afloat in Simpson's cut—report Spider bridge out, send—" And the current broke.

Callahan's hand closed rigidly over his pipe; Peeto sat speechless; Bucks read again at the broken message, but Hailey sprang like a man wounded and snatched the clip from his superintendent's hand.

He stared at the running words till they burned his eyes, and then, with an oath, frightful as the thunder that broke down the mountains, he dashed the clip to the floor. His eyes snapped greenish with fury and he cursed Omaha, cursed its messages and everything that came out of it. Slow at first, but bitter, then fast and faster until all the sting that poisoned his heart at his unjust discharge poured from his lips. It flooded the room like a spilling stream and no man put a word against it, for they knew he stood a wronged man. Out it came—all the rage—all the heart-burning—all the bitterness—and he dropped, bent, into a chair and covered his face with his hands: only the sounder clicking iron jargon and the thunder shaking the Wickiup like a reed filled the ears about him. They watched him slowly knot his fingers and loosen them, and saw his face rise dry and hard and old out of his hands.

"Get up an engine!"

"Not—you're not going down there tonight?" stammered Bucks.

"Yes. Now. Right off. Peeto! Get out your crew!"

The foreman jumped for the door; Bucks hesitated barely an instant, then turning where he sat cut a telephone plug into the roundhouse; Callahan saw him act and, leaning forward, spoke low to Duffy. The dispatcher snatching the train sheet began instantly clearing track for a bridge special.

In twenty minutes twenty men were running twenty ways through the storm and a live engine boomed under the Wickiup windows.

"Phil, I want you to be careful!" It was Bucks standing by the roadmaster's side at the window as they looked out into the storm. "It's a bad night." Hailey made no answer. "A wicked night," muttered Bucks as the lightning shot the yards in a blaze and a crash rolled down the gorge. But wicked as it was he could not bring himself to countermand; something forbade it. Evans, the conductor of the special, ran in.

"Here's your orders!" exclaimed Duffy. Evans pulling down his storm cap nodded as he took the tissue. Hailey buttoned his leather jacket and turned to Bucks.

"Good-by."

"Mind your track," said Bucks warningly to Evans as he took Hailey's hand. "What's your permit?"

"Forty miles an hour."

"Don't stretch it. Good-by, Phil," he added, speaking to Hailey. "I'll see you in the morning."

"In the morning," repeated Hailey. "Good-by. Nothing more in, Duffy?"

"Nothing more."

"Come on!" With the words he pushed the conductor through the door and was gone. The switch engine puffed up with the caboose. Ahead of it Ed Peeto had coupled in the pile driver. At the last minute Callahan asked to go, and as the bridge gang tumbled into the caboose, the assistant superintendent, Ed Peeto and Hailey climbed into the engine. Denis Mullenix sat on the right and with William Durden, fireman, they pulled out, five in the cab, for the Spider Water.

From Medicine Bend to the Spider Water is a ninety-mile run: down the gorge, through the foothills and into the Painted Desert that fills the jaw of the spur we intersect again west of Peace River. From the Peace to the Spider the crow flies twenty miles, but we take thirty for it: there is hardly a tangent between. Their orders set a speed limit, but from the beginning they crowded it. Hailey, moody at first, began joking and laughing the minute they got away. He sat behind Denis Mullenix on the right and poked at his ribs and taunted him with his heavy heels. After a bit he got down and threw coal for Durden, mile after mile, and crowded the boiler till the safety screamed. When Durden took the shovel Hailey put his hand on the shoulder of Callahan, who was trying to hang to big Ed Peeto on the fireman's seat.

"Callahan," he yelled in his ear, "a man's better off—" And Callahan, though he couldn't, in the pound and the roar, catch the words, nodded and laughed because Hailey fiercely laughed. Then going around to the right the roadmaster covered Denis Mullenix's finger on the throttle latch and the air with his big hands and good-naturedly coaxed them loose, pushed the engineer back and got the whip and the reins into his own keeping. It was what he wanted, for he smiled as he drew out the bar a notch and settled himself for the run across the flat country. They were leaving the foothills, and when the lightning opened the night they could see behind through the blasting rain the great hulking pile driver nod and reel out into the Painted Desert like a drunken man; for Hailey's schedule was the wind and his limit the wide throttle.

The storm shook them with freshening fury and drove the flanges into the south rail with a grinding shriek, as they sped from the shelter of the hills. The rain fell in a sheet, and the right of way ran a river. The wind, whipping the water off the ballast, dashed it like hail against the cab glass; the segment of desert caught in the yellow of the headlight rippled and danced and swam in the storm water, and Hailey pulled again at the straining throttle and latched it wider. Callahan hung with a hand to a brace and a hand to Peeto, and every little while looked back at the caboose dancing a hornpipe over the joints; Mullenix, working the injector, stared astonished at Hailey; but Durden grimly sprinkled new blood into the white furnace and eyed his stack.

Notch after notch Hailey drew, heedless of lurch and jump; heedless of bed or curve; heedless of track or storm; and with every spur at her cylinders the engine shook like a frantic horse. Men and monster alike lost thought of care and drank a frenzy in the deafening whirl that Hailey opened across the swimming plain.

The Peace River hills loomed into the headlight like moving pictures; before they could think it, the desert was behind. Callahan, white-faced, climbed down, and passed from hand to hand by Durden and Mullenix got his hands on Hailey's shoulders and his lips to his ear.

"For God's sake, Phil, let up!"

Hailey nodded and choked the steam a little, threw a

hatful of air on the shoes, but more as a test than a check: the
fire was in his blood and he slewed into the hills with a speed
unslackened. From the rocks it is a down grade all the way to
the canyon, and the wind blew them and the track pulled
them and a frenzied man sat at the throttle. Just where the
line crosses Peace River the track bends sharply in through
the Needles to take the bridge.

The curve is a ten-degree. As they struck it, the headlight
shot far out upon the river—and they in the cab knew they
were dead men. Instead of lighting the box of the truss the
lamp lit a black and snaky flood sweeping over the abutment
with yellow foam. The Peace had licked up Agnew's thirty-
foot piles and his bridge was not.

Whatever could be done—and Hailey knew all—meant
death to the cab. Denis Mullenix never moved; no man that
knew Hailey would think of trying to supplant him even
with death under the ponies. He did what a man could do.
There was no chance anyway for the cab: but the caboose
held twenty of his faithful men.

He checked—and with a scream from the flanges, the
special, shaking in the clutches of the air-brake, swung the
curve.

Again, the roadmaster checked heavily. The leads of the
pile driver swaying high above gravity center careened for
an instant wildly to the tangent; then the monster machine,
parting from the tender, took the elevation like a hurdle and
shot into the trees, dragging the caboose after it. But engine
and tender and five in the cab plunged head on into the
Peace.

Not a man in the caboose was killed: it was as if Hailey
had tempered the blow to its crew. They scrambled out of
the splinters and on their feet, men and ready to do. One
voice from below came to them through the storm, and they
answered its calling. It was Callahan; but Durden, Mullenix,
Peeto, Hailey, never called again.

At daybreak wreckers of the West End, swarming from mountain and plain, were heading for the Peace, and the McCloud gang crossed the Spider on Hailey's bridge— on the bridge the coward trainmen had reported out, quaking as they did in the storm at the Spider foaming over its approaches. But Hailey's bridge stood—stands today.

Yet three days the Spider raged, and then knew its master, while he, three whole days, sat at the bottom of the Peace clutching the engine levers in the ruins of Agnew's mistake.

And when the divers got them up, Callahan and Bucks tore big Peeto's arms from his master's body and shut his staring eye and laid him at his master's side. And only the Spider ravening at Hailey's caissons raged. But Hailey slept.

A LITTLE ACTION

By Harold Titus

Harold Titus

HAROLD TITUS was born on February 20, 1888, in Traverse City, Michigan, where he now resides. He obtained his higher education at the University of Michigan, which, in appreciation of his literary work, awarded him an honorary M.A. in 1931. Titus received his practical writing experience as a reporter for the Detroit *News*, from 1907 to 1910. His subsequent career seems to have veered between fruit-growing and writing.

Most of Titus' novels are concerned with logging camps in the northern woods of Michigan. Among his books are *Timber*, *Below Zero*, *Code of the North*, and other titles indicative of their rugged outdoor setting. Incidentally, he describes the operation of a lumber railroad in the Wolverine State. His other railroad stories include such top-notchers as *No Gift of Gab*, *Hot Engineer* and the selection included in this volume, *A Little Action*.

Much has been written about men out on the line—in cab or caboose, along the track, and in lonely wayside stations—which is all well and good. There are other men, though, never seen and rarely thought of, who have their indispensable part in keeping the trains running. Of such is the dispatcher, whose desk comes close to being the nerve center of his division. Mr. Titus' dispatcher in *A Little Action* is not of the old school of brass pounders described by Spearman and Packard. He sends his messages by telephone rather than by telegraph key, and receives them through office loudspeakers rather than through the chattering sounder. But that, as readers of the story will agree, does not lessen the action.

A LITTLE ACTION

By Harold Titus

GEORGE HOSKINS, small, spectacled, sixtyish, was relieved by the third-trick dispatcher at 4:01 P.M.

He went wearily down the hallway, right shoulder higher than his left from so many years at key and switchboard, turned into the washroom and emptied the coffee in his vacuum bottle down a drain. He wrapped the sandwiches in a newspaper and gave them to an aged redcap at the waiting-room entrance.

Ella always complained when he didn't eat, and today he didn't want any complaint, even if it was for his own good. Ella never had been able to understand a lot of things; among them, just how it was with a train dispatcher.

George arrived home at 4:34 P.M., and when Ella took his lunch box out to the kitchen, he dropped into a chair by the radio with a furtive sigh of relief. A violin solo was on, and, although he didn't care much about music, he leaned back and closed his eyes as though enjoying it instead of just resting.

Ella, large and brunette, returned, intently solicitous.

"You look all beat out!"

"Oh, no. Just a little hot downtown."

"But you look like a dishrag!"

George's scraggly mustache bristled in a slight grin.

"And married to a handsome woman like you!"

"Pshaw!" she said, but blushed a little. "You look— In that chair all day! And here you are in another chair! It's enough to wear you out! The back yard," she said, "could stand mowing."

"Wasn't it only Friday I mowed it?"

"Oh, all right!" Her surrender was easy, because she was not thinking about grass so much as George's own good.

She picked up the paper he had brought and glanced at the headlines. "See anybody or hear anything?"

"No. Pretty busy. Passenger special north. Boy scouts out of Chicago for their summer camp."

Ella turned pages and clicked her tongue deprecatingly.

"Cooped up all alone! And just sitting in a chair! A man your age, after all these years! Everybody needs change; any-body needs a little action now and then. Needs to get out. What's in the movies"—spreading the paper wide—"that might be relaxing? What's advertised that might give you a little action after all day in a chair?"

George Hoskins had entered the office at 7:36 A.M. The general superintendent and Cary, the chief dispatcher, were leaning over the first-trick man's shoulder, and the former was saying:

". . . means a revenue of six thousand dollars. Swell business!"

George approached and glanced at the Chicago Division train sheet. They were talking, he saw, about Special Passenger Extra 739, due out of Chicago at 7:30, but not yet reported. The special had twelve coaches and a baggage car. Nice train for such times.

"C. & G. L.'s had those Scouts for years," the superin-tendent said. "If we handle 'em right, we'll cinch the busi-ness." He scowled at the clock, and George knew he was thinking that passenger specials are always late getting on the road.

No. 19, the time freight, had seventy-eight loads out of Chicago. A lot more important than any passenger special, George might say, with its perishable and regular rush merchandise. But that tonnage was right up to the engine's capacity. Besides, he saw, rain was reported south, which meant a wet rail. Erickson, 19's engineer, would go his best to make the time and keep out of the Scouts' way. Maybe others would go their best, too, to handle both those important trains properly. Yes, indeed!

The Chicago operator came on, voice resonant in the amplifying receiver.

"No. 739 at 7:41!" he said, and the superintendent grunted. They'd make up those eleven minutes handily.

The man on trick recorded the time and began writing his transfer in the order book as George slid the Northern Division sheet from beneath the Chicago Division's for a look.

The superintendent started for the door and paused.

"Those Scouts," he said. "We've got to cinch that business."

"Sure," said George, catching his imperativeness.

He signed the transfer, and the other dispatcher stood up, handing over the telephone transmitter. George put his head through the loop and sat down. He didn't know it, but he wasn't going to get up until 4:01 P.M. Spiritually, he was going to be all over two divisions, but the narrow seat of his pants was going to stay right where it was put that moment.

Landon reported in a nasal singsong:

"Extra 1577 at 8:04."

"Going on, eh?"

"Yup."

George made the entry on his big yellow sheet, hitched his chair closer to the desk and shoved it back. He did that when annoyed. It was about the only way you'd ever know he was annoyed.

He was annoyed, now, at McBain, engineer on that extra. He was only twelve minutes ahead of 19's time at Landon and had ten miles to Stover, and the time freight would gain

with every wheel turn. McBain should have gone into clear
at Landon. You don't take chances delaying time freights
these days. Passenger trains go into holes for time freights
these days. And there was McBain, with a slop run, making
a holy show of himself.

This McBain, now. One of those pushers, always biting
off too much. But by 8:16, when Landon reported 19 on
time, McBain would know he was in wrong again and would
be beating the stack off his engine. The fireman would be
bailing coal for Stover Hill, working his back ragged to keep
steam on her. George moved his shoulders to stretch his own
back muscles in sympathy. You can't be on a job almost fifty
years without knowing what everybody else does, when, why
and how. George had gone railroading at sixteen and knew
the business from road maintenance up to finance. So he
knew what McBain's fireman's back felt like.

And in the extra's caboose they'd be talking it over, and,
when McBain finally shut off, the rear brakeman would pick
up his signals before McBain whistled out the flag. George
went out on the caboose platform and down the steps with
the man, and his one hand gripped a chair arm as the shack's
would be gripping the handrail; his eyes also watched the
ground ahead, and he felt his own body swinging outward
and down and his heels hitting the grit before McBain
stopped her.

McBain would open her again and beat her on toward
Stover, making a bad matter worse because he was rattled,
and the flagman would clamp his caution torpedoes on the
one rail and trot along the track and get his stop guns in
place and unfurl his flag and wait. He'd be muttering and
watching his caboose dwindle, and cock his eye and ear for 19.

George left the flagman and got into Erickson's cab, if you
understand. And he began to growl with Erickson when he
got the caution explosions, and shut off with Erickson for the
flagman, and hitched around with Erickson as the man

scrambled up the steps, and demanded to know what in the name of this-or-that was up. The shack would tell him, and Erickson would get them going again as fast as he dared and be asking what in the such-and-such chance a man with that tonnage and a wet rail had of making his time if these so-and-so's with extras kept gumming things up.

George stared at his switchboard, but didn't see it. He saw, instead, Erickson's reddening face and heard Erickson swear. Before long, Erickson would be seeing McBain's smoke; maybe looking right into the extra's caboose, with his time going to pot and the passenger special boring unhindered from behind.

He took a couple of train reports and rang Stover.

"Hear anything of 1577?"

"Not a whisper. . . . Yeah. Sure. I'll call soon's I do."

It was 8:40 when Stover called.

"Extra 1577's heading in now," he said. "And 19's whistling for the yard limits."

George nodded. Erickson would be redder than ever. He'd pull them down just enough to let the flagman fall off; then he'd give himself a sharp hitch in his seat and commence lacing it to 'em.

The operator stayed on the wire. A fuzzy roaring came over it, developed a steady rhythm, grew and clarified to the living beat of a hard-worked locomotive's exhaust.

The vigor of it sent a slow prickle along George's spine. Erickson certainly would pop it to her now! He'd be half out of the window, eyes straight ahead as he hammered past the sidetracked extra. George's head jerked slightly in the measure of that gathering rush. He could feel, beneath his worn chair, the drive and surge of big power. He could feel the wind, sort of fluttering, as it would be in Erickson's face. His right elbow was suddenly cool, in that stuffy room, as Erickson's would be, leaning on the padded arm-rest of the cab-window sash.

But Erickson was seven minutes late and, on toward the terminal, his time wasn't going to give him anything at all over the special. The Scouts had made up their eleven minutes' delay, and 19 certainly would have to keep wheeling.

No operator was between Stover and St. Thomas, where the next report would come from, but an iron operator—an amplifying telephone transmitter—hung on the depot wall at Selkirk, a flag stop; and when George hoped Erickson might have got that far, he turned its switch and listened.

It was 8:52 and no sound; and 8:53 and 8:54. The grade was stiff there, with a bad curve at the bottom, and she might have slipped a little. Erickson would have to ease her off, then, and blow sand under the wheels. George rang an operator on the Northern Division for a routine call, but in his mind's eye his hand reached for no switch on that board before him; instead, it turned the sander in Erickson's cab. He uttered a light grunt, too, as if he felt drivers fly up beneath his chair.

He leaned closer to the telephone on its flexible bracket and caught the first faint squall of Erickson's whistle, picked out the distant mutter of an engine. It came nearer, swelled louder, crashed and exploded and dwindled, and his mustache twitched as he glanced at the clock. No. 19 had lost two more minutes.

Up north, the local set out loads and picked up empties. The limited made up time lost handling express. But while George Hoskins' mind had to be on both divisions, concerned with all trains, his heart could be where it willed, and that was down below, in the cab with Erickson, while the man fought to get his train up to schedule and keep out of the passenger special's way.

But Erickson wasn't cutting it. Erickson kept losing time. It got to be 9:15, and the time freight had been due out of St. Thomas a minute before. It got to be 9:21, and still St.

Thomas made no report. George watched the long hand of the clock, crawling steadily down. He scowled, there alone in his chair.

Finally: "St. Thomas!" His head moved closer to the receiver as he responded, "Dispatcher." The voice said: "No. 19's stopped here. He's whistling out a flag."

"Is, eh?" You seldom could tell by George's voice what went on inside him. His voice was even now, but he was thinking "What in tunket?" and his skin was suddenly hot. "Get out there and find out what ails him," he said.

The stoker was what ailed them. The left elevator of the duplex was what ailed them. A block of wood jammed in the screw was what ailed them.

"Erickson says they'll do better to stop and get it working," the operator reported.

George shook his head. So that's what had happened! Fighting their tonnage, the wet rail and the grades, they'd seen the steam going back. The fireman had gone to work with his shovel to supplement the functioning of the one elevator, but still the steam had dropped. The average man just doesn't muzzle-load that big power, which is why they're equipped with mechanical stokers. And George knew that those twenty-one-hundreds, like 19's, were so drafted that nobody could get coal up to the front of the firebox with a shovel.

So they'd have got the head brakeman to take the inspection plate off the dead elevator while they kept going as best they could; and once that section of the big cylindrical casting, within which a great screw lifted coal from conveyor to firebox, was off, he'd pulled the wet coal out with a packing hook.

George, in retrospect, was on his knees with the shack in that engine cab. He handled the wrench himself, loosening the three nuts that held the plate in place. He worked with the brakeman, I say, just as he heaved coal with the fireman and struggled with Erickson to keep her going with the steam pressure down.

George had his head right down with those three, peering into the elevator, once the plate was off and the coal out. He even swayed to the engine's light roll as he made out that block of wood lodged between the edge of the screw and the cylinder wall. It was wet, and swelled, and jammed tighter than a drum.

That, in retrospect, understand. And then he went to work on it with them. Likely the packing hook wouldn't pull the chunk out, and Erickson would swear as he got a hammer and cold chisel out of his tool box. They'd be kneeling in that litter of coal and George could feel sharp chunks biting into his knees. He rubbed them and made a face as he took another report on the Scout special. They'd have their heads together, one setting the blade of the chisel, tapping carefully with the hammer. He could feel the warmth and smoothness of that hammer handle in his own palm.

He realized he hadn't been breathing properly. He'd held his breath as a man excited and in a hurry will, to set a chisel blade just right. He gasped through his mouth to relieve the gone feeling in his stomach and called St. Thomas. It was 9:33.

"How're they coming?"

"Still chipping away."

George's stomach commenced to ache. By the time the ache became pronounced the passenger special was due out of St. Thomas in eighteen minutes. If he had to delay it, or lay Erickson out— He rubbed his scraggly gray mustache vigorously with a knuckle.

No. 19 finally got out of town twenty-eight minutes late, only twelve minutes ahead of the Boy Scouts.

It was plenty hot in the dispatcher's office. Thick heat waves wriggled up from the train-shed roof outside and into the open windows, but that wasn't what set sweat on George's temples. Not much! It was working with Erickson to get them going.

Sitting in his chair, he hooked her up along with Erickson. He took it a notch at a time, his hand half closing and jerking when he thought about pulling up that reverse lever. George, back tense, got her into half stroke, along with Erickson. He, along with Erickson, got a swing on them and felt that big Mikado tremble under the beating she had to take, heard her exhaust shorten and sharpen and her drivers click faster over rail joints. He, along with Erickson, got her working smartly, easily, fast and faster, until she ran like a watch and a mill race.

Erickson's time gave him eighteen minutes to Brookville. He did it in sixteen, and George's mild blue eyes were almost glowing when the chief came in and asked about it.

George told him. "But he's got 'em going now," he said.

The chief spat and said, "Judas Priest!" as George began checking up on the southbound local. The local should be going into clear for the time freight at Lakeside, and when George called Lakeside, the operator said: "Yeah. Just heading in."

Then he cried: "Whoa! Hold on!" After a pause, he said: "Say, he broke 'em in two!"

"Where?" George hitched his chair up and shoved it back.

"Just got the first cars into the sidetrack. Drawbar, I guess."

George's stomach muscles tightened. "Where'd she let go?"

"Looks about six cars back."

"Judas Priest!" barked the chief. "Ask him—"

George knew what to ask, with 19 winding it northward and the main line likely to be tied up at Lakeside. Was there anybody around to help, was what he asked.

"Then get the baggageman up there!" he said, and his mild voice carried the suggestion of sharpness.

The flagman would be legging it up the track with his signals, see? The train crew might need help to get done what had to be done in the time they had to do it. They'd have to chain up that broken coupling, and Huston, the local's conductor, would be opening the caboose cellar and dragging the chain out alone. It would come a dozen or twenty links at a time, and George fought its rusty weight with Huston. The head brakeman would have to run back to where she'd broken in two, feet sliding in the ballast shoulder. The rain hadn't come that far north and it would be hot under the lee of those cars with the sun beating down, and the shack would sweat as he ran. George sweated and ran with him.

"Baggageman gone up?"

"On the run!"

George had to run with the baggageman too.

He was breathing rather fast, with all that running and chain lifting and hanging on to seventy-eight loads with Erickson less than twenty miles from the stalled local.

The head brakeman and the baggageman would be getting the broken drawbar out of the way. They'd have the air coupled and the engineer would be pumping it up as Athena came in to report 19 at 10:05. Erickson had gained two more minutes, and at the rate he was wheeling them, that local's crew wouldn't have any too much time to get into clear, and when George looked up at the chief, his mustache bristled because he shut his lips so tightly.

By then Huston would have the thirty feet of chain out on the ground and would be setting the brakes on the last two cars, so that when they backed the bad-order car up to where the chain lay and shut off, the rear wouldn't keep on going.

George heard three short whistle blasts. "Moving!" he said.

"Judas Priest!" said the chief, and spat and looked at the clock.

Minutes ticked off. "They're chaining her up," said Lakeside. "Baggageman's going to handle the switch, looks like."

Huston and his brakeman would be wrestling with the chain now. They'd uncouple the rear, so the chain wouldn't let go under the starting pull. They'd get the chained-up car into the house track with those ahead of it. The engine would go through, back down the side track and out onto the main line for the rest of them.

The engine backed past the Lakeside depot after the rest of them, just as Dollarton, eight miles away, reported 19.

"He's out there now!" said Lakeside. His eyes would be bunging, having caught the report on 19. He'd be expecting George to tell him to put the board out.

George hitched his chair up and shoved it back. He found his foot tapping rhythmically. It was like waiting for word that your first kid had finally been born. Something like that.

"Whistling in his flag!" said Lakeside.

George galloped for the caboose with the flagman. He lifted the pin with the brakeman. He stood beside the switch with the baggageman. He lifted his hand with Huston to give the highball and, with the engineer, opened the throttle.

"He's got 'em!" the Lakeside operator yelped. "They're into the switch!" he cried. "And 19's whistling at the mile board!" he said as George, out there with the baggageman, pulled on the switch handle and yanked it over and jammed it down into the groove and grabbed for the padlock dangling on its chain. After he set the hasp through the hole and squeezed the lock shut, he drew sort of a long breath.

"Judas Priest!" said the chief in a whisper, and made spitting motions as George took a report from up north.

Erickson had picked up ten full minutes, but, even so, was only sixteen minutes ahead of the special's time, and while the chief was saying everything'd ought to be all right now, George began to think about Bridge 127 and New Comfort Hill ahead of Erickson.

The chief could figure it was all right now to think about something else for a while. But George couldn't. He stayed in his chair, and his mind stayed on those two trains, and a drop of sweat trickled down the small of his back.

There was a slow order on Bridge 127, understand—fifteen miles an hour for freight trains, twenty-five for passenger. The order and the hill wouldn't bother the special, but Erickson, starting into four miles of climb at only fifteen an hour, would have to lug 'em. He'd just sit there and lug 'em clear to the top.

No. 19 picked up three more minutes in the dozen miles to Manchester, but that wasn't enough. The special, right on the dot and with faster time, was creeping up, with a chance of coming right up on his rear before New Comfort.

Erickson would be drifting down to that bridge now. He'd be drawing off six or eight pounds of air, setting the brakes screeching and pulling him down to his ordered speed by the time his engine trucks resounded hollowly on the trestle.

And then George bent forward in his chair, somewhat as Erickson would be doing, and opened her and commenced to fight. She'd roar and bark and shudder. Maybe she'd slip a little and he'd have to catch her up. Maybe he'd dust a little sand under her—just a little—and she'd commence to pick up slowly—oh, so slowly! George beat that engine with Erickson inch by inch, pole by pole, with never more than two minutes without a report coming in or having to call some operator on routine matters, understand. His head bobbed in painfully slow acceleration as the engine's exhaust would accelerate between the lug and the beating.

He called New Comfort. New Comfort had heard nothing of 19.

"And I can't help him," George said. He waited, considering. "Take an order," he said. "We'll have it if he can't make it. If he does, we'll annul."

And he dictated an order laying 19 out, writing in his order book as he spoke, putting Erickson into a hole after the try he'd made. The freight agent would roar, shippers

might squawk, but George had two important trains to con-
flict, a single track, and that was that.

But the operator, starting his X response, broke in:

"Can hear him now!" he said. "Can see him now!" he said,
and George knew the man could see only a mile down the
track.

It was 11:06. In two minutes Erickson would be on top and
have a chance. He was only eleven minutes ahead of the
Scouts, but he had a down grade and straight track in front
of him.

George made faces as Erickson got them on top, and when
Erickson would be settling back in his seat, George settled
back. Erickson could roll them until they whimpered, then,
and he would, and George chuckled a little as he recorded a
movement of the Northern Division's limited.

Erickson rolled them. He rolled them away from the pursuing special. He must have rolled them over sixty in places,
the way he made time. He ate up his lost minutes, two and
three between stations. He was a hogger from away back,
that Erickson. He rolled them to destination only six minutes late, and was probably washing up when the special
roared through the freight terminal, winging toward the
train shed which sent thick heat waves through George's
window.

The chief came in on his way to lunch and looked down
into the train shed as the special panted to a stop.

"So far, so good," he said. "Ought to be simple on the
Northern Division."

He turned away, grinning, from his glimpse of those twelve
coaches of kids. George couldn't see from his chair, but he
could hear them. Like a million or so happy crickets, they
sounded, he thought, as he took a report of a semaphore in
bad order.

The chief went out and George figured he'd eat as soon as
the hot shot got out of town, at 12:22. He was hungry after

all the heavy and fast work he'd done that forenoon. He
thought he'd eat, George did, and how wrong he was! How
wrong he was!

At 12:31 he reached for his transmitter plug to pull it out
and walk across the room for his lunch box, when Keenan
came on, the operator's voice shrill:

"Say, 448's just piled up right in front of here!"

George's eye went back to the clock, and lunch went out of
his mind. Keenan was seventy-four miles north; the Scout
special was four miles on its way, with a derailment staring
it in the face.

"How bad is it?"

"Looks tough. Main line's all torn to hell."

"Sidetrack?"

"Can see one gondola layin' half acrost it. Looks like more
on the other side."

"Get out there and look her over. We've got an hour and
fifty minutes before this blamed special. Move, now!"

His eyes went back to the clock, but his mind swept the
entire division, taking in trains, equipment, manpower.

A northbound extra freight would now be approaching
Florence, the next station below Keenan. The Keenan operator came back.

"It ain't so terrible bad," he said. "This gondola's on its
side and canted up over the sidetrack. There's a box car,
belly-up, restin' on the tie ends. The steel's all okay—"

"Get off the wire!" George's voice was just level. Dead
level.

He turned a black key switch down to call Florence. It
traveled slowly back to position. The Florence phone rang
as it traveled back. It took a second and a half to travel back,
but seemed to take, anyhow, a minute and a half. Goose
pimples came out on George's thin forearms as it traveled
back.

If those cars could be rolled out of the way at Keenan, he

could let his hot shot through the sidetrack without delay. To get a wrecker out from either terminal and not lay out the Scouts was impossible. But a tool car with a repair crew was at Savanna, thirty-three miles north of the special's position at the moment, thirty-seven miles south of the derailment.

But the nearest engine was pulling that northbound extra freight. That's why a second and a half seemed like a minute and a half, a week and a half, a month—

"Flor-ence!"—blithely, at his elbow.

"Seen anything of 1022?" That was the extra freight.

"Goin' by now. Just was goin' to—"

"Get him! Give him the board and get him!"

Over the wire George could distinguish the roll of wheels. Actually, he reached above his head as the operator would be doing to grasp the lever handle and throw the board for any eyes riding in the caboose to see—if there were eyes there to see.

And there were eyes there to see! George knew it before the operator yelped. He heard the note of free-rolling wheels change to the frit and scream of braked tires, heard the slack come out of her as air went on at the rear on the down grade: "Bunk, bunk, ka-bunk!"

There'd been eyes in the cupola. Conductor or brakeman was riding there and had caught the turn of the board. He'd leaned forward and grabbed the air valve, and George could feel the cool iron in his own sweating palm. He could feel, with the engineer, the sudden lag; his eyes, like the engineer's, went to the air gauge in the cab, and he, with the engineer, shut off and looked back.

"Got him!" the operator yelped, and before he'd said the two words, George had done all those things, felt, seen, heard them as if he were all over that distant train instead of right there in his chair.

"Let me talk to Cramer," he said, without excitement in

his voice. In his heart, understand, but not in his voice. The caboose couldn't be far from the depot then. Cramer, the extra's conductor, wouldn't have far to run when the operator called him. George's eye went to the clock, back to his train sheet.

"Listen, Cramer; 448's derailed at Keenan. 739's due there at 2:21. Set your train out and run back to Savanna for the tool car. Mebby they can open the sidetrack."

The operator, breathing audibly, came on for the order:

"Thirty-one; copy three. No. 47. To C. & E. Extra Freight 1022, t-e-n—" He gave the order calmly, and his hand, writing as he spoke, did not tremble. But inside—ah, inside! "Tell 'em to wheel it!" he said. "Little enough time!"

It would take five or six minutes to set the train out and get the light engine out of town, backing up on its nineteen-mile run for the tool car. Nothing was on the track ahead of the tool car, Savanna informed George. And they'd get the car-repair crew and any loose section men lined up.

It was hard waiting for 1022 to get out of Florence; harder just to sit there and take reports on other trains and issue other orders and watch the minutes zip off as that light engine backed up: 12:53 the Scout special rapped by Hillman, twenty-one miles south of Savanna. If the light engine could get down and get hold of that tool car without delay now; and if they could beat the special's time back to Keenan— And if everything went right just for once, today— Right, just for once! That's why it was hard for George to sit in his chair.

The engine made its first twelve miles in eighteen minutes, and George hitched forward and shoved back and rubbed his mustache. That was backing an engine up! Seven miles more into Savanna, and he breathed with only the upper part of his lungs as the minutes passed. He gulped and sort of moaned and took a lot of air through his mouth as Savanna reported them in at 1:16.

George, in his mind's eye, stood beside that tool car, ready to couple the air hose. He could see the repair crew hanging out the door, maybe some section men on the flat car behind it, straw hats in their laps because they were going for a ride.

He rode with them, pelting northward as, at 1:20, the Scout special passed Lee, forty-four miles from the tangle at Keenan. But the tool car did seventy down the grades, and the engineer hung onto it through Miller and Florence and on for Keenan, with George right behind him in the cab. They made the thirty-seven miles in that many minutes and had twenty-four to try to clear up the mess for the Scouts.

He gave Florence a 19 order for the special, putting them through the sidetrack at Keenan, and kept Keenan on the wire, getting news, word by word, move by move.

He could see men shucking from the tool car before it stopped. Two of them would have the end of the cable as it paid out; others would fall in, grabbing the inch-thick wire line. They'd strain against the lag of its reel, pulling it straight out for the first few feet, swinging up the tracks with it after they had a start. Heavy shoes would be digging into the cinders, shiny soles gleaming as men leaned their weight into the task. They'd hold the cable hard against their bellies as they strained, and they'd grunt while they toiled. George could feel that cable against his own belly. He grunted as they pulled up there at Keenan.

He didn't do only that. He trotted with two others across the tracks, carrying the heavy block and a length of chain. White oaks grew outside the fence there—good anchorage. With his own hands he passed the chain around a tree and helped rig the block.

Train reports came in and he marked them down, but all the same he could hear, if you understand, the car-repair foreman yelling orders and the excited shouts of the gang gathered there. He watched them, if you understand, as they fitted the cable's knuckle link into the front drawbar of the engine. He helped get it over to the block chained to the dead man, and then ran with the heavy hook over to the prostrate gondola.

The foreman would set that hook himself. His hands might tremble a little, being so short of time. George's hands trembled a little now. Quite a little.

They'd take out the slack slowly, engine exhaust little more than sighing as she backed. Maybe the hook would slip. Maybe the car would only slide instead of rolling over. George shuffled his feet and swallowed dryly. Maybe she'd even skid up on the side track and rip out a rail. He wiped his hands on his pants, they were so wet.

"Over she goes!" That was the Keenan operator, and George imagined the crash, the clank, the drifting dust, the assault on the box-car, with fourteen minutes before the special was due!

The chief sauntered in from lunch. He threw his cigar, third smoked, hard into the cuspidor and said, "Judas Priest!"

It was 2:11 before the chief found out all he wanted to know. As he talked, George got the cable over to the box-car —in a way, understand. He put the board out at Keenan, too, because the special was getting close. Then he went back to help set that hook.

"Taking out the slack," said the Keenan operator and, for an instant, George sat beside him, staring through the dusty depot windows. "Off she goes!" the operator cried. "And she's clear for 'em!"

"Take in your board. . . . Dispatcher." He marked down a report from the Chicago Division and wiped the sweat off his forehead with a wrist, and looked at the wrist and scowled oddly, and then his mustache bristled in a sort of sheepish grin. He'd expected to wipe coal dust and grease and rust off his forehead, but hadn't. He'd been right there in his chair, after all.

"Want to bring me a drink of water?" he asked the chief,

and began writing an order for the wrecker to clean up the main line.

It was 2:52 when he finished that, with the Scouts by Wells and rolling steadily on toward Lincolnville, the destination. He'd be glad when those kids got there and into trucks or busses for the run to camp. About all they had now which concerned him was the thirteen miles of Lincolnville hill, with no trains ahead of them for fifty miles and—

"Dispatcher." His voice was a trifle weary, as a man's has a right to be when he's been many places and done many things in seven short hours.

"This 's Kennedy! Lincolnville!" Kennedy was the yard foreman up there. "I'm in th' yard-limits booth. Gondola of scrap iron's out on the main line and 's goin' like a bat out of hell! We chased her this far, but couldn't catch it!"

George's stomach began to crawl. Something like an icicle traversed his spine.

He could see Kennedy's eyes popping, could see the fireman staring down into the booth and the engineer in the gangway, his face sort of gray, because a runaway was out there, starting down thirteen miles of grade with nothing between it and the Scout special.

Thirteen miles, understand, with no operator to help, no switchman to throw a derailer, no one to open a sidetrack and let the car go to the devil by itself. Thirteen miles, with plenty of curves around which to race, head-on into the special.

I'm giving it to you as it came to George. It takes time for me to give it as he saw it. It takes time, too, for me to tell how he remembered the Scouts at noon and thought their shrilling like that of happy crickets. It takes more time for me to write that his mustache bristled as he thought what those voices would sound like if that runaway met their engine.

It takes more time for me to tell you that the 871, switching at Lincolnville, was no small-wheeled switch engine, but a road engine, too light for modern heavy trains, but plenty fast. Plenty fast.

But all the time it took for all this to slip through George's head was the time it took to hitch his chair close up to his desk and jam it back—a split second.

"Take an order!" His voice was low, but, oh, so quick! He knew Kennedy grabbed for the pad. "Thirty-one; copy three. No. 52. To C. & E. Extra 871, e-i-g-h-t. . . . Leaving Lincolnville at 3:16, t-h-r-e-e—to work between Lincolnville and Milepost one-one-eight"—eyes narrowing.

If they couldn't pick it up by then; if they couldn't pick it up in fourteen miles, it was no use. If they couldn't stop that runaway before Milepost 118, there was no use sending that engine, its crew, Kennedy and the switchman, who surely would be there, into the mess that would be around the curve beyond that milepost.

"Complete!" he said, and pushed the buzzer for the chief, and began to pant a little, as if he'd run too far.

No operator was between that yard limits and the Scouts. No flesh-and-blood operator. Just an iron operator at Halfway, nine miles south of Lincolnville.

Sweat popped out on his forehead. He gripped his pen until his fingers ached to record a movement. "What now?" the chief asked, coming in grinning. His grin stayed, a ghastly thing, without any color in his face.

George tapped the Halfway key on his switchboard.

"Open," he said, and his voice was almost casual, though getting the word out was like lifting a great weight.

Their heads all but touched beside the telephone. The chief swallowed aloud as he got it—the hum of rails, the dull clang of running wheels, the sleek, slippery, slimy slink of the runaway as it slid past Halfway.

"Nine miles," George said, and held up his hand warningly.

He cocked his head closer to the phone. They'd be coming now. They'd have got that engine away like a racehorse. They'd be driving her until she rolled like a ship in a storm. They wouldn't be thinking she might throw herself off the track. They'd only be thinking that they must have it somewhere in them to make her roll even faster!

Kennedy and his switchman would be sitting on the pilot beam, fingers locked around the handrail. They'd be hunched forward, grimacing against the belch of wind, eyes half closed against the slap of wind. George winced sharply. That was when he thought how the ends of handkerchiefs, knotted about their throats, would bite as they snapped on cheeks or neck in the gush of wind. His torso was cold, as theirs would be, with the blast of wind bellying their shirts like balloons. His body was cold, either from that, or thought of the Scouts —like happy crickets—

They could hear that pursuing engine whistle a mile from Halfway. George got his eyes to the clock and to the train sheet and back to the clock.

"Eight minutes, twenty seconds; nine miles," he muttered as 871 crashed past Halfway, and let up on the clench of his teeth to stop the pain where his jaw muscles bulged.

Five miles, now, to Milepost 118. George could feel the chief tremble as he shoved himself away from the telephone.

A train movement was reported. "I'll get the boss," croaked the chief and went out quickly. Something cold and heavy lay at the pit of George's stomach, but somehow he answered the superintendent's sharp, biting questions.

He answered from the chair, but he wasn't there, understand? Queer, but he wasn't there. The part of him that felt and hoped and feared, I mean. That part of him was out, down on the footboard of 871. He had a grip on the handrail, his knees were bent, his eyes better than half closed to keep out the dust sucked up by the runaway, right ahead. Trucks clicked and snapped beneath him; the exhaust cannonaded above and behind.

That part of George which wasn't in the chair swayed forward, straining on the hand hold as if he'd lift her on faster. He had the knuckle open, one hand on its sun-warmed metal. He could feel the slackening of the speed, hear the dwindling bellow of the engine as they moved up on the runaway. He took the hand off the knuckle to reach out and lift the pin on the gondola if she didn't catch and couple on the bump— if she didn't catch and couple—

He sagged just a trifle against his desk. Perhaps, after all, the air was on. Perhaps, after all, the engine was coming to a stop within its working limits. Perhaps, after all, Kennedy was repeating the same despairing oath, over and over. Perhaps, after all, the runaway's start had been too great.

He didn't dare look at the superintendent. He stared at the clock. He leaned over to the telephone again, mouth working. Time seemed to be standing still. Or else flying so you couldn't mark its passage, as you can't see the spokes of a spinning wheel. He drew his shoulders up in a sort of a shrug. And stopped. And held his breath.

A long faint whistle blast came out of the transmitter. They waited. It came again, clearer, nearer. Was it a cry of triumph? Or a wail of defeat? Were they back at Halfway with that truant gondola? Or were they—well, just back?

An engine's exhaust rap became distinguishable. It came on smartly. Slowed. Stopped. Picked up laconically again. Stopped after a moment. No. 871 was into clear at Halfway.

"Jud—" began the chief, but couldn't finish. He looked almost beseechingly at George.

"Listen!" The superintendent's voice was a croak. "Lis—" he began again and, like the chief, couldn't finish. Then he straightened and made a funny sound in his throat. They all heard it, a chime whistle, blowing for a crossing. There'd be only one chime whistle on the Northern Division that afternoon! There'd be only one engine with such a whistle cracking it past Halfway that afternoon! That was the Scout special, on time, passing Extra 871 in its sidetrack, boring northward to destination, and as they heard her rip past the little depot, the chief began to laugh and the superintendent gripped George's shoulder.

Probably it was his grip which caused George to blot the time entry in the special's column at Halfway.

So, as I say, George arrived home at 4:34 P.M., and about 4:47 P.M., his wife, having scanned the amusement page of the evening newspaper said:

"Looks like a good Western picture at the Gem. Suppose we have an early supper and take in the seven-o'clock show? After all day in that blamed old chair, I'll bet a little action will do you good."

"It might, Ella," said George. "It might, at that."

THE STOLEN
RAILROAD TRAIN

By Marquis James

Marquis James

MARQUIS JAMES does not have to "fictionize" the characters whose biographies he writes. He can stick to facts, and carefully authenticated facts at that, and make them more absorbing, if not stranger, than most fiction.

He was born in Missouri; reared in the Cherokee Strip of Oklahoma; educated for a little while at Phillips University, and for a much longer while on various newspapers here and there. From a father who was a pioneering lawyer, from the other lawyers, the cattlemen and the frontier farmers whom he knew in and about Enid, Oklahoma, his boyhood home, he absorbed the lore and the color of the Southwest and of the older South from which it stemmed—much of which is distilled into his latest book, *The Cherokee Strip*. Besides important works on business history, his published works include *The Raven*, a life of Sam Houston, and *Andrew Jackson*, both of which won Pulitzer prizes for biography.

The selection here published, *The Stolen Railroad Train*, is from the volume *They Had Their Hour*.* It isn't railroad fiction but is straight fact—the facts about the most daring railroad episode in the War between the States, if not in entire railroad history, the seizure by Union soldiers of a train pulled by the engine *General*, and its recapture by Confederate forces after an incredible hundred-mile chase. It is included to show something of wartime railroading in those days, as well as something of the courage and determination of Americans on both sides of that struggle.

* Bobbs-Merrill.

THE STOLEN
RAILROAD TRAIN

By Marquis James

I

ON SUNDAY EVENING, the sixth of April, 1862, a tall, carefully dressed civilian with a heavy black beard and the
inflection of the South in his speech, presented himself to the
pickets of Mitchel's Division, encamped near Shelbyville,
Tennessee. His papers were in order and he was admitted.

Major General O. M. Mitchel and the spy sat down over a
map and it was daylight before they reached an agreement.
The scheme offered by the secret agent was such that even a
soldier as bold as Mitchel drew back. But step by step the
civilian justified the proposal. Audacity would promote its
success, he said, and success would be worth any risk. General
Mitchel's caller asked for thirty picked men from whom to
make his personal selections, and at length Mitchel agreed he
should have them.

That forenoon thirty volunteers were culled from the veteran Second, Twenty-first and Thirty-third Ohio Infantry
Regiments, the colonels passing upon the qualifications of
each man, who was told that a detail was being made up for
duty involving great personal peril. Though occupied with
plans for a military advance, General Mitchel himself took
the time to look over a few of the applicants. In the afternoon
the chosen thirty were sent to Shelbyville to purchase civilian

clothing and to report to J. J. Andrews, a tall civilian with a heavy beard who would be found on the streets of the town.

Shelbyville was full of soldiers, and, as soldiers often laid off their uniforms when going home on furlough, the thirty made their purchases without exciting comment. J. J. Andrews was easily identified. He sauntered about the streets, frequently entering a store to take an apparently idle interest in a soldier who was buying clothing. In the course of the afternoon all thirty approached him, singly or in small groups, for they were generally unknown to one another. He would ask what they were to report to him for. The soldiers would say that they did not know, or something of the sort. Andrews would ask them a few questions. Then in a casual tone he would say, "You may meet me tonight shortly after dark on the Wartrace Road a mile or so from town." To five or six he said, "There must be some mistake. I am not the man you are looking for." Their demeanor had not satisfied the Union spy.

Nor was Sergeant Major Marion Ross altogether satisfied with his interview. "A mile or so from town." "Shortly after dark." The instructions were so vague that he asked his friend Corporal William Pittenger what he thought of this Andrews. "I answered with enthusiasm," the Corporal related in after years. "The strong influence this singular man never failed to exert over those who were brought in contact with him was already at work. His pensive manner, his soft voice, not louder than a woman's, his grace and dignity made me at once declare him above the ordinary type of manhood. He was more like a poet than an adventurer, but I would have trusted him to the end of the earth."

2

Such whole-hearted endorsement put Ross in entire agreement with his friend's estimate. In fact, his curiosity was now aroused and he wished that he knew more about their new leader. And General Mitchel himself would have liked to know more about James J. Andrews, but all he knew or ever learned was that he was a good spy and described himself as a resident of Flemingsburg, Kentucky.

This town was equally unsatisfied with the scope of its knowledge. Andrews had come there two years before the war —from Virginia, as he said, but he gave no particulars. Something about the man suggested an interesting past. Flemingsburg believed he "had a story."

Perhaps one person in Flemingsburg really knew. She was Elizabeth Layton, to whom Mr. Andrews, after a long courtship, had just become engaged. They were to be married in two months, and a part of the bargain was that Andrews should abandon his perilous profession as a Union secret agent. The service he had proposed to Mitchel was intended to be his last. It was calculated to reveal to the world where his true loyalties lay, for in the South Andrews was known as a confidential agent of the Confederate armies.

The night following the interviews at Shelbyville was pitch dark and the rain fell in sheets. Twenty-four men, singly or in small parties, trudged through the mud of the Wartrace Road. Several of them were hopeless of meeting Andrews or anyone on such a night. Yet twenty-three of the twenty-four found him as readily as if they had had daylight and explicit directions to guide them. Andrews led them into a patch of woods near the road and began to speak in a quiet voice, stopping when the thunder was too loud for him to be heard distinctly.

He said that the expedition for which they had volunteered would take them into the enemy's country in disguise, which meant that anyone captured and detected would probably be hanged as a spy. Therefore, anyone unwilling to take the risk might now withdraw. Mr. Andrews paused. No one stirred and in a few sentences the speaker outlined the undertaking. In bands of two to four, the party would proceed to Marietta, Georgia, in the heart of the Confederacy, arriving on Thursday, four days hence. The following morning they would capture the north-bound mail train from Atlanta to Chattanooga, and run it to Bridgeport, Alabama, burning bridges behind them and rendering useless a hundred and thirty miles of railroad and telegraph. At Bridgeport, the party would meet Mitchel in the course of his southward advance. The destruction of these communications would paralyze the movement of Southern armies in the Central West and embarrass Lee's operations in Virginia.

"I shall be in Marietta with you or before you," said Mr. Andrews, "and there will tell each man what to do."

The route from Shelbyville to Marietta was long and difficult, and Andrews gave his men a few pointers on travel. If questioned, the best thing to say was that they were Kentuckians on their way to join the southern armies. But the men were to use their heads. They had been selected because they were thought capable of independent action.

"But what if they take us at our word and insist that we enlist?" asked one.

"Oh, be looking for a special regiment that is some place else. But if diplomacy fails, enlist any place."

"What if they won't take us?"

"No danger about that," replied Andrews. "The difficulty is not to get in but to stay out of the rebel army."

Andrews distributed seven hundred dollars of Confederate money and shook hands with each man. "Good-by. Good-by, Sergeant. Marietta not later than five, Thursday afternoon. Now, move out, men. Not more than four together."

3

On the appointed Thursday—April 10, 1862—two of the twenty-three reached Marietta. They strolled about town until late and went to bed uneasy. All day Friday they waited without a sign of one of their comrades, so far as they were able to recognize, the party having been together but once and then in the dark. The evening train from Chattanooga, however, brought Andrews and the remainder of his men, except two who were never heard from.

Incessant rain had made traveling difficult. When the party converged at Chattanooga to take the train for Marietta, Mr. Andrews had passed the word that the raid should be postponed one day. Thus all but the two men who had outstripped their schedule by a few hours had lain over at Chattanooga. Andrew's reason for the delay was that he felt it better to run the captured train into Bridgeport a day late than risk getting there ahead of Mitchel, whose advance, he figured, would be retarded by the weather.

At Marietta the men slept in different hotels and at dawn met Andrews in his room for final instructions. As usual the leader did not waste a word. "Buy tickets to different points up the line. Take seats in the same car. When the train stops at Big Shanty remain seated until I tell you to go. When the signal is given, if anybody interferes, shoot him."

The ranking soldier present was Sergeant Major Ross, whose courage was well known. Respectfully asking permission to speak, he suggested that the whole project be dropped or delayed for a reconsideration of all the factors involved. The delay of one day had altered everything, said Ross. Big Shanty was surrounded by troops; the line was congested by rolling stock being hurried out of Mitchel's reach; should Mitchel get to Bridgeport on time, the raiders, a day late, might miss him. Very courteously Mr. Andrews took up Ross's objections. He said the excitement and confusion caused by Mitchel's drive into Alabama would facilitate, not hinder, the flight of the fugitive train. "Boys," he concluded, after dismissing the last of the sergeant major's arguments, "I will succeed in this or leave my bones in Dixie."

That was the nearest to a heroic speech that J. J. Andrews ever made. He closed his watch and picked up his tall silk hat. The depot was just across the street and there was barely time before the train came in to buy tickets.

An hour later Conductor William A. Fuller walked through the coaches. Fuller was a wiry young fellow with a blond goatee and steady gray eyes.

"Big Shanty!" he called. "Twenty minutes for breakfast."

The sleepy passengers began to scramble toward the door. Andrews rose and beckoned to William Knight, who had been designated as engineer. The station was on the right side of the track. Four Georgia regiments were encamped on the left side and a bored sentry walked his post within a few feet of the cars. Andrews and Knight got off on the side next to the camp. They strolled forward and took a look at the engine. The cab was empty. Behind the tender were three empty freight cars. Andrews stopped beside the last one.

"Uncouple here," he told Knight.

He walked to the coach where the other men were waiting. Strolling part of the way down the aisle, Andrews paused and said in an ordinary tone, "Come on, boys, it's time to go."

4

Wilson W. Brown, the relief engineer, and George D. Wilson, the fireman, swung off and darted toward the locomotive. Knight was in the cab with his hand on the throttle. Andrews signaled the others to tumble into the box-cars—all the work of probably twelve seconds. Knight pulled the throttle half-way open. The wheels spun on the track but the train did not move. Then the wheels "bit" and the engine, the three box-cars attached, shot forward with a bound that piled the box-car passengers in a heap.

They scurried to their feet to look from the doors and

cheer. The start had been propitious beyond expectation. The picket, near enough to have used his bayonet, was staring in open-mouthed amazement—which, after all, was a fortunate negligence on the part of this green recruit, as each of Andrews' men carried a cocked pistol in his coat.

The feeling of triumph was short-lived, however. Less than a mile from the Confederate camp the engine began to falter, which was strange, for this locomotive, the *General*, was rated one of the best on the Western and Atlantic road. Shortly this excellent engine stopped dead, and Andrews, who was in the cab, called to the men in the cars to cut the telegraph wires. While John Scott, the smallest man in the party, was shinning up the telegraph pole, the trouble with the engine was located. The draft was shut off and the fire nearly out. Wood doused with oil soon had the fire-box roaring and they were on their way again.

Nothing now, said Andrews, who was not given to strong statements, could defeat them. Cutting the wires at this point was an excess precaution. There was no need for it so soon as Big Shanty lacked a telegraph office. Pursuit would be a matter of hours, the nearest engines available for this purpose being at Atlanta on the south and Kingston on the north, each about thirty miles from Big Shanty. Three south-bound trains from Chattanooga must be dealt with, but Andrews had arranged for that. He would adhere to the regular time on the mail train until Kingston was reached, and pass there a local freight, the first of these trains. After burning some eleven bridges beyond Kingston and keeping the wires cut to prevent word from getting ahead of them, the raiders could skirt Chattanooga by means of the "Y" below the town, and dash westward into Alabama where Mitchel would be waiting.

The schedule of the fast mail from Atlanta was sixteen miles an hour, and Andrews had difficulty in holding his engineers down to that speed, even though the track was crooked and soft from the rains, and the rails light and worn by the constant travel of military trains. The local freight must be passed at Kingston and it would be better to take it easy en route than to get to Kingston early and have to wait. So they jogged along, stopping once to relieve a track repair gang of its tools, and again to cut wires and lift a rail. The rail-lifting was slow work, as the tools they had taken were not the proper ones.

Half-way to Kingston Andrews received a surprise. Slowing up for a private switch that led to the Etowah Iron Works, five miles off the main line, he saw a locomotive fired up not forty feet from the main track. It was the veteran *Yonah*, owned by the iron works, and, carefully as he had explored the road, Andrews had not learned of its existence until now. Knight put on the brakes.

"We had better get rid of them," he suggested.

Andrews hesitated. "No," he said, "go ahead. It won't make any difference."

Andrews did not wish to risk a delay in meeting the freight at Kingston. Beyond Kingston he could destroy track and thwart pursuit by the *Yonah* as effectively as by attacking its crew and the iron works gang at the switch. The decision reveals an important difference in temperament between Andrews and his men. The men would have preferred to disable the *Yonah* on the spot. They were soldiers, the pick of a first-class division, and accustomed to direct methods. Andrews' way was otherwise—to avoid clashes and to finesse his way through tight places where the flick of an eyelash might mean death.

5

Seven miles from Kingston was Cassville, a wood and water stop. The box-car doors were closed while the engine crew replenished the tender. The wood-yard foreman strolled up, curious to know about the small train running on the schedule of the morning mail, with the mail's locomotive but none of the regular hands. Mr. Andrews had put on his silk hat in place of the cap he wore while the train was under way. This was a powder train, he said, being taken to General Beauregard, who was in a bad way for ammunition. The wood-yard foreman wished the powder-bearers luck.

Kingston was a good-sized town. The station platform was filled with people. The branch train for Rome was there, waiting for the Atlanta mail. Knight stopped alongside it and the Rome engineer called out:

"What's up? Fuller's engine and none of his men on board."

"I have taken this train by Government authority," said Andrews, "to run powder through to Beauregard." He waved his hand toward the box-cars in which his men were shut up.

The local freight was late. Andrews could get no information beyond that. Five minutes passed. Ten, fifteen minutes. To the men in the dark box-cars they seemed like hours.

Mr. Andrews walked up and down the station platform. One or two persons recognized him and saluted respectfully. He would stop and chat for a moment, belittling the alarming stories of Mitchel's advance into Alabama. People spoke of his poise during the vexatious delay of the powder train.

Finally the freight came in. Andrews hastened to ask the conductor to pull up so that the powder train could move. The conductor was willing to oblige, but indicated a red flag on the end of his train. Another train was behind, made up, the freight conductor said, of everything on wheels that could be gleaned out of Mitchel's path. "And where," asked the conductor, "did you say you were to deliver this powder to Beauregard?" "At Corinth, Mississippi," repeated Andrews. "Why, you can't get through," explained the conductor. "Mitchel is on the line at Huntsville." Andrews said he did not believe it, but the trainman said he knew, having just come from there.

Twenty minutes, thirty minutes dragged by. Andrews patrolled the station platform within earshot of the telegraph key. With one hand he raised his tall hat in polite greeting. The other hand enclosed the butt of a pistol in the pocket of his long black coat. Any attempt to send a suspicious message and the telegraph operator would be a dead man. Andrews told Knight to get word to the men in the cars as to how the land lay and have them ready to fight.

Knight and his crew oiled their engine. An old switch tender who had spent a lifetime on Southern railroads hung around asking questions. The powder-train story did not concern him. The strange crew in the General's cab interested the veteran, whose mind was an encyclopedia of Southern railway personnel. Where had they worked? Road? Division? Knight and his helpers answered in monosyllables. Fortunately Brown had once run a locomotive on the Mobile and Ohio, but there was no evading a certain discomfort in the old-timer's boring cross-examination.

Forty minutes is a long time to wait for a train under any circumstances. There was a whistle around the curve and Andrews met the refugee train as it pulled in, shouting directions for it to take its place on the already crowded sidings. This conductor also pointed to a red flag on his last car. The refugee train was running in two sections.

Fifty minutes. One hour—and a whistle that was music to the ears of twenty-two men. Section two rumbled in. Two regular trains from the north were now overdue. A prudent conductor would not have entertained a notion of leaving Kingston then. But Andrews said he would have to take the chance of passing the trains at Adairsville, ten miles farther on.

He waved for the switch admitting his train to the main line to be opened. But the old switch tender refused to budge. He had hung up his keys in the station and said that Andrews would have to show his authority to get them. The men inside the box-cars heard the old man's defiance and got their pistols ready. Not so the mannerly Mr. Andrews, whose life was filled with escapes from apprehensive moments. He laughed at the veteran's distemper and said he would get the keys. He did so, and the *General* was off after a delay of one hour and five minutes at Kingston, making in all an elapse of three hours and fifteen minutes from Big Shanty, thirty-two miles away.

"Push her, boys, push her," Andrews urged, and the *General* simply flew.

6

Well for Mr. Andrews that he had taken a chance and left for Adairsville. Four minutes after the *General* cleared the Kingston yards, a screaming whistle was heard from the south. The impatient passengers thought Fuller's train was coming and picked up their valises. It was Fuller—but he had not brought his train. The old *Yonah* rolled in, wheezing and blowing. Fuller swung off with the stunning story of the capture of the *General* at Big Shanty, and while the tracks were being cleared of the four trains congesting them, he managed to give a few of the details of his almost incredible pursuit.

At Big Shanty—now the town of Kenesaw—Fuller had just sat down to breakfast when a shout went up that his train had been stolen. He was on the platform in time to see the *General* and three box-cars glide around a curve. The station and camp were in an uproar. The dumfounded sentry stammered his story. It flashed on Fuller that the engine had been seized by deserters who would run it up the track for a few miles and take to the woods.

Let's get her back before we are badly out of time," he shouted and, with Engineer Cain and Superintendent Murphy of the machine shops, started up the track at a dead run.

Two miles out the three were winded and about to give up when they met the track gang whose tools Andrews had appropriated.

"If we can find the old *Yonah* at our end of the branch, we will get the scoundrels at Kingston where those extras will hold them up," said Fuller.

Before anyone could reply to this observation, push-car and riders, sailing down a grade, were pitched into a ditch, having struck a lifted rail.

The *Yonah* was overtaken just as she started to leave the main line. This old engine was full of complaints, but she had had her day, and on this day she turned back the calendar. The sixteen miles to Kingston were covered in thirteen minutes.

The crowd at the station told Fuller that his quarry had eluded him by four minutes. The conductor dashed into the telegraph office and sent a message north. He came back to the platform to hear the powder story, but, of course, did not learn that the "powder" cars were filled with armed men. Otherwise, he and his few helpers would have proceeded much more cautiously. The trains still were in a snarl on the tracks and, rather than lose any more time in switching, Fuller decided to abandon the *Yonah*. He uncoupled the engine of the Rome train and was off in a little better than six minutes, or about eleven minutes behind the Yankees.

The message telegraphed from Kingston did not get through because Andrews had stopped above the town in a blinding rain and cut the wires. Here the men also started to lift a rail, but their ineffective tools made clumsy work of it. Two-thirds of the rail was loose from the ties and the fugitives were about to give it up as a bad job, when the unmistakable whistle of a locomotive was heard from the south. Pursuit! It could be nothing else. The lifting of the rail became a matter of life or death. Most of the members of the party were large muscular men. They grasped the loose end of the rail, and with the strength born of peril heaved and pulled and heaved and pulled again. The iron rail snapped and the men tumbled in a heap. In an instant they were on their feet, in the cars and away.

At Adairsville the raiders were cheered by the sight of the south-bound freight waiting on the siding. At the depot Andrews received positive information that Mitchel held several miles of the railroad in Alabama. To Andrews, the Yankee raider, this was welcome news. To Andrews, the Confederate powder-train official, it presented complications. The story of the powder-train was rendered absurd on its face, but the marvelous address of the spy covered up the inconsistency long enough for him to get away. This took a little time, too. He tarried to reassure the freight crew and send them south with their trains. With the pursuers coming north, the freight going south, and a broken rail between them, Andrews expected his adversaries to be delayed long enough to give him the lead he needed.

To accomplish this he took further risks. The south-bound passenger train, following the freight, was overdue. The station officials advised Andrews to wait for it. Quite truthfully Andrews said he could not afford to wait, but he promised to run slowly, sending a flagman ahead on curves. Thus Andrews hoped to reach Calhoun, nine miles farther on, and deal with the passenger train there.

So as not to arouse suspicion, the *General* rolled cautiously away from the Adairsville depot. A quarter of a mile of this and Andrews told Knight to let her go.

7

The *Yonah*, ancient as she was, had been a faster locomotive than the engine Fuller took from the Rome train, but it was this fact—and an element of luck, as the conductor him-

self admitted—that averted disaster to the pursuit. Having
struck one broken rail, he was on the lookout for others, although the rain made it almost impossible to see anything.
Nevertheless Fuller did see, or thought he saw, where the
track had been tampered with in time to have his engineer
throw the engine into reverse and stop it on the brink of
the gap.

The conductor leaped from the useless locomotive and,
motioning to his men to follow again, started another foot-
race up the track, sliding and slipping in the mud. He had
not gone far when he saw the through freight headed toward
him. He flagged it down and backed it into Adairsville. The
freight engine was the *Texas* and there was no better locomotive on the line. It was detached and with a small party of
armed men started, tender forward, toward Calhoun.

Fuller believed he had the Yankees now. Andrews was
thought to be running slowly for fear of colliding with the
south-bound passenger train. If so, Fuller's quarry was boxed
between two trains. But if Andrews had succeeded in reaching Calhoun before the passenger left, Fuller himself would
risk a collision—unless he took care. Fuller did not take care.
The scent was hot and he sent the *Texas* racing ahead.

8

To this day Knight probably holds the speed record between Adairsville and Calhoun, Georgia. The nine miles
were behind the stolen engine in seven and one-half minutes
—over a track on which safe running was reckoned to be sixteen miles an hour. At that the Andrews party escaped destruction by thirty seconds. The passenger train had just
pulled out from the station when the wild *General* was seen
roaring toward it. The two locomotives, screaming under the
pressure of their brakes, were stopped within a few yards of

each other. The passenger engineer was trembling with fright—and he was angry. He refused to back up and let Andrews pass. A crisis seemed at hand, for Andrews literally did not have a minute to lose, as he had not yet cut the wires beyond Adairsville.

The rain still fell. The passenger conductor came up to see what was the trouble. Andrews addressed him in a tone of authority. He said he had requested the removal of his passenger train in order that powder for the front might not be delayed. Now he had no alternative but to issue orders. Without a word the conductor obeyed.

The spraddling hamlet of Calhoun diminished in the distance and the Yankees breathed more easily. Sergeant Major Ross had been right about a day's delay altering things. Yesterday it would have been smooth sailing—no extra trains, no excitement on the line, the powder-train story perfection itself. By now the raiders should have been near their triumphant journey's end. But today difficulties had been encountered only to be overcome. Five trains passed, a pursuit shaken off by a matter of minutes, and now they were on the main line once more with an open road ahead and a broken track behind.

9

Fuller covered the nine miles to Calhoun in ten minutes— which still leaves the Yankee Knight in possession of the record, however. The passenger train was still waiting. One scare in a day had been enough for the engineer. Andrews had tried vainly to send him on his way, which would certainly have been the end of Conductor Fuller. Instead, the raider's Nemesis, saved by another stroke of luck, rushed the *Texas*, running backward, out of Calhoun. Fuller himself perched on the tender where he could get a better view of the track.

The *General* and crew were within a few minutes of the first bridge to be burned—a covered wooden structure over the Oostanaula River. Here Andrews planned to render his success secure. He stopped a couple of miles in front of the bridge to cut wires and take up track. While some of the men tugged at a rail, others collected wood to fire the bridge. This would not be easy as the downpour continued and everything was soaking wet. The toiling rail crew was having its usual difficulties when they saw a sight that would not have startled them more had it been a ghost. A locomotive whistled and hove in view, burning up the track from the south. For the first time during the chase, Fuller sighted his quarry. Those at the rail yanked like men possessed. They could not break the rail, but they bent a yard of it some inches out of line. That seemed sufficient to wreck any train and the men jumped into the box-cars and the *General* started off.

It did not, however, wreck the mysterious pursuer. As far as the fugitives could see the oncoming engine shot over the bent rail as if nothing was wrong. On the tender Fuller had been so engrossed in observing the men in possession of the *General* that he overlooked the rail until it was too late to stop. Actually the rail had nearly thrown the pursuing crew from the cab and they thought they were lost. Not until afterward did they learn how fortunate they had been. The bent rail was on the inside of a curve and the weight of the swiftly moving engine was on the outside rail. The bent rail simply straightened and the train kept on the track.

As for the Yankees, all their chances of getting away now depended on firing the bridge, and Andrews attempted a dramatic expedient to gain time for that. He reversed the *General* and charged his pursuers. When going full tilt the rear box-car was uncoupled, and the *General* was started forward leaving the box-car to continue the assault.

The bridge was reached. On a fair day a little oil and a

faggot or two would have finished it, but it was raining harder than ever. Every stick of wood was soaked and the men kept their pistol ammunition dry with difficulty. Nevertheless a fire was kindled and coaxed to burn in one of the remaining cars. The plan was to leave the car in flames on the covered wooden bridge, but before the fire seemed the least encouraging here came the pursuers—pushing the raider's box-car in front of them. The Southerners had had some more luck. On a down grade the flying box-car might have driven them back for miles. But the hard-pressed Andrews was compelled to let it go on a level stretch. Fuller had simply reversed the *Texas* for a short distance, and, when the car slowed down, coupled it on and renewed the chase. When he came in sight of the bridge, Andrews was forced to flee, and, for the first time, a feeling that the fates were not on their side overtook the Union adventurers.

Certainly all the advantages of chance had gone against Andrews. Still, Fuller's pursuit had been intelligent and daring and he had made no mistakes. None can question the daring of Andrews, but he had made a grave mistake in not destroying the *Yonah*.

On the bridge the *Texas* picked up the smoking car that Andrews had tried to convert into a firebrand. Both cars were sidetracked at Reseca, a station a few hundred yards beyond the bridge.

Passing Reseca the *General* did not run very fast. It was plain that there was no eluding the *Texas* by speed alone. The Yankees tried wrecking her. As there was no time to stop and dismantle the track, a hole was rammed in the rear end of the remaining box-car, and ties and sticks of fire-wood were dropped out in the hope of obstructing a rail. The wood showed a maddening disposition to roll off the track, but now and then a piece stayed on and Fuller was forced by the protests of his men to slow up.

The desperate expedient was effective as long as the wood

lasted, but presently it was all gone, except a few sticks which were crammed into the fire-box for a sprint to the next wood-yard. There about half a load had been thrown aboard when the *Texas* hove in sight, but fuel was so precious that the men continued to pile it on and Fuller had to check speed to avert a collision. Before the hard-pressed *General* pulled out, Andrews' men had made a barrier of ties across the track, and, while Fuller removed it, the fugitives gained a few minutes' headway in their race to the water tank a few miles farther, for the *General's* boilers were almost dry. When the *General* left the water tank, the *Texas* was again in view.

Andrews was now ten or twelve miles from Dalton, which was a large town with a complicated arrangement of switches. Somehow the hard-pressed Yankees must gain a few minutes to take care of possible delays there. It was also equally important to cut the wires before a message could get into Dalton to raise enemies in his path. A tremendous spurt was made. Then a sudden stop by throwing the engine into reverse. Before the wheels had ceased to revolve, the diminutive Scott was out of the car and up a pole. Another party was building a barrier across the track. Another was frantically trying to wrench up a rail. Corporal Pittenger, a young law student who had got in the army with difficulty because of his thick spectacles, approached Mr. Andrews.

"We can capture that train if you are willing," said he.

"How?" asked Andrews.

Without hesitating for a word the corporal outlined an excellent plan of attack. "Block the track and place our party in ambush. Run our engine out of sight to disarm suspicion. When they stop to remove the obstruction we'll seize their engine and reverse it against any other trains that may be in this pursuit."

Mr. Andrews said nothing for a moment. "It is a good plan," he conceded. "It is worth trying." He glanced about as if studying the landscape. His survey was interrupted by the inevitable whistle of the pursuers. His glance shifted to the men who were vainly straining to force the rail.

"All aboard, boys," he called, and the dash to Dalton began.

10

The *Texas* was not in sight when the *General* halted a hundred yards in front of the Dalton depot, which was a large structure with a shed enclosing the track. Several local railwaymen came up. The powder story was useless now—what with one battered car which had been literally peeled for fire-wood and a company of correspondingly battered men. Andrews dropped from the cab to see if the switches were set for a clear track. They appeared to be. "I am running this train through to Corinth," he called out in general acknowledgement of a flood of inquiries, and, signaling Knight to proceed, caught on the engine step as it passed.

The *General* tore through the station shed and through the town to the great consternation of the citizens of Dalton. This consternation had not diminished when, five minutes later, Fuller's *Texas* rolled in, merely slowing up to drop a man who bolted like a shot from a gun and literally fell upon the telegrapher's key.

At the same instant, a mile from Dalton, in plain sight of a Confederate regiment, John Scott was climbing a telegraph pole. One minute later the wire was cut, putting a period where no period was intended in Conductor Fuller's message from Dalton. But this much got through:

"GEN LEADBETTER COMMANDER AT CHATTANOOGA. MY TRAIN CAPTURED THIS A M AT BIG SHANTY EVIDENTLY BY FEDERAL SOLDIERS IN DISGUISE. THEY ARE MAKING RAPIDLY FOR CHATTANOOGA POSSIBLY WITH THE IDEA OF BURNING . . ."

The Chattanooga commandant understood. What chance now for Andrews and his band? Every mile of flight from Fuller brought them a mile nearer to the open arms of the waiting Leadbetter.

Some distance from Dalton the road passed through a tunnel. Here was the place to turn and fight if they were ever to do it. But Andrews signaled to keep on. He meant to stake everything on the destruction of the Chickamauga River bridge. He ordered a fire built in the remaining box-car. This was hard to do. The car had been picked clean. Inside and out it was wet, and rain was still falling in torrents.

By drawing on the last quart of oil and almost the last stick of fire-wood a blaze was started. It crackled encouragingly and the spirits of the men rose with it. The little train stopped under the shelter of the bridge. As the oil burned from the surface of the wet wood the fire drooped a little. Still, the interior of the bridge shed was fairly dry, and given time the flames in the car would do their work.

A fire always holds an attraction, and, as this fire meant so much to its guardians, they half forgot their peril, and tarried to watch it. It was midday and the strain since dawn had been great. It was worth the price to relax. If the fire failed a few minutes would not matter.

The blaze picked up again. It took possession of the car, and tongues of flame licked the half-dry timbers of the bridge. No one had said a word for what might have been a full moment when the lookout called that the smoke of the *Texas* was in sight.

The burning car was uncoupled rather deliberately, and one of Andrews's men, who was brave enough to tell the truth, said that his heart sank. The *General* limped through the village of Ringgold. Wood was gone and oil was gone, but Andrews dared not stop.

Fuller picked up the blazing car on the bridge and dropped

it at Ringgold. A few miles from there he sighted the Yankees drilling along at fifteen miles an hour. They were burning their clothing to keep moving, and the journals on their
engine were melting from want of oil. Their last fragment of
hope was a wood-yard several miles away.

Fuller guessed their straits and their plan, but he lagged
behind. He knew that he was dealing with men who would
be desperate at bay. With the whole country behind him
aroused and other engines in pursuit by now, Fuller felt no
call to precipitate a battle.

The *General's* speed fell to eight miles an hour and Fuller
slacked accordingly, keeping a good quarter to half a mile in
the rear.

Knight said he could not make the wood-yard. Andrews did
not delay his decision.

"Jump and scatter, men, and be quick."

The men began to jump, rolling over and over until they
vanished in the dripping woods beside the right-of-way.
When all were off Knight reversed the engine and jumped.
The old *General* moved off toward the pursuers, but the
steam was too low for it to obtain any speed. Fuller simply
reversed, ran back away and let the *General* come up gradually and couple on.

A troop train which had joined the pursuit was soon on
the spot and the country was smothered with searchers under
orders to take the "train thieves," dead or alive.

All were taken, the captures requiring from a few hours
to ten days.

Nothing the soldiers of the North did during the war
aroused the South to a greater pitch than the exploit of these
twenty-one men. The newspaper *Southern Confederacy* of
Atlanta declared the preservation of the railroad bridges a
victory equal to Bull Run. "The mind and heart sink back at
the bare contemplation of the consequences that would have

followed the success" of the raid. It resulted in a reorganization of railroad administration in the South.

Mr. Andrews left his bones in Dixie. He was hanged in Atlanta, ten days before the date set for his wedding. When his Kentucky fiancée read an account of it in a newspaper, the shock killed her.

The following week seven others were executed, but the sudden thrust of a Federal column interrupted the court-martial of their fourteen comrades, eight of whom eventually escaped and reached the Union pickets. By this time the cry for vengeance had modulated and a few Southerners went so far as to show publicly their admiration for the Yankees' valor. A year later the six who remained in Confederate hands were exchanged for their weight in important political prisoners held by the North. President Lincoln received them at the White House and listened to an account of their adventures.

"A little luck with the battles now and the war will be over," he said.

AN ENGINEER'S
CHRISTMAS STORY

By John Alexander Hill

John Alexander Hill

FEW RAILROADERS WRITE, and fewer writers "railroad." John Alexander Hill did both. Like Warman and Hamblen he could pull the throttle as well as push the pen.

Born near Bennington, Vermont, on February 22, 1858, he started to work in a print shop at the age of fourteen. Later he turned to railroading and became an engineman for eight years. Like his contemporary Cy Warman, also a "hogger," Hill subsequently entered newspaper work and in 1885 founded and edited the Pueblo, Colorado, *Daily Press*. Again like Warman he became editor of a railroad periodical—*Locomotive Engineering*. In later life he was president of the Hill Publishing Company, the predecessor of the well-known McGraw-Hill Publishing Company.

While editing *Locomotive Engineering*, Hill wrote little story-essays of advice to enginemen which, because of their popularity, were put in book form under the title of *Jim Skeever's Object Lessons*. His next volume, *Stories of the Railroad*, was well received by rail workers and the layman. Mr. Hill's only other book was called *Progressive Examinations for Locomotive Engineers and Firemen*. It was for many years regarded as a standard textbook for men on both sides of the cab. John A. Hill died on January 24, 1916.

An Engineer's Christmas Story is improbable as an account of New England domestic relations, but it does present a picture of life in the cab in the 1860's, when engines bore names, firemen cleaned them and engineers helped to keep them in repair.

AN ENGINEER'S CHRISTMAS STORY

By John Alexander Hill

IN THE SUMMER, fall, and early winter of 1863, I was tossing chips into an old Hinkley insider up in New England for an engineer by the name of James Dillon. Dillon was considered as good a man as there was on the road: careful, yet fearless, kindhearted, yet impulsive, a man whose friends would fight for him and whose enemies hated him right royally.

Dillon took a great notion to me, and I loved him as a father; the fact of the matter is, he was more of a father to me than I had at home, for my father refused to be comforted when I took to railroading, and I could not see him more than two or three times a year at the most—so when I wanted advice I went to Jim.

I was a young fellow then, and being without a home at either end of the run, was likely to drop into pitfalls. Dillon saw this long before I did. Before I had been with him three months, he told me one day, coming in, that it was against his principles to teach locomotive-running to a young man who was likely to turn out a drunkard or gambler and disgrace the profession, and he added that I had better pack up my duds and come up to his house and let "mother" take care of me—and I went.

I was not a guest there: I paid my room rent and board just as I should have done anywhere else, but I had all the comforts of a home, and enjoyed a thousand advantages that money could not buy. I told Mrs. Dillon all my troubles, and found kindly sympathy and advice; she encouraged me in all my ambitions, mended my shirts, and went with me when I bought my clothes. Inside of a month, I felt like one of the family, called Mrs. Dillon "mother," and blessed my lucky stars that I had found them.

Dillon had run a good many years, and was heartily tired of it, and he seldom passed a nice farm that he did not call my attention to it, saying: "Jack, now there's comfort; you just wait a couple of years—I've got my eye on the slickest little place, just on the edge of M——, that I am saving up my pile to buy. I'll give you the *Roger William* one of these days, Jack, say good evening to grief, and me and mother will take comfort. Think of sleeping till eight o'clock—and no poor steamers, Jack, no poor steamers!" And he would reach over, and give my head a gentle duck as I tried to pitch a curve to a front corner with a knot: those Hinkleys were powerful on cold water.

In Dillon's household there was a "system" of financial management. He always gave his wife just half of what he earned; kept ten dollars for his own expenses during the month, out of which he clothed himself; and put the remainder in the bank. It was before the days of high wages, however, and even with this frugal management, the bank account did not grow rapidly. They owned the house in which they lived, and out of her half "mother" had to pay all the household expenses and taxes, clothe herself and two children, and send the children to school. The oldest, a girl of some sixteen years, was away at normal school, and the boy, about thirteen or fourteen, was at home, going to the public school and wearing out more clothes than all the rest of the family.

Dillon told me that they had agreed on the financial plan followed in the family before their marriage, and he used to say that for the life of him he did not see how "mother" got along so well on the allowance. When he drew a small month's pay he would say to me, as we walked home: "No cream in the coffee this month, Jack." If it was unusually large, he would say: "Plum duff and fried chicken for a Sunday dinner." He insisted that he could detect the rate of his pay in the food, but this was not true—it was his kind of fun. "Mother" and I were fast friends. She became my banker, and when I wanted an extra dollar, I had to ask her for it and tell what I wanted it for, and all that.

Along late in November, Jim had to make an extra one night on another engine, which left me at home alone with "mother" and the boy—I had never seen the girl—and after swearing me to be both deaf, dumb, and blind, "mother" told me a secret. For ten years she had been saving money out of her allowance, until the amount now reached nearly $2000. She knew of Jim's life ambition to own a farm, and she had the matter in hand, if I would help her. Of course I was head over heels into the scheme at once. She wanted to buy the farm near M——, and give Jim the deed for a Christmas present; and Jim mustn't even suspect.

Jim never did.

The next trip I had to buy some underclothes: would "mother" tell me how to pick out pure wool? Why, bless your heart, no, she wouldn't, but she'd just put on her things and go down with me. Jim smoked and read at home.

We went straight to the bank where Jim kept his money, asked for the President, and let him into the whole plan. Would he take $2100 out of Jim's money, unbeknown to Jim, and pay the balance of the price of the farm over what "mother" had?

No, he would not; but he would advance the money for the purpose—have the deeds sent to him, and he would pay the price. That was fixed.

Then I hatched up an excuse and changed off with the fireman on the M—— branch, and spent the best part of two lay-overs fixing up things with the owner of the farm and arranging to hold back the recording of the deeds until after

Christmas. Every evening there was some part of the project to be talked over, and "mother" and I held many whispered conversations. Once Jim, smiling, observed that, if I had any hair on my face, he would be jealous.

I remember that it was the fourteenth of December, 1863, that payday came. I banked my money with "mother," and Jim, as usual, counted out his half to that dear old financier.

"Uncle Sam'd better put that 'un in the hospital," observed Jim, as he came to a ragged ten-dollar bill. "Goddess of Liberty pretty near got her throat cut there; guess some Reb has had hold of her," he continued, as he held up the bill. Then laying it down, he took out his pocket-book and cut off a little three-cornered strip of pink court-plaster, and made repairs on the bill.

"Mother" pocketed her money greedily, and before an hour I had that very bill in my pocket to pay the recording fees in the courthouse at M——.

The next day Jim wanted to use more money than he had in his pocket, and asked me to lend him a dollar. As I opened my wallet to oblige him, that patched bill showed up. Jim put his finger on it, and then turning me around toward him, he said: "How came you by that?"

I turned red—I know I did—but I said, cool enough, " 'Mother' gave it to me in change."

"That's a lie," he said, and turned away.

The next day we were more than two-thirds of the way home before he spoke; then, as I straightened up after a fire, he said: "John Alexander, when we get in, you go to Aleck [the foreman] and get changed to some other engine."

There was a queer look on his face: it was not anger, it was not sorrow—it was more like pain. I looked the man straight in the eye, and said: "All right, Jim; it shall be as you say—but, so help me God, I don't know what for. If you will tell me what I have done that is wrong, I will not make the same mistake with the next man I fire for."

He looked away from me, reached over and started the pump, and said: "Don't you know?"

"No, sir, I have not the slightest idea."

"Then you stay, and I'll change," said he, with a determined look, and leaned out of the window, and said no more all the way in.

I did not go home that day. I cleaned the *Roger William* from the top of that mountain of sheet-iron known as a wood-burner stack to the back casting on the tank, and tried to think what I had done wrong, or not done at all, to incur such displeasure from Dillon. He was in bed when I went to the house that evening, and I did not see him until breakfast. He was in his usual spirits there, but on the way to the station, and all day long, he did not speak to me. He noticed the extra cleaning, and carefully avoided tarnishing any of the cab fittings—but that awful quiet! I could hardly bear it, and was half sick at the trouble, the cause of which I could not understand. I thought that, if the patched bill had anything to do with it, Christmas morning would clear it up.

Our return trip was the night express, leaving the terminus at 9:30. As usual, that night I got the engine out, oiled, switched out the cars, and took the train to the station, trimmed my signals and headlight, and was all ready for Jim to pull out. Nine o'clock came, and no Jim; at 9:10 I sent to his boarding-house. He had not been there. He did not come at leaving time—he did not come at all. At ten o'clock the conductor sent to the engine-house for another engineer, and at 10:45, instead of an engineer, a fireman came, with orders for John Alexander to run the *Roger William* until further orders. I never fired a locomotive again.

I went over that road the saddest-hearted man that ever made a maiden trip. I hoped there would be some tidings of Jim at home—there were none. I can never forget the blow it was to "mother"; how she braced up on account of her children but—oh, that sad face! Christmas came, and with it the daughter, and then there were two instead of one; the boy was frantic the first day, and playing marbles the next.

Christmas Day there came a letter. It was from him—brief and cold enough—but it was such a comfort to "mother." It was directed to Mary J. Dillon, and bore the New York postmark. It read:

> Uncle Sam is in need of men, and those who lose with Venus may win with Mars. Enclosed papers you will know best what to do with. Be a mother to the children—you have *three* of them.
>
> JAMES DILLON

He underscored the three—he was a mystery to me. Poor "mother"! She declared that no doubt "poor James's head was affected." The papers with the letter were a will, leaving her all, and a power of attorney, allowing her to dispose of or use the money in the bank. Not a line of endearment or love for that faithful heart that lived on love, asked only for love, and cared for little else.

That Christmas was a day of fasting and prayer for us. Many letters did we send, many advertisements were printed, but we never got a word from James Dillon, and Uncle Sam's army was too big to hunt in. We were a changed family: quieter and more tender of one another's feelings, but changed.

In the fall of '64 they changed the runs around, and I was booked to run in to M——. Ed, the boy, was firing for me. There was no reason why "mother" should stay in Boston, and we moved out to the little farm. That daughter, who was a second "mother" all over, used to come down to meet us at the station with the horse, and I talked "sweet" to her; yet at a certain point in the sweetness I became dumb.

Along in May, '65, "mother" got a package from Washington. It contained a tintype of herself; a card with a hole in it (made evidently by having been forced over a button), on which was her name and the old address in town; then there was a ring and a saber, and on the blade of the saber was etched, "Presented to Lieutenant Jas. Dillon, for bravery on the field of battle." At the bottom of the parcel was a note in a strange hand, saying simply, "Found on the body of Lieutenant Dillon after the battle of Five Forks."

Poor "mother"! Her heart was wrung again, and again the scalding tears fell. She never told her suffering, and no one ever knew what she bore. Her face was a little sadder and sweeter, her hair a little whiter—that was all.

I am not a bit superstitious—don't believe in signs or presentiments or prenothings—but when I went to get my pay the fourteenth of December, 1866, it gave me a little start to find in it the bill bearing the chromo of the Goddess of Liberty with the little three-cornered piece of court-plaster that Dillon had put on her wind-pipe. I got rid of it at once, and said nothing to "mother" about it; but I kept thinking of it and seeing it all the next day and night.

On the night of the sixteenth, I was oiling my Black Maria to take out a local leaving our western terminus just after dark, when a tall, slim old gentleman stepped up to me and asked if I was the engineer. I don't suppose I looked like the president, I confessed, and held up my torch, so I could see his face—a pretty tough-looking face. The white mustache was one of that military kind, reinforced with whiskers on the right and left flank of the mustache proper. He wore glasses, and one of the lights was ground glass. The right cheek-bone was crushed in, and a red scar extended across the eye and cheek; the scar looked blue around the red line because of the cold.

"I used to be an engineer before the war," said he. "Do you go to Boston!"

"No, to M——."

"M——! I thought that was on a branch."

"It is, but is now an important manufacturing point, with regular trains from there to each end of the main line."

"When can I get to Boston?"

"Not till Monday now; we run no through Sunday trains. You can go to M—— with me tonight, and catch a local to Boston in the morning."

He thought a minute, and then said, "Well, yes; guess I had better. How is it for a ride?"

"Good; just tell the conductor that I told you to get on."

"Thanks; that's clever. I used to know a soldier who used to run up in this country," said the stranger, musing. "Dillon; that's it, Dillon."

"I knew him well," said I. "I want to hear about him."

"Queer man," said he, and I noticed he was eying me pretty sharp.

"A good engineer."

"Perhaps," said he.

I coaxed the old veteran to ride on the engine—the first coal-burner I had had. He seemed more than glad to comply. Ed was as black as a negro, and swearing about coal-burners in general and this one in particular, and made so much noise with his fire-irons after we started, that the old man came over and sat behind me, so as to be able to talk.

The first time I looked around after getting out of the yard, I noticed his long slim hand on the top of the reverse-lever. Did you ever notice how it seems to make an ex-engineer feel better and more satisfied to get his hand on the reverse-lever and feel the life-throbs of the great giant under him? Why, his hand goes there by instinct—just as an ambulance surgeon will feel for the heart of the boy with a broken leg.

I asked the stranger to "give her a whirl," and noticed with what eager joy he took hold of her. I also observed with surprise that he seemed to know all about "four-mile hill," where most new men got stuck. He caught me looking at his face, and touching the scar, remarked: "A little love pat, with the compliments of Wade Hampton's men." We talked on a good many subjects, and got pretty well acquainted before we were over the division, but at last we seemed talked out.

"Where does Dillon's folks live now?" asked the stranger, slowly, after a time.

"M——," said I.

He nearly jumped off the box. "M——? I thought it was Boston!"

"Moved to M——."

"What for?"

"Own a farm there."

"Oh, I see; married again?"

"No."

"No!"

"Widow thought too much of Jim for that."

"No!"

"Yes."

"Er—what became of the young man that they—er—adopted?"

"Lives with 'em yet."

"So!"

Just then we struck the suburbs of M——, and, as we passed the cemetery, I pointed to a high shaft, and said: "Dillon's monument."

"Why, how's that?"

"Killed at Five Forks. Widow put up monument."

He shaded his eyes with his hand, and peered through the moonlight for a minute.

"That's clever," was all he said.

I insisted that he go home with me. Ed took the Black Maria to the house, and we took the street-cars to the end of the line, and then walked. As we cleaned our feet at the door, I said: "Let me see, I did not hear your name?"

"James," said he, "Mr. James."

I opened the sitting-room door, and ushered the stranger in.

"Well, boys," said "mother," slowly getting up from before the fire and hurriedly taking a few extra stitches in her knitting before laying it down to look up at us, "you're early."

She looked up, not ten feet from the stranger, as he took off his slouched hat and brushed back the white hair. In another minute her arms were around his neck, and she was murmuring "James" in his ear, and I, like a dumb fool, wondered who told her his name.

Well, to make a long story short, it was James Dillon himself, and the daughter came in, and Ed came, and between the three they nearly smothered the old fellow.

You may think it funny he didn't know me, but don't forget that I had been running for three years—that takes the fresh off a fellow; then, when I had the typhoid, my hair laid off, and was never reinstated, and when I got well, the whiskers—that had always refused to grow—came on with a rush, and they were red. And again, I had tried to switch with an old hook-motion in the night and forgot to take out the starting-bar, and she threw it at me, knocking out some teeth; and taking it altogether, I was a changed man.

"Where's John?" he said finally.

"Here," said I.

"No!"

"Yes."

He took my hand and said, "John, I left all that was dear to me once because I was jealous of you. I never knew how you came to have that money or why, and don't want to. Forgive me."

"That is the first time I ever heard of that," said "mother."

"I had it to buy this farm for you—a Christmas present—if you had waited," said I.

"That is the first time I ever heard of that," said he.

"And you might have been shot," said "mother," getting up close.

"I tried my darndest to be. That's why I got promoted so fast."

"Oh, James!" and her arms were around his neck again.

"And I sent that saber home myself, never intending to come back."

"Oh, James, how could you!"

"Mother, how can you forgive me?"

"Mother" was still for a minute, looking at the fire in the grate. "James, it is late in life to apply such tests, but love is like gold; ours will be better now—the dross has been burned away in the fire. I did what I did for love of you, and you did what you did for love of me; let us all commence to live again in the old way," and those arms of hers could not keep away from his neck.

Ed went out with tears in his eyes, and I beckoned the daughter to follow me. We passed into the parlor, drew the curtain over the doorway—and there was nothing but that rag between us and heaven.

RUN TO SEED

By Thomas Nelson Page

Thomas Nelson Page

THOMAS NELSON PAGE was born on April 23, 1853, at "Oakland," a plantation near Beaver Dam Station in Hanover County, and spent his early life in the Old Dominion listening to tales "befo' de War," observing the havoc and destruction resulting from near-by battles, and finally witnessing the lean, grinding years of Reconstruction.

He wrote about many phases of life in the South, and it is only natural that he should bring in the railroad, a vital part of life on both sides of the Mason and Dixon line. We find, for example, in *The New Agent* a delightful sketch of a station master in a small southern town. This selection is incorporated in his book *Under the Crust*. And his tale called *Old Sue* in *Pastime Stories* describes a refractory mule on a little village tramway.

Among his better-known works are a novel *Red Rock*, stories under the title of *The Old Gentleman of the Black Stock*, and his biography of Robert E. Lee. In 1913 Page was appointed by President Wilson as ambassador to Italy. He died on November 1, 1922.

Run to Seed is a story characteristic of the struggles of the post-war South, told with sympathy and understanding in the manner so typical of Page's writings. In the under-manned, under-powered, over-driven railways of the South in the years after what, in that region, is still known simply as "the War," it is hard to see the ancestors of today's great rail systems in the Southern states—but, as the story says, the seed was "damned good seed."

RUN TO SEED

By *Thomas Nelson Page*

I

JIM'S FATHER DIED at Gettysburg, up against the Stone Fence; went to Heaven in a chariot of fire on that fateful day when the issue between the two parts of the country was decided, when the slaughter on the Confederate side was such that after the battle a lieutenant was in charge of a regiment, and a major commanded a brigade.

This fact was much to Jim, though no one knew it: it tempered his mind, ruled his life. He never remembered the time when he did not know the story his mother, in her worn black dress and with her pale face, used to tell him of the bullet-dented sword and faded red sash which hung on the chamber wall.

They were the poorest people in the neighborhood. Everybody was poor, for the country lay in the track of the armies, and the war had swept the country as clean as a floor. But the Uptons were the poorest even in that community. Others recuperated, pulled themselves together, and began after a time to get up. The Uptons got flatter than they were before. The fences (the few that were left) rotted; the fields grew up in sassafras and pines; the barns blew down; the houses decayed; the ditches filled; the chills came.

"They're the shiftlesses' people in the worl'," said Mrs. Wagoner with a shade of asperity in her voice (or was it satisfaction?). Mrs. Wagoner's husband had been in a bombproof during the war, when Jim Upton, Jim's father, was with his company. He had managed to keep his teams from the quartermasters, and had turned up after the war the richest man in the neighborhood. He lived on old Colonel Duval's place, which he bought for Confederate money.

"They're the shiftlesses' people in the worl'," said Mrs. Wagoner. "Mrs. Upton ain't got any spirit; she jus' sets still and cries her eyes out."

This was true, every word of it. And so was something else that Mrs. Wagoner said in a tone of reprobation, about "people who made their beds having to lay on them," this process of incubation being too well known to require further discussion. But what could Mrs. Upton do? She could not change the course of Destiny. One—especially if she is a widow with bad eyes, and in poor health, living on the poorest place in the state—cannot stop the stars in their courses. She could not blot out the past, nor undo what she had done. She would not if she could. She could not undo what she had done when she ran away with Jim and married him. She would not if she could. At least the memory of those three years was hers, and nothing could take it from her—not debts, nor courts, nor anything. She knew he was wild when she married him. Certainly Mrs. Wagoner had been careful enough to tell her so, and to tell everyone else so, too. She would never forget the things she had said. Mrs. Wagoner never forgot the things the young girl said either—though it was more the way she had looked than what she had said. And when Mrs. Wagoner descanted on the poverty of the Uptons she used to end with the declaration: "Well, it ain't any fault of mine: she can't blame me, for Heaven knows I warned her: I did my duty!" Which was true. This was a duty Mrs. Wagoner seldom omitted. Mrs. Upton never thought of blaming her, or anyone else. Not all her poverty ever drew one complaint from her lips. She simply sat down under it, that was all. She did not expect anything else. She had given Jim to the South as gladly as any woman ever gave her heart to her love. She would not undo it if she could—not even to have him back, and God knew how much she wanted him. Was not his death glorious—his name a heritage for his son? She could not undo the debts which encumbered the land; nor the interest which swallowed it up; nor the suit which took it from her—that is, all but the old house and the two poor worn old fields which were her dower. She would have given up those, too, if it had not been for her children, Jim and Kitty, and for the little old enclosure on the hill under the big thorn-trees where they had laid him when they brought him back. No, she could not undo the past, nor alter the present, nor change the future. So what could she do?

In her heart Mrs. Wagoner was glad of the poverty of the Uptons; not merely glad in the general negative way which warms the bosoms of most of us as we consider how much better off we are than our neighbors—the "Lord-I-thank-thee-that-I-am-not-as-other-men-are" way—but Mrs. Wagoner was glad, positively. She was glad that any of the Uptons and the Duvals were poor. One of her grandfathers had been what Mrs. Wagoner (when she mentioned the matter at all) called "Manager" for one of the Duvals. She was aware that most people did not accept that term. She remembered old Colonel Duval—the *old* Colonel—tall, thin, white, grave, aquiline. She had been dreadfully afraid of him. She had had a feeling of satisfaction at his funeral. It was like the feeling she had when she learned that Colonel Duval had not forgiven Betty nor left her a cent. Mrs. Wagoner used to go to see Mrs. Upton—she went frequently. She carried her things —especially advice. There are people whose visits are like spells of illness. It took Mrs. Upton a fortnight to get over one of her visits—to convalesce. Mrs. Wagoner was a mother to her: at least she herself said so. In some respects it was rather akin to the substance of that name which forms in vinegar. It was hard to swallow: it galled. Even Mrs. Upton's gentleness was overtaxed—and rebelled. She had stood all the homilies—all the advice. But when Mrs. Wagoner, with her lips drawn in, after wringing her heart, recalled to her the warning she had given her before she married, she stopped standing it. She did not say much; but it was enough to make Mrs. Wagoner's stiff bonnet-bows tremble. Mrs. Wagoner walked out feeling chills down her spine, as if Colonel Duval were at her heels. She had meant to talk about sending Jim to school; at least she said so. She condoled with everyone in the neighborhood on the "wretched ignorance" in which Jim was growing up, "working like a common nigger." She called him "that ugly boy."

Jim was ugly—very ugly. He was slim, red-headed, freckle-faced, weak-eyed; he stooped and he stammered. Yet there was something about him, with his thin features, which made one look twice. Mrs. Wagoner used to say she did not know where that boy got all his ugliness from, for she must admit his father was rather good-looking before he became so bloated, and Betty Duval would have been "passable" if she had any "vivacity." She was careful in her limitations, Mrs. Wagoner was. Some women will not admit others are pretty, no matter what the difference in their ages: they feel as if they were making admissions against themselves.

Once when he was a boy Mrs. Wagoner had the good taste to refer in Jim's presence to his "homeliness," a term with which she sugar-coated her insult. Jim grinned and shuffled his feet, and then said, "Kitty's pretty." It was true. Kitty was pretty: she had eyes and hair. You could not look at her without seeing them—big brown eyes, and brown, tumbled hair. Kitty was fifteen—two years younger than Jim.

Jim never went to school. They were too poor. All he knew his mother taught him and he got out of the few old books in the bookcase left by the war—odd volumes of the Waverley novels, and *The Spectator, Don Quixote,* and a few others, stained and battered. He could not have gone to school if there had been a school to go to: he had to work; work, as Mrs. Wagoner had truthfully said, "like a common nigger." He did not mind it; a bird born in a cage cannot mind it much. The pitiful part is, it does not know anything else. Jim did not know anything else. He did not mind anything much—except chills. He even got used to them; would just lie down and shake for an hour and then go to plowing again as soon as the ague was over, with the fever on him. He had to plow, for corn was necessary. He had this compensation: he was worshiped by two people—his mother and Kitty. If other people thought him ugly, they thought him beautiful. If others thought him dull, they thought him wonderfully clever; if others thought him ignorant, they knew how wise he was.

Mrs. Upton's eyes were bad; but she saw enough to see Jim; the light came into the house with him. Kitty sat and gazed at him with speechless admiration; hung on his words, which were few; watched for his smile, which was rare. He repaid it to her by being—Jim. He slaved for her; waited for her (when a boy waits for his little sister it is something); played with her when he had time (this also was something); made traps for her; caught her young squirrels; was at once her slave and her idol. As he grew up he did not have time to play. He had to plow, "just like a common nigger," Mrs. Wagoner said. In this she spoke the truth.

It is a curious thing that farming paid better shortly after the war than it did later. Lands fell. Times grew harder. They were always growing harder with Jim. The land was worked out. Guano was necessary to make anything grow. Guano was bought on credit. The crops would not pay. Several summers there was drouth; crops failed. One of the two old mules he had died; Jim plowed with one. Then he broke his leg. When he got about again he was lame; the leg had shortened.

"They're the shiftlesses' folks in the worl'," said Mrs. Wagoner; "they can't blame me. Heaven knows I told—" etc. Which was true—more than true.

Jim plowed on, only slower than ever, thinner than ever, sleepier than ever.

One day something happened which waked him up. It was a Sunday. They went to church; they always went to church —old St. Ann's—whenever there was service. There was service there since the war only every first and third Sunday, and every other fifth Sunday. The Uptons and the Duvals had been vestrymen from the time they had brought the bricks over from England, generations ago. They had sat, one family in one of the front semicircular pews on one side of the chancel, the other family in the other. Mrs. Upton, after the war, had her choice of the pews; for all had gone but herself, Jim, and Kitty. She had changed, the Sunday after her marriage, to the Upton side, and she clung loyally to it ever after. Mrs. Wagoner had taken the other pew—a cold, she explained at first, had made her deaf. She always spoke of it afterward as "our pew." (The Billings, from which Mrs. Wagoner came, had not been Episcopalians until Mrs. Wagoner married.) Carrie Wagoner, who was a year older than Kitty, used to sit by her mother, with her big hat and brown hair. Jim, in right of his sex, sat at the end of his pew.

On this Sunday in question Jim drove his mother and Kitty to church in the horse cart. The old carriage was a wreck, slowly dropping to pieces. The chickens roosted in it. The cart was the only vehicle remaining which had two sound wheels, and even one of these "wabbled" a good deal, and the cart was "shackling." But straw placed in the bottom made it fairly comfortable. Jim always had clean straw in it. His mother and Kitty noticed it. Kitty looked so well. They reached church. The day was warm, Mr. Bickersteth was dry. Jim went to sleep during the sermon. He frequently did this. He had been up since four. When service was over he partially waked—about half-waked. He was standing in the aisle moving toward the door with the rest of the congregation. A voice behind him caught his ear.

"What a lovely girl Kitty Upton is." It was Mrs. Harrison, who lived at the other end of the parish. Jim knew the voice. Another voice replied.

"If she only were not always so shabby!" Jim knew this one also. It was Mrs. Wagoner's. Jim waked.

"Yes, but even her old darned dress cannot hide her. She reminds me of—" Jim did not know what it was to which Mrs. Harrison likened her. But he knew it was something beautiful.

"Yes," said Mrs. Wagoner; then added, "Poor thing, she's got no education, and never will have. To think that old Colonel Duval's fam'bly's come to this! Well, they can't blame me. They're clean run to seed."

Jim got out into the air. He felt sick. He had been hit vitally. This was what people thought! and it was true. He went to get his cart. (He did not speak to Kitty.) His home came before his eyes like a photograph: fences down, gates gone, houses ruinous, fields barren. It came to him as if stamped on the retina by a lightning-flash. He had worked— worked hard. But it was no use. It was true: they were "clean run to seed." He helped his mother and Kitty into the cart silently—doggedly. Kitty smiled at him. It hurt him like a blow. He saw every worn place, every darn in her old dress and little faded jacket. Mrs. Wagoner drove past them in her carriage, leaning out of the window and calling that she took the liberty of passing as she drove faster than they. Jim gave his old mule a jerk which made him throw up his head and wince with pain. He was sorry for it. But he had been jerked up short himself. He was quivering, too.

2

On the following Friday the President of one of the great railway lines which cross Virginia was in his office when the door opened after a gentle knock and someone entered. (The offices of presidents of railroads had not then become the secret and mysterious sanctums which they have since become.) The President was busily engaged with two or three of the directors, wealthy capitalists from the North, who had come down on important business. He was very much engrossed, and he did not look up directly. When he did he saw standing inside the door a queer figure—long, slim, angular—a man who looked a boy, or a boy who looked like a man, red-headed, freckle-faced, bashful, in a coat too tight even for his thin figure, breeches too short for his long legs; his hat was old and brown; his shirt was clean.

"Well, what do you want?" The President was busy.

It was Jim. His face twitched several times before any sound came:

"I w-w-w-want t-t-t-to ge-get a place."

"This is not the place to get it; I have no place for you." The President turned back to his friends. At the end of ten minutes, seeing one of his visitors look toward the door, he stopped in the middle of a sentence and glanced around.

The figure was still there—motionless. The President thought he had gone out. He had not.

"Well?" His key was high.

"I w-w-want to—to get a place."

"I told you I had no place for you. Go to the Superintendent."

"I—I've b-b-b-been to him."

"Well, what did he say?"

"Si-si-si-says he ain't got any place."

"Well, I haven't any. Go to Mr. Blake."

"I've b-been to him."

"Well, go to—to—" The President was looking for a paper. It occupied his mind. He did not think any further of Jim. But Jim was there.

"Go—go where?"

"Oh, I don't know—go anywhere—go out of here."

Jim's face worked. He turned and went slowly out. As he reached the door he said:

"Go-go-good evening, g-gentleman."

The President's heart relented: "Go to the Superintendent," he called.

Next day he was engaged with his directors when the door opened and the same apparition stepped within—tall, slim, red-haired, with his little, tight coat, short trousers, and clean shirt.

The President frowned.

"Well, what is it?"

"I—I—I w-w-w-went to—to the S-s-superintendent."

"Well, what about it?"

"Y-y-you told me to—to go—go to him. H-e-e ain't got any place." The directors smiled. One of them leaned back in his chair, took out a cigar and prepared to cut the end.

"Well, I can't help it. I haven't anything for you. I told you that yesterday. You must not come here bothering me; get out."

Jim stood still—perfectly motionless. He looked as if he had been there always—would be there always. The director with the cigar, having cut it, took out a gold match-box, and opened it slowly, looking at Jim with an amused smile. The President frowned and opened his mouth to order him out. He changed his mind.

"What is your name?"

"J-j-james Upton."

"Where from?"

Jim told him.

"Whose son are you?"

"C-c-c-captain J-j-james Upton's."

"What! You don't look much like him!"

Jim shuffled one foot. One corner of his mouth twitched up curiously. It might have been a smile. He looked straight at the blank wall before him.

"You are not much like your mother, either—I used to know her as a girl. How's that?"

Jim shuffled the other foot a little.

"R-r-run to seed, I reckon."

The President was a farmer—prided himself on it. The reply pleased him. He touched a bell. A clerk entered.

"Ask Mr. Wake to come here."

"Can you carry a barrel of flour?" he asked Jim.

"I—I'll get it there," said Jim. He leaned a little forward.

"Or a sack of salt? They are right heavy."

"I—I—I'll get it there," said Jim.

Mr. Wake appeared.

"Write Mr. Day to give this man a place as brakeman."

"Yes, sir. Come this way." This to Jim.

Jim electrified them all by suddenly bursting out crying. The tension had given way. He walked up to the wall and leaned his head against it with his face on his arm, shaking from head to foot, sobbing aloud.

"Thank you. I—I'm ever so much obliged to you," he sobbed.

The President rose and walked rapidly about the room.

Suddenly Jim turned and, with his arm over his eyes, held out his hand to the President.

"Good-by." Then he went out.

There was a curious smile on the faces of the directors as the door closed.

"Well, I never saw anything like that before," said one of them. The President said nothing.

"Run to seed," quoted the oldest of the directors; "rather good expression!"

"Damned good seed, gentlemen," said the President, a little shortly. "Duval and Upton—that fellow's father was in my command. Died at Gettysburg. He'd fight hell."

Jim got a place—brakeman on a freight-train. That night Jim wrote a letter home. You'd have thought he had been elected president.

It was a hard life: harder than most. The work was hard; the time was hard; the fare was hard; the life was hard. Standing on top of rattling cars as they rushed along in the night around curves, over bridges, through tunnels, with the rain and snow pelting in your face, and the tops as slippery as ice. There was excitement about it, too: a sense of risk and danger. Jim did not mind it much. He thought of his mother and Kitty.

There was a freemasonry among the men. All knew each other; hated or liked each other; nothing negative about it.

It was a bad road. Worse than the average. Twice the amount of traffic was done on the single track that should have been done. Result was men were ground up—more than on most roads. More men were killed in proportion to the number employed than were in service during the war. The *esprit de corps* was strong. Men stood by their trains and by each other. When a man left his engine in sight of trouble, the authorities might not know about it, but the men did. Unless there was cause he had to leave. Sam Wray left his engine in sight of a broken bridge after he reversed. The engine stopped on the track. The officers never knew of it; but Wray and his fireman both changed to another road. When a man even got shaky and began to run easy, the superintendent might not mind it, but the men did; he had to go. A man had to have not only courage but nerve.

Jim was not especially popular among men. He was reserved, slow, awkward. He was "pious" (that is, did not swear). He was "stuck up" (did not tell "funny things," by which was meant vulgar stories; nor laugh at them either). And according to Dick Rail, he was "stingy as h—l."

These things were not calculated to make him popular, and he was not. He was a sort of butt for the free and easy men who lived in their cabs and cabooses, obeyed their "orders," and owned nothing but their overalls and their shiny Sunday clothes. He was good-tempered, though. Took all their gibes and "dev'ling" quietly, and for the most part silently. So, few actually disliked him. Dick Rail, the engineer of his crew, was one of those few. Dick "despised" him. Dick was big, brawny, coarse: coarse in feeling, and when he had liquor in him he was mean. Jim "bothered" him, he said. He made Jim's life a burden to him. He laid himself out to do it. It became his occupation. He thought about it when Jim was not present; laid plans for it. There was something about Jim that was different from most others. When Jim did not laugh at a "hard story," but just sat still, some men would stop; Dick always told another harder yet, and called attention to Jim's looks. His stock was inexhaustible. His mind was like a spring which ran muddy water; its flow was perpetual. The men thought Jim did not mind. He lost three pounds, which, for a man who was six feet (and would have been six feet two if he had been straight) and who weighed 122 pounds, was considerable.

It is astonishing how one man can create a public sentiment. One woman can ruin a reputation as effectually as a churchful. One bullet can kill a man as dead as a bushel, if it hits him right. So Dick Rail injured Jim, for Dick was an authority. He swore the biggest oaths, wore the largest watch-chain, knew his engine better and sat it steadier than any man on the road. He had had a passenger train again and again, but he was too fond of whisky. It was too risky. Dick affected Jim's standing; told stories about him; made his life a burden to him. "He shan't stay on the road," he used to say. "He's stingier'n— Carries his victuals about with him— I b'lieve he sleeps with one o' them I-talians in a goods box." This was true—at least about carrying his food with him. (The rest was Dick's humor.) Messing cost too much. The first two months' pay went to settle an old guano bill; but the third month's was Jim's. The day he drew that he fattened a good deal. At least, he looked so. It was eighty-two dollars (for Jim ran extra runs—made double time whenever he could). Jim had never had so much money in his life; had hardly ever seen it. He walked about the streets that night till nearly midnight, feeling the wad of notes in his breast-pocket. Next day a box went down the country, and a letter with it, and that night Jim could not have bought a chew of tobacco. The next letter he got from home was heavy. Jim smiled over it a good deal, and cried a little, too. He wondered how Kitty looked in her new dress, and if the barrel of flour made good bread, and if his mother's shawl was warm.

One day he was changed to the passenger service, the express. It was a promotion, paid more, and relieved him from Dick Rail. He had some queer experiences being ordered around, but he swallowed them all. He had not been there three weeks when Mrs. Wagoner was a passenger on the train. Carrie was with her. They had moved to town. (Mr. Wagoner was interested in railroad development.) Mrs. Wagoner called him to her seat, and talked to him—in a loud voice. Mrs. Wagoner had a loud voice. It had the "carrying" quality. She did not shake hands; Carrie did, and said she was so glad to see him; she had been down home the week before —had seen his mother and Kitty. Mrs. Wagoner said they still kept their plantation as a country place. Carrie said Kitty looked so well. Her new dress was lovely. Mrs. Wagoner said his mother's eyes were worse. She and Kitty had walked over to see them to show Kitty's dress. She had promised that Mr. Wagoner would do what he could for him on the road.

Next month Jim went back to the freight service. He preferred Dick Rail. He got him. Dick was worse than ever:
his appetite was whetted by abstinence; he returned to his
attack with renewed zest. He never tired—never flagged. He
was perpetual; he was remorseless. He made Jim's life a
wilderness. Jim said nothing, just slouched along silenter
than ever, quieter than ever, closer than ever. He took to
going to another church on Sunday than the one he had attended, a more fashionable one than that. The Wagoners
went there. Jim sat far back in the gallery, very far back,
where he could just see the top of Carrie's head, her big hat
and her face, and could not see Mrs. Wagoner, who sat nearer
the gallery. It had a curious effect on him; he never went to
sleep there. He took to going uptown, walking by the stores
—looking in at the windows of tailors and clothiers. Once he
actually went into a shop and asked the price of a new suit of
clothes. (He needed them badly.) The tailor unfolded many
rolls of cloth and talked volubly: talked him dizzy. Jim
looked wistfully at them, rubbed his hand over them softly,
felt the money in his pocket; and came out. He said he
thought he might come in again. Next day he did not have
the money. Kitty wrote him she could not leave home to go
to school on their mother's account, but she would buy
books, and she was learning; she would learn fast, her mother
was teaching her; and he was the best brother in the world,
the whole world; and they had a secret, but he must wait.

One day Jim got a bundle. It was a new suit of clothes.
On top was a letter from Kitty. This was the secret. She and
her mother had sent for the cloth and made them; hoped
they would fit. They had cried over them. Jim cried a little,
too. He put them on. They did not fit, were much too large.
Under Dick Rail's fire Jim had grown even thinner than before. But he wore them to church. He felt that it would have
been untrue to his mother and Kitty not to wear them. He
was sorry to meet Dick Rail on the street. Dick had on a

black broadcloth coat, a velvet vest, and large-checked trousers. Dick looked Jim over. Jim winced, flushed a little; he was not so sunburned now. Dick saw it. Next week Dick caught Jim in a crowd in the "yard" waiting for their train. He told about the meeting. He made a double shot. He said, "Jim's in love, he's got new clothes! You ought to see 'em!" Dick was graphic; he wound up: "They hung on him like breechin' on his old mule. By—! I believe he was too—stingy to buy 'em, and made 'em himself." There was a shout from the crowd. Jim's face worked. There was a handspike lying near and he seized it. Someone grabbed him, but he shook him off as if he had been a child. Why he did not kill Dick no one ever knew. He meant to do it. For some time they thought he was dead. He laid off for a month. After that Jim wore what clothes he chose: no one ever troubled him.

So he went on in the same way: slow, sleepy, stuttering, thin, stingy, ill-dressed, lame, the butt of his tormentors.

He was made a fireman; preferred it to being a conductor. It led to being an engineer, which paid more. He ran extra trips whenever he could, up and double straight back. He could stand an immense amount of work. If he got sleepy he put tobacco in his eyes to keep them open. It was bad for the eyes, but waked him up. Kitty was going to take music next year, and that cost money. He had not been home for several months, but was going at Christmas.

They did not have any sight tests then. But the new directory meant to be thorough. Mr. Wagoner had become a director, had his eye on the presidency. Jim was one day sent for, asked about his eyes; they were bad. There was not a doubt about it. They were inflamed; he could not see a hundred yards. He did not tell them about the extra trips and putting the tobacco in them. Dick Rail must have told about him. They said he must go. Jim turned white. He went to his little room, close up under the roof of a little house in a back street, and sat down in the dark; thought about his mother and Kitty, and dimly about someone else; wrote his mother and Kitty a letter, said he was coming home—called it "a visit"; cried over the letter, but was careful not to cry on it. He was a real cry-baby—Jim was.

"Just run to seed," he said to himself, bitterly, over and over, "just run to seed." Then he went to sleep.

The following day he went down to the railroad. That was the last day. Next day he would be "off." The trainmaster saw him and called him. A special was just going out. The directors were going over the road in the Officers' car. Dick Rail was the engineer, and his fireman had been taken sick. Jim must take the place. Jim had a mind not to do it. He hated Dick. He thought of how he had pursued him. But he heard a voice behind him and turned. Carrie was standing down the platform, talking with some elderly gentlemen. She had on a traveling cap and ulster. She saw him and came forward—a step.

"How do you do?" She held out her little gloved hand. She was going out over the road with her father. Jim took off his hat and shook hands with her. Dick Rail saw him, walked around the other side of the engine, and tried to take off his hat like that. It was not a success; Dick knew it. Jim went.

"Who was that?" one of the elderly gentlemen asked Carrie.

"An old friend of mine—a gentleman," she said.

"Rather run to seed—hey?" the old fellow quoted, without knowing exactly why; for he only half recognized Jim, if he recognized him at all.

They started. It was a bad trip. The weather was bad, the road was bad, the engine bad; Dick bad—worse than all. Jim had a bad time: he was to be off when he got home. What would his mother and Kitty do?

Once Carrie came (brought by the President), and rode in the engine for a little while. Jim helped her up and spread his coat for her to sit on, put his overcoat under her feet; his heart was in it. Dick was sullen, and Jim had to show her about the engine. When she got down to go back to the car she thanked him—she "had enjoyed it greatly"—she "would like to try it again." Jim smiled. He was almost good-looking when he smiled.

Dick was meaner than ever after that, sneered at Jim—swore; but Jim didn't mind it. He was thinking of someone else, and of the rain which would prevent her coming again.

They were on the return trip, and were half-way home when the accident happened. It was just "good dusk," and it had been raining all night and all day, and the road was as rotten as mud. The special was behind and was making up. She had the right of way, and she was flying. She rounded a curve just above a small "fill," under which was a little stream, nothing but a mere "branch." In good weather it would never be noticed. The gay party behind were at dinner. The first thing they knew was the sudden jerk which came from reversing the engine at full speed, and the grind as the wheels slid along under the brakes. Then they stopped with a bump which spilled them out of their seats, set the lamps to swinging, and sent the things on the table crashing on the floor. No one was hurt, only shaken, and they crowded out of the car to learn the cause. They found it. The engine was half buried in wet earth on the other side of the little washout, with the tender jammed up into the cab. The whole was wrapped in a dense cloud of escaping steam. The noise was terrific. The big engineer, bare-headed and covered with mud, and with his face deadly white, was trying to get down to the engine. Someone was in there.

They got him out after a while (but it took some time) and laid him on the ground, while a mattress was got. It was Jim.

Carrie had been weeping. She sat down and took his head in her lap, and wiped his blackened and bleeding face with her lace handkerchief; and smoothed his wet hair.

The newspaper accounts, which are always reflections of

what public sentiment is, or should be, spoke of it—some, as "a providential"; others, as "a miraculous"; and yet others as "a fortunate" escape on the part of the President and the directors of the road, according to the tendencies, religious or otherwise, of their paragraphists.

They mentioned casually that "only one person was hurt —an employee, name not ascertained." And one or two had some gush about the devotion of the beautiful young lady, the daughter of one of the directors of the road, who happened to be on the train, and who, "like a ministering angel, held the head of the wounded man in her lap after he was taken from the wreck." A good deal was made of this picture, which was extensively copied.

Dick Rail's account, after he had come back from carrying the broken body down to the old place in the country, and helping to lay it away in the old enclosure under the big trees on the hill, was this:

"By ——!" he said, when he stood in the yard, with a solemn-faced group around him, "we were late, and I was just shaking 'em up. I had been meaner'n hell to Jim all the trip (I didn't know him, and you all didn't neither), and I was workin' him for all he was worth, I didn't give him a minute. The sweat was rolling off him, and I was damnin' him with every shovelful. We was runnin' under orders to make up, and we were just rounding the curve this side of Ridge Hill, when Jim hollered. He saw it as he raised up with the shovel in his hand to wipe the sweat off his face, and hollered to me, 'My God! Look, Dick! Jump!'

"I looked and Hell was right there. He caught the lever and reversed, and put on the air before I saw it, and then grabbed me and flung me clean out of the cab. 'Jump!' he says, as he give me a swing. I jumped, expectin' of course he was comin', too; and as I lit, I saw him turn and catch the lever and put on the sand. The old engine was jumpin' nigh off the track. But she was too near. In she went, and the tender right on her. You may talk about his eyes bein' bad; but when he gave me that swing, they looked to me like coals of fire. When we got him out 'twarn't Jim. He warn't nothin' but mud and ashes. He warn't quite dead; opened his eyes, and breathed oncet or twicet; but I don't think he knew anything, he was so smashed up. We laid him out on the grass, and that young lady took his head in her lap and cried over him (she had come and seed him in the engine), and said she knew his mother and sister down in the country (she used to live down there); they was gentlefolks; that Jim was all they had. And when one of them old director-fellows who had been swilling himself behind there come aroun', with his kid gloves on and his hands in his great-coat pockets, lookin' down, and sayin' something about, 'Poor fellow, couldn't he 'a' jumped? Why didn't he jump?' I let him have it; I said, 'Yes, and if it hadn't been for him, you and I'd both been frizzin' this minute.' And the President standin' there said to some of them, 'That was the same young fellow who came into my office to get a place last year when you were down, and said he had "run to seed." But,' he says, 'gentlemen, it was d—d good seed!' "

How good it was no one knew but two weeping women in a lonely house.

THE
NIGHT OPERATOR

By Frank L. Packard

Frank L. Packard

THE CREATOR OF Jimmie Dale and Shanghai Jim is seldom thought of as a railroad writer. Yet the late Frank L. Packard was not only a railway author in his own right, but also an ex-employee of a great railroad—the Canadian Pacific—in the Carleton Junction, Ontario, shops.

Frank Lucius Packard was born of American parents at Montreal, Quebec, on February 7, 1877. After receiving an education in Canadian and European universities he spent several years in railway and engineering work. With some five years of book learning, and several more of practical experience, Packard was well fitted to launch a new career: writing. It is only natural, too, that his first book, *On the Iron at Big Cloud,* should be on railroading. He had drawn on his own experience and that of his fellow workmen out on the line. After a hiatus of several years, Packard wrote *The Night Operator;* then after another interval he produced *Running Special*—all first-rate short stories of Canadian railway life.

Packard, however, is best known to the general public as the author of a score of detective or mystery stories. Among the most popular books are: *The Adventures of Jimmie Dale, Shanghai Jim, The Gold Skull Murders, Jimmie Dale and the Missing Hour,* and *The Dragon's Jaws.* His volume called *The Wire Devils* is a mystery tale concerning railroad telegraphy.

Toddles was a news "butch" who learned Morse—just as young Tom Edison did. Toddles was no Edison, but he didn't want to be. All he wanted was to railroad. How he got his wish is the story of *The Night Operator.* It might be the story of any fighting youngster of the time, forty or fifty years ago, and of any railroad, south or north of the border.

THE NIGHT OPERATOR

By Frank L. Packard

TODDLES, IN THE BEGINNING, wasn't exactly a railroad man
—for several reasons. First, he wasn't a man at all; second, he wasn't, strictly speaking, on the company's payroll;
third, which is apparently irrelevant, everybody said he was
a bad one; and fourth—because Hawkeye nicknamed him
Toddles.

Toddles had another name—Christopher Hyslop Hoogan
—but Big Cloud never lay awake at nights losing any sleep
over that. On the first run that Christopher Hyslop Hoogan
ever made, Hawkeye looked him over for a minute, said,
"Toddles," short-like—and, short-like, that settled the matter
so far as the Hill Division was concerned. His name was
Toddles.

Piecemeal, Toddles wouldn't convey anything to you to
speak of. You'd have to see Toddles coming down the aisle
of a car to get him at all—and then the chances are you'd
turn around after he'd gone by and stare at him, and it
would be even money that you'd call him back and fish for
a dime to buy something by way of excuse. Toddles got a
good deal of business that way. Toddles had a uniform and
a regular run all right, but he wasn't what he passionately
longed to be—a legitimate, dyed-in-the-wool railroader. His
paycheck, plus commissions, came from the News Company
down East that had the railroad concession. Toddles was a
newsboy. In his blue uniform and silver buttons, Toddles
used to stack up about the height of the back of the car seats

as he hawked his wares along the aisles; and the only thing that was big about him was his head, which looked as though it had got a whopping big lead on his body—and didn't intend to let the body cut the lead down any. This meant a big cap, and, as Toddles used to tilt the visor forward, the tip of his nose, bar his mouth, which was generous, was about all one got of his face. Cap, buttons, magazines and peanuts, that was Toddles—all except his voice. Toddles had a voice that would make you jump, if you were nervous, the minute he opened the car door, and if you weren't nervous you would be before he had reached the other end of the aisle— it began low down somewhere on high G and went through you shrill as an east wind and ended like the shriek of a brake-shoe with everything the Westinghouse equipment had to offer cutting loose on a quick stop.

Hawkeye? That was what Toddles called his beady-eyed conductor in retaliation. Hawkeye used to nag Toddles every chance he got, and, being Toddles' conductor, Hawkeye got a good many chances. In a word, Hawkeye, carrying the punch on the local passenger, that happened to be the run Toddles was given when the News Company sent him out from the East, used to think he got a good deal of fun out of Toddles—only his idea of fun and Toddles' idea of fun were as divergent as the poles, that was all.

Toddles, however, wasn't anybody's fool, not by several degrees—not even Hawkeye's. Toddles hated Hawkeye like poison; and his hate, apart from daily annoyances, was deep-seated. It was Hawkeye who had dubbed him "Toddles." And Toddles repudiated the name with his heart, his soul— and his fists.

Toddles wasn't anybody's fool, whatever the division thought, and he was right down to the basic root of things from the start. Coupled with the stunted growth that nature in a miserly mood had doled out to him, none knew better than himself that the name of "Toddles," keeping that nature stuff patently before everybody's eyes, damned him in his aspirations for a bona fide railroad career. Other boys got a job and got their feet on the ladder as call-boys, or in the roundhouse; Toddles got—a grin. Toddles pestered everybody for a job. He pestered Carleton, the super. He pestered Tommy Regan, the master mechanic. Every time that he saw anybody in authority Toddles spoke up for a job: he was in deadly earnest—and got a grin. Toddles with a basket of unripe fruit and stale chocolates and his "best-seller" voice was one thing; but Toddles as anything else was just—Toddles.

Toddles repudiated the name, and did it forcefully. Not that he couldn't take his share of a bit of guying, but because he felt that he was face to face with a vital factor in the career he longed for—he fought. And if nature had been niggardly in one respect, she had been generous in others: Toddles, for all his size, possessed the heart of a lion and the strength of a young ox, and he used both, with black and bloody effect, on the eyes and noses of the call-boys and younger element who called him Toddles. He fought it all along the line—at the drop of the hat—at a whisper of "Toddles." There wasn't a day went by that Toddles wasn't in a row; and the women, the mothers of the defeated warriors whose eyes were puffed and whose noses trickled crimson, denounced him in virulent language over their washtubs and the back fences of Big Cloud. You see, they didn't understand him, so they called him a "bad one," and, being from the East and not one of themselves, "a New York gutter snipe."

But, for all that, the name stuck. Up and down through the Rockies it was—Toddles. Toddles, with the idea of getting a lay-over on a siding, even went to the extent of signing himself in full—Christopher Hyslop Hoogan—every time his signature was in order; but the official documents in which he was concerned, being private matters between himself and the News Company, did not, in the very nature

of things, have much effect on the Hill Division. Certainly
the big fellows never knew he had any name but Toddles—
and cared less. But they knew him as Toddles, all right! All
of them did, every last one of them! Toddles was everlastingly and eternally bothering them for a job. Any kind of
job, no matter what, just so it was real railroading, and so a
fellow could line up with everybody else when the paycar
came along, and look forward to being something some day.

Toddles, with time, of course, grew older, up to about
seventeen or so, but he didn't grow any bigger—not enough
to make it noticeable. Even Toddles' voice wouldn't break—
it was his young heart that did all the breaking there was
done. Not that he ever showed it. No one ever saw a tear in
the boy's eyes. It was clenched fists for Toddles, clenched
fists and passionate attack. And therein, while Toddles had
grasped the basic truth that his nickname militated against
his ambitions, he erred in another direction that was equally
fundamental, if not more so.

And here, it was Bob Donkin, the night dispatcher, as
white a man as his record after years of train-handling was
white, a railroad man from the ground up if there ever was
one, and one of the best, who set Toddles— But we'll come
to that presently. We've got our "clearance" now, and we're
off with "rights" through.

No. 83, Hawkeye's train—and Toddles'—scheduled Big
Cloud on the eastbound run at 9:05; and, on the night the
story opens, they were about an hour away from the little
mountain town that was the divisional point, as Toddles, his
basket of edibles in the crook of his arm, halted in the forward end of the second-class smoker to examine again the
fistful of change that he dug out of his pants pocket with his
free hand.

Toddles was in an unusually bad humor, and he scowled.
With exceeding deftness he separated one of the coins from

the others, using his fingers like the teeth of a rake, and dropped the rest back jingling into his pocket. The coin that remained he put into his mouth, and bit on it—hard. His scowl deepened. Somebody had presented Toddles with a lead quarter.

It wasn't so much the quarter, though Toddles' salary wasn't so big as some people's who would have felt worse over it, it was his *amour propre* that was touched—deeply. It wasn't often that any one could put so bald a thing as lead money across on Toddles. Toddles' mind harked back along the aisles of the cars behind him. He had made only two sales that round, and he had changed a quarter each time —for the pretty girl with the big picture hat, who had giggled at him when she bought a package of chewing gum; and the man with the three-carat diamond tie-pin in the parlor car, a little more than on the edge of inebriety, who had got on at the last stop, and who had bought a cigar from him.

Toddles thought it over for a bit; decided he wouldn't have a fuss with a girl anyway, balked at a parlor-car fracas with a drunk, dropped the coin back into his pocket and went on into the combination baggage and express car. Here, just inside the door, was Toddles', or, rather, the News Company's chest. Toddles lifted the lid; and then his eyes shifted slowly and traveled up the car. Things were certainly going badly with Toddles that night.

There were four men in the car: Bob Donkin, coming back from a holiday trip somewhere up the line; MacNicoll, the baggage-master; Nulty, the express messenger—and Hawkeye. Toddles' inventory of the contents of the chest had been hurried—but intimate. A small bunch of six bananas was gone, and Hawkeye was munching them unconcernedly. It wasn't the first time the big, hulking, six-foot conductor had pilfered the boy's chest, not by many—and never paid for the pilfering. That was Hawkeye's idea of a joke.

Hawkeye was talking to Nulty, elaborately simulating ignorance of Toddles' presence—and he was talking about Toddles.

"Sure," said Hawkeye, his mouth full of banana, "he'll be a great railroad man some day! He's the stuff they're made of! You can see it sticking out all over him! He's only selling peanuts now till he grows up and—"

Toddles put down his basket and planted himself before the conductor.

"You pay for those bananas," said Toddles in a low voice —which was high.

"When'll he grow up?" continued Hawkeye, peeling more fruit. "I don't know—you've got me. The first time I saw him two years ago, I'm hanged if he wasn't bigger than he is now—guess he grows backwards. Have a banana?" He offered one to Nulty, who refused it.

"You pay for those bananas, you big stiff!" squealed Toddles belligerently.

Hawkeye turned his head slowly and turned his little beady, black eyes on Toddles, then he turned with a wink to the others, and for the first time in two years offered payment. He fished into his pocket and handed Toddles a twenty-dollar bill—there always was a mean streak in Hawkeye: he was more or less of a bully, none too well liked. His name on the payroll, by the way, was Reynolds.

"Take fifteen cents out of that," he said, with no idea that the boy could change the bill.

For a moment Toddles glared at the yellowback; then a thrill of unholy glee came to Toddles. He could just about make it: business all around had been pretty good that day, particularly on the run west in the morning.

Hawkeye went on with the exposition of his idea of humor at Toddles' expense; and Toddles went back to his chest and his reserve funds. Toddles counted out eighteen dollars in bills, made a neat pile of four quarters—the lead one on the bottom—another neat pile of the odd change, and returned to Hawkeye. The lead quarter wouldn't go very far toward liquidating Hawkeye's long-standing indebtedness—but it would help some.

Hawkeye counted the bills carefully, and crammed them into his pocket. Toddles dropped the neat little pile of quarters into Hawkeye's hand—they counted themselves—and Hawkeye put those in his pocket. Toddles counted out the odd change piece by piece, and as Hawkeye put *that* in his pocket—Toddles put his fingers to his nose.

Queer, isn't it—the way things happen? Think of a man's whole life, aspirations, hopes, ambitions, everything, pivoting on—a lead quarter! But then they say that opportunity knocks once at the door of every man; and, if that be true, let it be remarked in passing that Toddles wasn't deaf!

Hawkeye, making Toddles a target for a parting gibe, took up his lantern and started through the train to pick up the fares from the last stop. In due course he halted before the inebriated one with the glittering tie-pin in the smoking compartment of the parlor car.

"Ticket, please," said Hawkeye.

"Too busy to buysh ticket," the man informed him, with heavy confidence. "Whash fare Loon Dam to Big Cloud?"

"One-fifty," said Hawkeye curtly.

The man produced a roll of bills, and from the roll extracted a two-dollar note.

Hawkeye handed him back two quarters, and started to punch a cash-fare slip. He looked up to find the man holding out one of the quarters insistently, if somewhat unsteadily.

"What's the matter?" demanded Hawkeye brusquely.

"Bad," said the man.

A drummer grinned; and an elderly gentleman, from his magazine, looked up inquiringly over his spectacles.

"Bad!" Hawkeye brought his elbow sharply around to

focus his lamp on the coin; then he leaned over and rang it on the window sill—only it wouldn't ring. It was indubitably bad. Hawkeye, however, was dealing with a drunk—and Hawkeye always did have a mean streak in him.

"It's perfectly good," he asserted gruffly.

The man rolled an eye at the conductor that mingled a sudden shrewdness and anger, and appealed to his fellow travelers. The verdict was against Hawkeye, and Hawkeye ungraciously pocketed the lead piece and handed over another quarter.

"Shay," observed the inebriated one insolently, "shay, conductor, I don't like you. You thought I was—hic!—s'drunk I wouldn't know—eh? Thash where you fooled yerself!"

"What do you mean?" Hawkeye bridled virtuously for the benefit of the drummer and the old gentleman with the spectacles.

And then the other began to laugh immoderately.

"Same ol' quarter," said he. "Same—hic!—ol' quarter back again. Great system—peanut boy—conductor—hic! Pass it off on one—other passes it off on some one else. Just passed it off on—hic!—peanut boy for a joke. Goin' to give him a dollar when he comes back."

"Oh, you did, did you!" snapped Hawkeye ominously. "And you mean to insinuate that I deliberately tried to—"

"Sure!" declared the man heartily.

"You're a liar!" announced Hawkeye, spluttering mad. "And what's more, since it came from you, you'll take it back!" He dug into his pocket for the ubiquitous lead piece.

"Not—hic!—on your life!" said the man earnestly. "You hang onto it, old top. I didn't pass it off on *you*."

"Haw!" exploded the drummer suddenly. "Haw—haw, haw!"

And the elderly gentleman smiled.

Hawkeye's face went red, and then purple.

"Go 'way!" said the man petulantly. "I don't like you. Go 'way! Go an' tell peanuts I—hic!—got a dollar for him."

And Hawkeye went—but Toddles never got the dollar. Hawkeye went out of the smoking compartment of the parlor car with the lead quarter in his pocket—because he couldn't do anything else—which didn't soothe his feelings any, and he went out mad enough to bite himself. The drummer's guffaw followed him, and he thought he even caught a chuckle from the elderly party with the magazine and spectacles.

Hawkeye was mad; and he was quite well aware, painfully well aware that he had looked like a fool, which is about one of the meanest feelings there is to feel; and, as he made his way forward through the train, he grew madder still. That change was the change from his twenty-dollar bill. He had not needed to be told that the lead quarter had come from Toddles. The only question at all in doubt was whether or not Toddles had put the counterfeit coin over on him knowingly and with malice aforethought. Hawkeye, however, had an intuition deep down inside of him that there wasn't any doubt even about that, and as he opened the door of the baggage car his intuition was vindicated. There was a grin on the faces of Nulty, MacNicoll and Bob Donkin that disappeared with suspicious celerity at sight of him as he came through the door.

There was no hesitation then on Hawkeye's part. Toddles, equipped for another excursion through the train with a stack of magazines and books that almost hid him, received a sudden and vicious clout on the side of the ear.

"You'd try your tricks on me, would you?" Hawkeye snarled. "Lead quarters—eh?" Another clout. "I'll teach you, you blasted little runt!"

And with the clouts, the stack of carefully balanced periodicals went flying over the floor; and with the clouts, the

nagging, and the hectoring, and the bullying, that had ran-
kled for close on two years in Toddles' turbulent soul, rose
in a sudden all-possessing sweep of fury. Toddles was a
fighter—with the heart of a fighter. And Toddles' cause was
just. He couldn't reach the conductor's face—so he went for
Hawkeye's legs. And the screams of rage from his high-
pitched voice, as he shot himself forward, sounded like a
cageful of Australian cockatoos on the rampage.

Toddles was small, pitifully small for his age; but he wasn't
an infant in arms—not for a minute. And in action Toddles
was as near to a wild cat as anything else that comes handy
by way of illustration. Two legs and one arm he twined and
twisted around Hawkeye's legs; and the other arm, with a
hard and knotty fist on the end of it, caught the conductor a
wicked jab in the region of the bottom button of the vest.
The brass button peeled the skin off Toddles' knuckles, but
the jab doubled the conductor forward, and coincident with
Hawkeye's winded grunt, the lantern in his hand sailed ceil-
ingwards, crashed into the center lamps in the roof of the
car, and down in a shower of tinkling glass, dripping oil and
burning wicks, came the wreckage to the floor.

There was a yell from Nulty; but Toddles hung on like
grim death. Hawkeye was bawling fluent profanity and seeing red. Toddles heard one and sensed the other—and he
clung grimly on. He was all doubled up around Hawkeye's
knees, and in that position Hawkeye couldn't get at him very
well; and, besides, Toddles had his own plan of battle. He
was waiting for an extra heavy lurch of the car.

It came. Toddles' muscles strained legs and arms and back
in concert, and for an instant across the car they tottered,
Hawkeye staggering in a desperate attempt to maintain his
equilibrium—and then down—speaking generally, on a het-
erogeneous pile of express parcels; concretely, with an elo-
quent squnch, on a crate of eggs, thirty dozens of them, at
forty cents a dozen.

Toddles, over his rage, experienced a sickening sense of disaster, but still he clung; he didn't dare let go. Hawkeye's fists, both in an effort to recover himself and in an endeavor to reach Toddles, were going like a windmill; and Hawkeye's threats were something terrifying to listen to. And now they rolled over, and Toddles was underneath; and then they rolled over again; and then a hand locked on Toddles' collar, and he was yanked, terrier-fashion, to his feet.

His face white and determined, his fists doubled, Toddles waited for Hawkeye to get up—the word "run" wasn't in Toddles' vocabulary. He hadn't long to wait.

Hawkeye lunged up, draped in the broken crate—a sight. The road always prided itself on the natty uniforms of its train crews, but Hawkeye wasn't dressed in uniform then— mostly egg yolks. He made a dash for Toddles, but he never reached the boy. Bob Donkin was between them.

"Cut it out!" said Donkin coldly, as he pushed Toddles behind him. "You asked for it, Reynolds, and you got it. Now cut it out!"

And Hawkeye "cut it out." It was pretty generally understood that Bob Donkin never talked much for show, and Bob Donkin was bigger than Toddles, a whole lot bigger, as big as Hawkeye himself. Hawkeye "cut it out."

Funny, the egg part of it? Well, perhaps. But the fire wasn't. True, they got it out with the help of the hand extinguishers before it did any serious damage, for Nulty had gone at it on the jump; but while it lasted the burning oil on the car floor looked dangerous. Anyway, it was bad enough so that they couldn't hide it when they got into Big Cloud —and Hawkeye and Toddles went on the carpet for it the next morning in the super's office.

Carleton, "Royal" Carleton, reached for a match, and, to keep his lips straight, clamped them firmly on the amber mouthpiece of his brier, and stumpy, big-paunched Tommy Regan, the master mechanic, who was sitting in a chair by the window, reached hurriedly into his back pocket for his chewing and looked out of the window to hide a grin, as the two came in and ranged themselves in front of the super's desk—Hawkeye, six feet and a hundred and ninety pounds, with Toddles trailing him, mostly cap and buttons and no weight at all.

Carleton didn't ask many questions—he'd asked them before, of Bob Donkin—and the dispatcher hadn't gone out of his way to invest the conductor with any glorified halo. Carleton, always a strict disciplinarian, said what he had to say and said it quietly; but he meant to let the conductor have the worst of it, and he did—in a way that was all Carleton's own. Two years' picking on a youngster didn't appeal to Carleton, no matter who the youngster was. Before he was half through he had the big conductor squirming. Hawkeye was looking for something else—besides a galling and matter-of-fact impartiality that accepted himself and Toddles as being on exactly the same plane and level.

"There's a case of eggs," said Carleton at the end. "You can divide up the damage between you. And I'm going to change your runs, unless you've got some good reason to give me why I shouldn't?"

He waited for an answer.

Hawkeye, towering, sullen, his eyes resting bitterly on Regan, having caught the master mechanic's grin, said nothing; Toddles, whose head barely showed over the top of Carleton's desk, and the whole of him sizing up about big enough to go into the conductor's pocket, was equally silent —Toddles was thinking of something else.

"Very good," said Carleton suavely, as he surveyed the ridiculous incongruity before him. "I'll change your runs, then. I can't have you two *men* brawling and prize-fighting every trip."

There was a sudden sound from the window, as though

Regan had got some of his blackstrap juice down the wrong way.

Hawkeye's face went black as thunder.

Carleton's face was that of a sphinx.

"That'll do, then," he said. "You can go, both of you."

Hawkeye stamped out of the room and down the stairs. But Toddles stayed.

"Please, Mr. Carleton, won't you give me a job on—" Toddles stopped.

So had Regan's chuckle. Toddles, the irrepressible, was at it again—and Toddles after a job, any kind of job, was something that Regan's experience had taught him to fly from without standing on the order of his flight. Regan hurried from the room.

Toddles watched him go—speculatively, rather reproachfully. Then he turned to Carleton.

"Please give me a job, Mr. Carleton," he pleaded. "Give me a job, won't you?"

It was only yesterday on the platform that Toddles had waylaid the super with the same demand—and about every day before that as far back as Carleton could remember. It was hopelessly chronic. Anything convincing or appealing about it had gone long ago—Toddles said it parrot-fashion now. Carleton took refuge in severity.

"See here, young man," he said grimly, "you were brought into this office for a reprimand and not to apply for a job! You can thank your stars and Bob Donkin you haven't lost the one you've got. Now, get out!"

"I'd make good if you gave me one," said Toddles earnestly. "Honest, I would, Mr. Carleton."

"Get out!" said the super, not altogether unkindly. "I'm busy."

Toddles swallowed a lump in his throat—but not until after his head was turned and he'd started for the door so the super couldn't see it. Toddles swallowed the lump—and got out. He hadn't expected anything else, of course. The re- fusals were just as chronic as the demands. But that didn't make each new one any easier for Toddles. It made it worse.

Toddles' heart was heavy as he stepped out into the hall, and the iron was in his soul. He was seventeen now, and it looked as though he never would get a chance—except to be a newsboy all his life. Toddles swallowed another lump. He loved railroading; it was his one ambition, his one desire. If he could ever get a chance, he'd show them! He'd show them that he wasn't a joke, just because he was small!

Toddles turned at the head of the stairs to go down, when somebody called his name.

"Here—Toddles! Come here!"

Toddles looked over his shoulder, hesitated, then marched in through the open door of the dispatchers' room. Bob Don- kin was alone there.

"What's your name—Toddles?" inquired Donkin, as Tod- dles halted before the dispatcher's table.

Toddles froze instantly—hard. His fists doubled; there was a smile on Donkin's face. Then his fists slowly uncurled; the smile on Donkin's face had broadened, but there wasn't any malice in the smile.

"Christopher Hyslop Hoogan," said Toddles, unbending.

Donkin put his hand quickly to his mouth—and coughed.

"Um-m!" said he pleasantly. "Super hard on you this morning—Hoogan?"

And with the words Toddles' heart went out to the big dispatcher: "Hoogan"—and a man-to-man tone.

"No," said Toddles cordially. "Say, I thought you were on the night trick."

"Double-shift—short-handed," replied Donkin. "Come from New York, don't you?"

"Yes," said Toddles.

"Mother and father down there still?"

It came quick and unexpected, and Toddles stared for a moment. Then he walked over to the window.

"I haven't got any," he said.

There wasn't any sound for an instant, save the clicking of the instruments; then Donkin spoke again—a little gruffly.

"When are you going to quit making an ass of yourself?"

Toddles swung from the window, hurt. Donkin, after all, was like all the rest of them.

"Well?" prompted the dispatcher.

"You go to blazes!" said Toddles bitterly, and started for the door.

Donkin halted him.

"You're only fooling yourself, Hoogan," he said coolly. "If you wanted what you call a real railroad job as much as you pretend you do, you'd get one."

"Eh?" demanded Toddles defiantly; and went back to the table.

"A fellow," said Donkin, putting a little sting into his words, "never got anywhere by going around with a chip on his shoulder fighting everybody because they called him Toddles, and making a nuisance of himself with the Big Fellows until they got sick of the sight of him."

It was a pretty stiff arraignment. Toddles choked over it, and the angry blood flushed to his cheeks.

"That's all right for you!" he spluttered out hotly. "You don't look too small for the train crews or the roundhouse, and they don't call you Toddles so's nobody'll forget it. What'd *you* do?"

"I'll tell you what I'd do," said Donkin quietly. "I'd make everybody on the division wish their own name was Toddles before I was through with them, and I'd *make* a job for myself."

Toddles blinked helplessly.

"Getting right down to a cash fare," continued Donkin, after a moment, as Toddles did not speak, "they're not so far wrong, either, about you sizing up pretty small for the train crews or the roundhouse, are they?"

"No-o," admitted Toddles reluctantly, "but—"

"Then why not something where there's no handicap hanging over you?" suggested the dispatcher—and his hand reached out and touched the sender. "The key, for instance?"

"But I don't know anything about it," said Toddles, still helplessly.

"That's just it," returned Donkin smoothly. "You never tried to learn."

Toddles' eyes widened, and into Toddles' heart leaped a sudden joy. A new world seemed to open out before him in which aspirations, ambitions, longings all were a reality. A key! That *was* real railroading, the top-notch of railroading, too. First an operator, and then a dispatcher, and—and—and then his face fell, and the vision faded.

"How'd I get a chance to learn?" he said miserably. "Who'd teach me?"

The smile was back on Donkin's face as he pushed his chair from the table, stood up, and held out his hand—man-to-man fashion.

"I will," he said. "I liked your grit last night, Hoogan. And if you want to be a railroad man, I'll make you one—before I'm through. I've some old instruments you can have to practice with, and I've nothing to do in my spare time. What do you say?"

Toddles didn't say anything. For the first time since Toddles' advent to the Hill Division, there were tears in Toddles' eyes for someone else to see.

Donkin laughed.

"All right, old man, you're on. See that you don't throw me down. And keep your mouth shut; you'll need all your wind. It's work that counts, and nothing else. Now chase yourself! I'll dig up the things you'll need, and you can drop in here and get them when you come off your run tonight."

Spare time! Bob Donkin didn't have any spare time those days! But that was Donkin's way. Spence sick, and two men handling the dispatching where three had handled it before, didn't leave Bob Donkin much spare time—not much. But a boost for the kid was worth a sacrifice. Donkin went at it as earnestly as Toddles did—and Toddles was in deadly earnest.

When Toddles left the dispatcher's office that morning with Donkin's promise to teach him the key, Toddles had a hazy idea that Donkin had wings concealed somewhere under his coat and was an angel in disguise; and at the end of two weeks he was sure of it. But at the end of a month Bob Donkin was a god! Throw Bob Donkin down! Toddles would have sold his soul for the dispatcher.

It wasn't easy, though; and Bob Donkin wasn't an easy-going taskmaster, not by long odds. Donkin had a tongue, and on occasions could use it. Short and quick in his explanations, he expected his pupil to get it short and quick; either that, or Donkin's opinion of him. But Toddles stuck. He'd have crawled on his knees for Donkin anywhere, and he worked like a major—not only for his own advancement, but for what he came to prize quite as much, if not more, Donkin's approval.

Toddles, mindful of Donkin's words, didn't fight so much as the days went by, though he found it difficult to swear off all at once; and on his runs he studied his Morse code, and he had the "calls" of every station on the division off by heart right from the start. Toddles mastered the "sending" by leaps and bounds; but the "taking" came slower, as it does for everybody—yet even at that, at the end of six weeks, if it wasn't thrown at him too fast and hard, Toddles could get it after a fashion.

Take it all around, Toddles felt like whistling most of the time; and, pleased with his own progress, looked forward to starting in presently as a full-fledged operator. He mentioned the matter to Bob Donkin—once. Donkin picked his words and spoke fervently. Toddles never brought the subject up again.

And so things went on. Late summer turned to early fall, and early fall to still sharper weather, until there came the night that the operator at Blind River muddled his orders and gave No. 73, the westbound fast freight, her clearance against the second section of the eastbound Limited that doomed them to meet somewhere head-on in the Glacier Canyon; the night that Toddles—but there's just a word or two that comes before.

When it was all over, it was up to Sam Beale, the Blind River operator, straight enough. Beale blundered. That's all there was to it; that covers it all—he blundered. It would have finished Beale's railroad career forever and a day—only Beale played the man, and the instant he realized what he had done, even while the tail lights of the freight were disappearing down the track and he couldn't stop her, he was stammering the tale of his mistake over the wire, the sweat beads dripping from his wrist, his face gray with horror, to Bob Donkin under the green-shaded lamp in the dispatchers' room at Big Cloud, miles away.

Donkin got the miserable story over the chattering wire—got it before it was half told—cut Beale out and began to pound the Gap call. And as though it were before him in reality, that stretch of track, fifteen miles of it, from Blind River to the Gap, unfolded itself like a grisly panorama before his mind. There wasn't a half mile of tangent at a single stretch in the whole of it. It swung like the writhings of a snake, through cuts and tunnels, hugging the canyon walls, twisting this way and that. Anywhere else there might be a chance, one in a thousand even, that they would see each other's headlights in time—here it was disaster quick and absolute.

Donkin's lips were set in a thin, straight line. The Gap answered him; and the answer was like the knell of doom.

He had not expected anything else; he had only hoped against hope. The second section of the Limited had pulled out of the Gap, eastbound, two minutes before. The two trains were in the open against each other's orders.

In the next room, Carleton and Regan, over their pipes, were at their nightly game of pedro. Donkin called them—and his voice sounded strange to himself. Chairs scraped and crashed to the floor, and an instant later the super and the master mechanic were in the room.

"What's wrong, Bob?" Carleton flung the words from him in a single breath.

Donkin told them. But his fingers were on the key again as he talked. There was still one chance, worse than the thousand-to-one shot; but it was the only one. Between the Gap and Blind River, eight miles from the Gap, seven miles from Blind River, was Cassil's Siding. But there was no night man at Cassil's, and the little town lay a mile from the station. It was ten o'clock—Donkin's watch lay face up on the table before him. The day man at Cassil's went off at seven—the chance was that the day man MIGHT have come back to the station for something or other!

Not much of a chance? No—not much! It was a possibility, that was all; and Donkin's fingers worked—the Seventeen, the life and death—calling, calling on the night trick to the day man at Cassil's Siding.

Carleton came and stood at Donkin's elbow, and Regan stood at the other; and there was silence now, save only for the key that, under Donkin's fingers, seemed to echo its stammering appeal about the room like the sobbing of a human soul.

"CS—CS—CS," Donkin called; and then, "Seventeen," and then, "Hold second Number Two." And then the same thing over and over again.

And there was no answer.

It had turned cold that night and there was a fire in the

little heater. Donkin had opened the draft a little while before, and the sheet-iron sides now began to purr red-hot. Nobody noticed it. Regan's kindly, good-humored face had the stamp of horror in it, and he pulled at his scraggly brown mustache, his eyes seemingly fascinated by Donkin's fingers. Everybody's eyes, the three of them, were on Donkin's fingers and the key. Carleton was like a man of stone, motionless, his face set harder than face was ever carved in marble.

It grew hot in the room; but Donkin's fingers were like ice on the key, and, strong man though he was, he faltered.

"Oh, my God!" he whispered—and never a prayer rose more fervently from lips than those three broken words.

Again he called, and again, and again. The minutes slipped away. Still he called—with the life and death, the Seventeen—called and called. And there was no answer save that echo in the room that brought the perspiration streaming now from Regan's face, a harder light into Carleton's eyes, and a chill like death into Donkin's heart.

Suddenly Donkin pushed back his chair; and his fingers, from the key, touched the crystal of his watch.

"The second section will have passed Cassil's now," he said in a curious, unnatural, matter-of-fact tone. "It'll bring them together about a mile east of there—in another minute."

And then Carleton spoke—master railroader, "Royal" Carleton, it was up to him then, all the pity of it, the ruin, the disaster, the lives out, all the bitterness to cope with as he could. And it was in his eyes, all of it. But his voice was quiet. It rang quick, peremptory, his voice—but quiet.

"Clear the line, Bob," he said. "Plug in the roundhouse for the wrecker—and tell them to send uptown for the crew."

Toddles? What did Toddles have to do with this? Well, a good deal, in one way and another. We're coming to Toddles now. You see, Toddles, since his fracas with Hawkeye, had been put on the Elk River local run that left Big Cloud at 9:45 in the morning for the run west, and scheduled Big Cloud again on the return trip at 10:10 in the evening.

It had turned cold that night, after a day of rain. Pretty cold—the thermometer can drop on occasions in the late fall in the mountains—and by eight o'clock, where there had been rain before, there was now a thin sheeting of ice over everything, very thin—you know the kind—rails and telegraph wires glistening like the decorations on a Christmas tree, very pretty—and also very nasty running on a mountain grade. Likewise, the rain, in a way rain has, had dripped from the car roofs to the platforms—the local did not boast any closed vestibules—and had also been blown upon the car steps with the sweep of the wind, and, having frozen, it stayed there. Not a very serious matter; annoying, perhaps, but not serious, demanding a little extra caution, that was all.

Toddles was in high fettle that night. He had been getting on famously of late; even Bob Donkin had admitted it. Toddles, with his stack of books and magazines, an unusually big one, for a number of the new periodicals were out that day, was dreaming rosy dreams to himself as he started from the door of the first-class smoker to the door of the first-class coach. In another hour now he'd be up in the dispatcher's room at Big Cloud for his nightly sitting with Bob Donkin. He could see Bob Donkin there now; and he could hear the big dispatcher growl at him in his bluff way: "Use your head—use your head—HOOGAN!" It was always "Hoogan," never "Toddles." "Use your head"—Donkin was everlastingly drumming that into him; for the dispatcher used to confront him suddenly with imaginary and hair-raising emergencies, and demand Toddles' instant solution. Toddles realized that Donkin was getting to the heart of things, and that some day he, Toddles, would be a great dispatcher—like Donkin. "Use your head, Hoogan"—that's the way Donkin talked—"anybody can learn a key, but that doesn't make a railroad man out of him. It's the man when trouble comes who can think quick and think *right*. Use your—"

Toddles stepped out on the platform—and walked on ice. But that wasn't Toddles' undoing. The trouble with Toddles was that he was walking on air at the same time. It was treacherous running, they were nosing a curve, and in the cab, Kinneard, at the throttle, checked with a little jerk at the "air." And with the jerk, Toddles slipped; and with the slip, the center of gravity of the stack of periodicals shifted, and they bulged ominously in the middle. Toddles grabbed at them—and his heels went out from under him. He ricocheted down the steps, snatched desperately at the handrail, missed it, shot out from the train, and, head, heels, arms and body going every which way at once, rolled over and over down the embankment. And, starting from the point of Toddles' departure from the train, the right of way for a hundred yards was strewn with "the latest magazines" and "new books just out today."

Toddles lay there, a little, curled, huddled heap, motionless in the darkness. The tail lights of the local disappeared. No one aboard would miss Toddles until they got into Big Cloud—and found him gone. Which is Irish for saying that no one would attempt to keep track of a newsboy's idiosyncrasies on a train: it would be asking too much of any train crew; and, besides, there was no mention of it in the rules.

It was a long while before Toddles stirred; a very long while before consciousness crept slowly back to him. Then he moved, tried to get up—and fell back with a quick, sharp cry of pain. He lay still, then, for a moment. His ankle hurt him frightfully, and his back, and his shoulder, too. He put his hand to his face where something seemed to be trickling warm—and brought it away wet. Toddles, grim little warrior, tried to think. They hadn't been going very fast when he fell off. If they had, he would have been killed. As it was, he was hurt, badly hurt, and his head swam, nauseating him.

Where was he? Was he near any help? He'd have to get help somewhere, or—or with the cold and—and everything he'd probably die out here before morning. Toddles shouted out—again and again. Perhaps his voice was too weak to carry very far; anyway, there was no reply.

He looked up at the top of the embankment, clamped his teeth, and started to crawl. If he got up there, perhaps he could tell where he was. It had taken Toddles a matter of seconds to roll down; it took him ten minutes of untold agony to get up. Then he dashed his hand across his eyes where the blood was, and cried a little with the surge of relief. East, down the track, only a few yards away, the green eye of a switch lamp winked at him.

Where there was a switch lamp there was a siding, and where there was a siding there was promise of a station. Toddles, with the sudden uplift upon him, got to his feet and started along the track—two steps—and went down again. He couldn't walk, the pain was more than he could bear—his right ankle, his left shoulder, and his back. Hopping only made it worse—it was easier to crawl.

And so Toddles crawled.

It took him a long time even to pass the switch light. The pain made him weak, his senses seemed to trail off giddily every now and then, and he'd find himself lying flat and still beside the track. It was a white, drawn face that Toddles lifted up each time he started on again—miserably white, except where the blood kept trickling from his forehead.

And then Toddles' heart, stout as it was, seemed to snap. He had reached the station platform, wondering vaguely why the little building that loomed ahead was dark—and now it came to him in a flash, as he recognized the station. It was Cassil's Siding—*and there was no night man at Cassil's Siding!* The switch lights were lit before the day man left, of course. Everything swam before Toddles' eyes. There—there was no help here. And yet—yet perhaps—desperate hope came again—

perhaps there might be. The pain was terrible—all over him. And—and he'd got so weak now—but it wasn't far to the door.

Toddles squirmed along the platform, and reached the door finally—only to find it shut and fastened. And then Toddles fainted on the threshold.

When Toddles came to himself again, he thought at first that he was up in the dispatcher's room at Big Cloud with Bob Donkin pounding away on the battered old key they used to practice with: only there seemed to be something the matter with the key, and it didn't sound as loud as it usually did—it seemed to come from a long way off somehow. And then, besides, Bob was working it faster than he had ever done before when they were practicing. "Hold second"—second something—Toddles couldn't make it out. Then the Seventeen—yes, he knew that—that was the life and death. Bob was going pretty quick, though. Then "CS—CS—CS"—Toddles' brain fumbled a bit over that—then it came to him. CS was the call for Cassil's Siding. *Cassil's Siding!* Toddles' head came up with a jerk.

A little cry burst from Toddles' lips—and his brain cleared. He wasn't at Big Cloud at all—he was at Cassil's Siding—and he was hurt—and that was the sounder inside calling, calling frantically for Cassil's Siding—where he was.

The life and death—*the Seventeen*—it sent a thrill through Toddles' pain-twisted spine. He wriggled to the window. It, too, was closed, of course, but he could hear better there. The sounder was babbling madly.

"Hold second—"

He missed it again—and as, on top of it, the Seventeen came pleading, frantic, urgent, he wrung his hands.

"Hold second"—he got it this time—"Number Two."

Toddles' first impulse was to smash in the window and reach the key. And then, like a dash of cold water over him, Donkin's words seemed to ring in his ears: "Use your head."

With the Seventeen it meant a matter of minutes, per-

haps even seconds. Why smash the window? Why waste the
moment required to do it simply to answer the call? The
order stood for itself—"Hold second Number Two." That
was the second section of the Limited, eastbound. Hold her!
How? There was nothing—not a thing to stop her with. "Use
your head," said Donkin in a far-away voice to Toddles'
wobbling brain.

Toddles looked up the track—west—where he had come
from—to where the switch light twinkled green at him—and,
with a little sob, he started to drag himself back along the
platform. If he could throw the switch, it would throw the
light from green to red, and—and the Limited would take
the siding. But the switch was a long way off.

Toddles half fell, half bumped from the end of the platform to the right of way. He cried to himself with low moans
as he went along. He had the heart of a fighter, and grit to
the last tissue; but he needed it all now—needed it all to
stand the pain and fight the weakness that kept swirling
over him in flashes.

On he went, on his hands and knees, slithering from tie
to tie—and from one tie to the next was a great distance. The
life and death, the dispatcher's call—he seemed to hear it yet
—throbbing, throbbing on the wire.

On he went, up the track; and the green eye of the lamp,
winking at him, drew nearer. And then suddenly, clear and
mellow through the mountains, caught up and echoed far
and near, came the notes of a chime whistle ringing down
the gorge.

Fear came upon Toddles then, and a great sob shook him.
That was the Limited coming now! Toddles' fingers dug into
the ballast, and he hurried—that is, in bitter pain, he tried
to crawl a little faster. And as he crawled, he kept his eyes
strained up the track—she wasn't in sight yet around the
curve—not yet, anyway.

Another foot, only another foot, and he would reach the

siding switch—in time—in plenty of time. Again the sob—but now in a burst of relief that, for the moment, made him forget his hurts. He was in time!

He flung himself at the switch lever, tugged upon it—and then, trembling, every ounce of remaining strength seeming to ooze from him, he covered his face with his hands. It was *locked*—padlocked.

Came a rumble now—a distant roar, growing louder and louder, reverberating down the canyon walls—louder and louder—nearer and nearer. "Hold second Number Two. Hold second Number Two"—the Seventeen, the life and death, pleading with him to hold Number Two. And she was coming now, coming—and—and—the switch was locked. The deadly nausea racked Toddles again; there was nothing to do now—nothing. He couldn't stop her—couldn't stop her. He'd—he'd tried—very hard—and—and he couldn't stop her now. He took his hands from his face, and stole a glance up the track, afraid almost, with the horror that was upon him, to look. She hadn't swung the curve yet, but she would in a minute—and come pounding down the stretch at fifty miles an hour, shoot by him like a rocket to where, somewhere ahead, in some form, he did not know what, only knew that it was there, death and ruin and—

"*Use your head!*" snapped Donkin's voice to his consciousness.

Toddles' eyes were on the light above his head. It blinked *red* at him as he stood on the track facing it; the green rays were shooting up and down the line. He couldn't swing the switch—but the *lamp* was there—and there was the red side to show just by turning it. He remembered then that the lamp fitted into a socket at the top of the switch stand, and could be lifted off—if he could reach it!

It wasn't very high, for an ordinary-sized man—for an ordinary-sized man had to get at it to trim and fill it daily—

only Toddles wasn't an ordinary-sized man. It was just nine or ten feet above the rails—just a standard siding switch.

Toddles gritted his teeth and climbed upon the base of the switch—and nearly fainted as his ankle swung against the rod. A foot above the base was a footrest for a man to stand on and reach up for the lamp, and Toddles drew himself up and got his foot on it—and then at his full height the tips of his fingers only just touched the bottom of the lamp. Toddles cried aloud, and the tears streamed down his face now. Oh, if he weren't hurt—if he could only shin up another foot—but—but it was all he could do to hang there where he was.

What was that! He turned his head. Up the track, sweeping in a great circle as it swung the curve, a headlight's glare cut through the night—and Toddles "shinned" the foot. He tugged and tore at the lamp, tugged and tore at it, loosened it, lifted it from its socket, sprawled and wriggled with it to the ground—and turned the red side of the lamp against second Number Two.

The quick, short blasts of a whistle answered, then the crunch and grind and scream of biting brake-shoes—and the big mountain racer, the 1012, pulling the second section of the Limited that night, stopped with its pilot nosing a diminutive figure in a torn and silver-buttoned uniform, whose hair was clotted red, and whose face was covered with blood and dirt.

Masters, the engineer, and Pete Leroy, his fireman, swung from the gangways; Kelly, the conductor, came running up from the forward coach.

Kelly shoved his lamp into Toddles' face—and whistled low under his breath.

"Toddles!" he gasped; and then, quick as a steel trap: "What's wrong?"

"I don't know," said Toddles weakly. "There's—there's something wrong. Get into the clear—on the siding."

"Something wrong," repeated Kelly, "and you don't—"

But Masters cut the conductor short with a grab at the other's arm that was like the shutting of a vise—and then bolted for his engine like a gopher for its hole. From down the track came the heavy, grumbling roar of a freight. Everybody flew then, and there was quick work done in the next half minute—and none too quickly done. The Limited was no more than on the siding when the fast freight rolled her long string of flats, boxes and gondolas thundering by.

And while she passed, Toddles, on the platform, stammered out his story to Kelly.

Kelly didn't say anything—then. With the express messenger and a brakeman carrying Toddles, Kelly kicked in the station door and set his lamp down on the operator's table.

"Hold me up," whispered Toddles—and, while they held him, he made the dispatcher's call.

Big Cloud answered him on the instant. Haltingly, Toddles reported the section "in" and the freight "out"—only he did it very slowly, and he couldn't think very much more, for things were going black. He got an order for the Limited to run to Blind River and told Kelly, and got the "complete" —and then Big Cloud asked who was on the wire, and Toddles answered that in a mechanical sort of way without quite knowing what he was doing—and went limp in Kelly's arms.

And as Toddles answered, back in Big Cloud, Regan, the sweat still standing out in great beads on his forehead, fierce now in the revulsion of relief, glared over Donkin's left shoulder, as Donkin's left hand scribbled on a pad what was coming over the wire.

Regan glared fiercely—then he spluttered.

"Who in hell's Christopher Hyslop Hoogan—h'm?"

Donkin's lips had a queer smile on them.

"Toddles," he said.

Regan sat down heavily in his chair.

"*What?*" demanded the super.

"Toddles," said Donkin. "I've been trying to drum a little railroading into him—on the key."

Regan wiped his face. He looked helplessly from Donkin to the super, and then back again at Donkin.

"But—but what's he doing at Cassil's Siding? How'd he get there—h'm? H'm? How'd he get there?"

"I don't know," said Donkin, his fingers rattling the Cassil's Siding call again. "He doesn't answer any more. We'll have to wait for the story till they make Blind River, I guess."

And so they waited. And presently at Blind River, Kelly, dictating to the operator—not Beale, Beale's day man—told the story. It lost nothing in the telling—Kelly wasn't that kind of man: he told them what Toddles had done, and he left nothing out; and he added that they had Toddles on a mattress in the baggage car, with a doctor they had discovered amongst the passengers looking after him.

At the end, Carleton tamped down the dottle in the bowl of his pipe thoughtfully with his forefinger—and glanced at Donkin.

"Got along far enough to take a station key somewhere?" he inquired casually. "He's made a pretty good job of it as the night operator at Cassil's."

Donkin was smiling.

"Not yet," he said.

"No?" Carleton's eyebrows went up. "Well, let him come in here with you, then, till he has; and when you say he's ready, we'll see what we can do. I guess it's coming to him; and I guess"—he shifted his glance to the master mechanic—"I guess we'll go down and meet Number Two when she comes in, Tommy."

Regan grinned.

"With our hats in our hands," said the big-hearted master mechanic.

Donkin shook his head.

"Don't you do it," he said. "I don't want him to get a swelled head."

Carleton stared; and Regan's hand, reaching into his back pocket for his chewing, stopped midway.

Donkin was still smiling.

"I'm going to make a railroad man out of Toddles," he said.

A GHOST TRAIN ILLUSION

By Cy Warman

Cy Warman

Cy WARMAN was probably America's first all-railroad writer of any importance. Indeed, his books are now regarded as top-notch railroadiana and are much in demand by collectors throughout the country. But by many older folks Warman will be remembered for his lyric, "Sweet Marie," which was put to music by Raymond Moore, and which in six months' time sold more than a million copies.

Warman was born near Greenup, Illinois, on June 22, 1855. After a meager education he turned to railroading and for many years was employed by the Denver and Rio Grande (now the Denver and Rio Grande Western) as an engineman. In 1888 he edited a semi-monthly paper called the *Western Railway*. Two years later found him editor-in-chief of the *Chronicle*, a newspaper in the mining town of Creede, Colorado. Not content with his success at journalism, Warman wanted to write poetry, and write poetry he did at every available opportunity. Finally he published a little book of verse called *Mountain Melodies* which sold by the thousands on Denver and Rio Grande trains. But once a railroader always a railroader, and Warman, even though he earned the title of "The Poet of the Rockies," could hardly forget the iron way. Nor did he.

The Warman who is remembered today, at least in the hearts of railroad enthusiasts, is not the poet, journalist or song-writer: he is the author who told about the men in the cab, in the caboose and out on the line. It happened by chance, as such things do, that he was reading a railroad story in *McClure's Magazine* by a writer who obviously was not familiar with the industry. Warman, then and there, decided he would submit a story on railroading which would be accurate and at the same time make a "hit" with the reading public. His story—*A Thousand-Mile Ride on the Engine of the Swiftest Train in the World (McClure's Magazine*, January, 1894)—met with instant approval. From that time on Warman continued railroad writing.

In later life Warman was assistant to the president of the Grand Trunk, now part of the Canadian National System. As a lasting tribute to the memory of their author-railroader, the Maple Leaf System has named a town in his honor—the important railroad junction of WARMAN located in the province of Saskatchewan about fifteen miles northeast of Saskatoon. Cy Warman died on April 7, 1914.

Among the better-known books by Warman are: *Tales of an Engineer, Short Rails,* and *The Last Spike*—all short stories; *The White Mail* and *Snow on the Headlight*—novels; and *The Story of the Railroad*—a historical sketch. His book of verse called *Songs of Cy Warman* contains several railway selections.

A Ghost Train Illusion from the volume entitled *The Express Messenger* is like most of Warman's tales—a true account of an actual event, although such a derailment as is described in the narrative must have been rare indeed, even before the days of "Believe It or Not" items. The operation described was on the original narrow-gauge line of the Denver & Rio Grande, as laid by General William Jackson Palmer. The particular line referred to has long since been converted to the standard gauge of four feet eight and one-half inches, but the D&RGW even today has some hundreds of miles of lines of three-foot six-inch gauge in the Rocky Mountains in Colorado and New Mexico.

A GHOST TRAIN ILLUSION

By Cy Warman

WHEN THE Rio Grande Western was a narrow-gauge road it was very crooked. Even in the Utah desert there were many curves among the sand hills that have been piled up during the last few thousand years. A locomotive—one of a type known as "sewing machines," because all their machinery was in sight—was trying to make a spur for the general manager's special, against which she had a time order. The time was growing alarmingly short, and the driver of the light engine knew that the man on the special, with the G.M. behind him, would be crowding the limit. These "sewing machines" were famous riders. The springs were so light and so perfectly adjusted that one of these locomotives would ride as easily to the engineer as a Pullman car does to a commercial traveler, with one seat for himself and another for his feet. As the little machine rocked around the corners, screaming at every curve, the engineer and fireman kept a sharp lookout ahead, at the same time counting the minutes and reckoning the miles that lay between them and the spur.

Down the desert one of the swiftest engines on the road was trembling away toward the sewing machine, and at the end of each minute the two locomotives were a mile and a half nearer each other.

To be allowed to "pull" the general manager is an honor earnestly striven for by engineers, and when once obtained it is carefully guarded. Whatever record a man makes at the head of such a train is sure to count for or against him, since he is then directly under the eye of the management. The chances are always in favor of a good run, for the train dispatcher, with his own reputation at stake, can be depended upon to keep the track clear. He will hold a passenger train ten minutes rather than hold the special five. Another point in favor of the special engineer is the fact that he is due at no particular point at any specified time, and having no time-card to hold him down, he may regulate the speed of the train to suit himself. He is always an experienced runner who knows the road—knows every low joint and high center, every curve and sag on his division. Consequently the officials put no limit upon the speed of the train, but leave it all to the good judgment of the engineer. It was a clear, dry day in the early autumn, the very best time of the year for a fast run, and "Old Sam" had been gauging his speed for fifty miles back so as to hit Coyote spur on the dot, and break the record for fast running on the Alkali division.

By the rules of the road, five minutes were allowed for the variation of watches, but the rule is not always respected, and as the man on the special was known to be a daring driver, the sewing-machine crew saw that they were in a close place long before the smoke of the approaching locomotive was seen. Now they had barely five minutes left, and nothing for the variation, and the coveted siding four miles away. At last there remained but a single mile, and only a minute to do it in. The throttle was wide open, and the little engine was rolling so that the bell rang continually. The fireman had put in his last fire, and was now straining his eyes to catch the smoke of the special. The engineer, with his left hand on the whistle-rope, clung to the side of the cab to keep from being thrown out of the right of way.

The wheels under the sewing machine were so small that the best she could do was forty-five miles, and now when she came down to the very last second, there was still a quarter of a mile between her and the meeting point, but at that moment the flying wheels of the special engine crashed over the switch and shut her out. The sewing machine, hidden among the sand hills, was straining every nerve to reach the passing point at which she was already overdue. The man on the special was just beginning to feel sure of his position when he rounded a curve and saw the light engine emerging from a shallow cut. Of course, he shut off and tried to lessen the force of the collision, but to stop was out of the question.

The fireman on the light engine saw the special and warned his companion, for they were curving to the left and the driver could not see, but the four men knew that nothing short of a miracle could prevent a dreadful collision, and that in a few seconds' time they would all be piled up in a heap. Both drivers had called to their firemen to jump, and the firemen had turned to their windows. The special engineer was in the act of reversing, that he might take the good opinion of the official with him. The other driver only shoved the throttle lever in, braced himself, and awaited the shock.

A man who has never lived up to what he thought his last moment on earth, and survived to tell about it afterward, can never know how much business one can transact, in his mind, during that moment in which he waits and listens for the swish of the scythe. But one does not always review his past life at such a moment; often he wastes time thinking upon a mere trifle. Lafe Pence was in a wreck the next day after his election to Congress, and, although he had been a Democrat, and had become a Populist, he gave no thought to the past or the future, but said to himself, as the sleeper plunged down an embankment, "Now, what the devil was I elected for?"

The driver of the special engine had a boy, and this boy had climbed up on a picket fence to kiss his father good-by that morning at their home in Salt Lake, but he slipped, fell, and hung there with a fence picket through the seat of his first pair of trousers, and it was all so funny that, now as the engineer recalled the circumstance, he threw back his head and laughed as heartily as he had ever laughed in this life. The fireman, casting a farewell glance at his companion, saw him laughing, and concluded, in his last moment, that the driver had suddenly become insane, but as he glanced ahead where death was waiting, he was not sure that he was sane himself.

The driver, having finished his laugh and still feeling no shock, looked ahead. The track was clear! He unlatched the reverse lever and threw the engine in the forward motion, and the speed of the train, which had been but little checked, carried them away down among the sand hills. The driver looked at the fireman and asked, "Did you see anything?"

"No," said the fireman. "Did you?" And the driver said no, tried his water and opened the throttle, and the engine whirled away, while the fireman returned to his place at the furnace door.

The two men scarcely glanced at each other again until they stopped for water at Green River, but each in his own mind was recalling all the wild tales of ghost trains he had ever heard. Each was firm in the belief that he had seen a ghost, but he would never tell it—not for his job.

The officials in the special train felt the resistance of the engine when the engineer shut off and reversed, and the general manager, turning to the superintendent, asked, with surprise, "When did you put in that siding?"

"What, back there? That's Coyote spur, and has been there for six months," was the reply.

"I know very well," said the manager, "where Coyote spur is, for we waited there fifteen minutes for Number Eight going down the other day, but we just passed a siding on the north."

The superintendent was inclined to be funny, but the

Colonel, stroking his long gray Peffers, remarked that he had seen a locomotive standing at the point mentioned, and "as trains are not in the habit of meeting and passing between stations, I take it that there must be a siding there." There was just a twinkle of mirth in the Colonel's eyes, which, despite the fingermarks left about them by the touch of time, are still bright with the sparkle of youth, but the superintendent was utterly unable to understand the general manager.

There was silence for a little while, but the general manager was by no means satisfied. He pressed the button, and when the black porter came in he asked: "Did you see an engine on a siding back a ways, George?"

"No, sah, I haven't saw no engine: d'ain't no sidin' 'cept Ci-ote spur, an' dat was clear."

"Send the conductor to me," said the official, and when the conductor came in the manager asked to look at the running orders.

"Run special to Grand Junction, avoiding all regular trains. Extra engine 57 has until 5:55 to make Coyote spur against you."

"What time did you pass the spur?" demanded the Colonel.

"Precisely at 5:55," said the conductor, now somewhat alarmed at the manager's air.

"Is there a siding between here and Coyote?" asked the Colonel, and the superintendent, being at a loss to make out what the manager was driving at, started to leave the car, but was called back.

"There is not," was the conductor's reply.

"Perhaps," said the Colonel, "there was not when we went down, but there is now, for I saw a locomotive standing there."

The conductor laughed as the superintendent had done, but the Colonel offered to risk a case of champagne that he had seen no ghost train, and the superintendent took the bet as the easiest way of settling an argument which was about to become embarrassing.

When the special reached Green River the party went into the eating-house, where supper had been ordered, and, as was his habit, the Colonel sat at the same table with the train and engine crew.

"What did you shut off for just this side of Coyote spur, Sam?" asked the Colonel, looking the engineer in the eye, and instantly the eyes of the whole party were upon the driver's dusky face. The engineer was speechless. Not that the circumstances had escaped his mind, for as a matter of fact he had thought of little else, but he knew not how to answer.

"Did you think that engine was on the main line?" asked the general manager, noticing the embarrassment of the engine crew.

"What engine?" asked the engineer, trying to look and speak naturally.

"There was only one engine there besides your own," was the Colonel's response. "Will you be good enough to answer my question?"

"Well," thought the driver, "if I've got 'em the G.M.'s got 'em," and he answered, "I did think she was on the main stem."

"What did you think, Harry?" asked the superintendent of the fireman, who was staring at the engineer. The fireman only closed his eyes and shook his head slowly, as if he considered them all crazy, and his long lashes, dark with coal dust, lay upon his newly washed face like the lashes of a chorus girl.

"Did you see anything on your side?" asked the Colonel, who was determined to unlock the lips of the fireman.

"Not a thing," said Harry. "I don't believe in ghosts."

"It will not be necessary for you to take out Sixty-three [an accident report], but I wish you would tell me what you saw and how it affected you," said the general manager to the engineer.

"May I ask you first if you saw anything, Colonel?" said the driver.

"I saw a locomotive standing on a spur or siding just east of Coyote."

"When I see her first," said Sam, taking courage from the Colonel's confession, "she was bang in front of us, coming out of a cut like a ball out of a cannon. I saw it was all up with us, but I naturally shut off—mechanically, so to speak. I think I hooked her over, but I didn't whistle, open the sand valve, or set the air—they wa'n't no use—no time; but just then I thought of little Sammie as I saw him last, hangin' on the fence by the seat of his pants, an' it seemed to me that I never see anything quite so funny, and I laughed that hard that the tears came in my eyes and blinded me. Then the thought came to me that we were a long time coming together, so I looks ahead, an' there wa'n't a thing in sight. I asked Harry if he see anything, an' he lied an' asked if I see anything, an' I lied, too, an' opened up the throttle again. That's all I know about it."

There was a noticeable increase in the attention of the company, and Tim Flarrity, the flagman, leaning low toward the table, crossed himself and ventured the prediction that they would have a head-end collision before they reached the junction. "I never see a ghost train show up yet that didn't mean something," he added, but the burst of laughter that followed closed his circuit, and he said no more.

Now the agent came in with a number of messages for the superintendent, and as the official began reading the first of the lot, he began to smile.

"Read it out," said the Colonel. "Perhaps it will tell us something about the ghost." The superintendent read:

"Engine 57 is off the track and nearly off the right of way 1,000 yards east of Coyote spur, but still on her feet."

That explained the ghost engine. At the instant when the engineer shut off, the "sewing machine," just then rounding a sharp curve, jumped the track, lit square on her wheels, and went plowing out over the hard adobe of the desert. She rolled and rocked for a few seconds, and then came to a stop with the enginemen still standing in the cab. The engine had been working hard, and if the throttle had remained open, she might have made the curve all right, but the sudden relaxation of all her tension caused a jar that threw her off her feet, and it was a lucky jar for her crew.

Since that time, however, old Sam has been in hard luck. He has already lost three legs. The last one, being caught under an engine, was chopped off by the conductor with an ordinary ax to prevent the engineer being roasted alive. Those who witnessed the operation say that Sam rested on one elbow and smoked a cigar while the conductor hacked away at his ankle. It was a wooden leg.

THE ANGEL OF CANYON PASS

By Charles W. Tyler

Charles W. Tyler

CHARLES W. TYLER was born in North Hinsdale, New Hampshire, September 1, 1887. He learned telegraphy at nineteen, working as a Western Union messenger. In 1911 he turned to railroading as an engine wiper on the Boston and Maine's Fitchburg Division and later took up firing. On the very day that he married Alice McKenzie, April 23, 1916, he was called to fire a switcher. His wife brought his lunch at midnight.

Tyler broke into print with a story called *On First 303* for the old *Railroad Man's Magazine* back in 1913. Since that year he has written over seventy tales for that periodical and its successors, *Railroad Stories* and *Railroad Magazine*. All in all he has placed more than three hundred short stories and novelettes in nearly a score of magazines. Many of his own personal experiences are embodied in these stories. He is also the author of two books, *Quality Bill's Girl* and *Blue Jean Billy*—both detective stories.

Among his stories which have appeared in *Railroad Magazine* or its predecessors are: *The Road to Yesterday, When Hobos Ride, Railroad Drummer, Clear Iron* and *God of High Iron*.

The Angel of Canyon Pass is reminiscent of the early days of railroading when trackside burials were common. Even today section men will show you graves located along the right of way where pioneer railroaders are laid at rest. The story is from *Railroad Magazine*.

THE ANGEL OF CANYON PASS

By Charles W. Tyler

THE SANGRE DEL SALVADORS rise from the high desert floor of the Llanos Pintado like a wavy purple barrier on a flaming carpet. Far to the east of Del Rosa, serrated rims trace their hazy outlines against the horizon.

Of these, one deep slash stands out between towering peaks like the notched V of a gun sight. Clearly defined, the eye finds it, a full seventy miles distant. They call it Canyon Pass.

A mighty gorge, with bold ramparts hewn when the world was in the making, Canyon Pass has been shackled by steel but never fully conquered. Ceaseless warfare is forever waged there. Many pages in the history of the Pacific Coast & Transcontinental's Canyon Division are today written in red, grim entries in the ledger of life.

Stories of Canyon Pass have been told and retold wherever railroad men gather. In sandhouse and switch shanty and dispatcher's office; in engine cab and caboose, even in those stiff sanctuaries where heavy-jowled brass hats sit on their mahogany thrones.

Of these tales one has become legend. It concerns Bill Carnegan and "the Angel of Canyon Pass."

Just over the hump, in the Sangre del Salvadors, are six miles of track that railroad men consider the most dangerous on the division. Long ago the P. C. & T. built a shanty at Milepost 104, on a little flat an eighth of a mile east of the trestle over Big Stormy Canyon, and stationed a track-walker there.

A tiny hut, far from the nearest habitation and surrounded by jagged peaks. It was almost a place of exile. Men called that job "the sheepherder's trick."

Now and then the section boss and his Mexican crew from Paraje had work to do in the vicinity. At intervals a freight stopped to leave supplies. Occasionally wandering Indians broke the monotony. Sometimes folks waved from observation platforms of speeding trains, or there was a shout and a hand raised in salute from cab or caboose. Perhaps a late paper came fluttering off, or a magazine.

Always there were Frowsy Head and Thunder Mountain scowling down from their lofty heights, as though debating what particular kind of hell they would hurl next at Canyon Pass.

Bill Carnegan was big, cleancut and fine-looking. Superintendent McCuen eyed the man speculatively. Something stamped him as a railroader. McCuen judged him to be about thirty-two.

"Well? What is it?" There was scant encouragement in the flat, hard tone.

Bill said, a hint of desperation in his voice: "I'm looking for a job"—he hesitated—"any kind."

"Jobs are scarce," McCuen announced briefly. "What can you do?"

"I—I was an engineer."

The super shook his head. "We got a list as long as your arm of men set back firing."

"I know," said Bill despondently. "I've tried every roundhouse between here and Trinidad. But I've *got* to get something. Can't you fit me in anywhere? Wages don't matter, just as long as there is enough for my wife and me to get by on."

"So you're married, eh?"

Bill nodded. "We had to come West for her health. I had

rights on the Central Valley, back in New England. She had a bad attack of flu and her lungs are affected."

"Kind of tough, wasn't it—quitting back there when you had seniority?"

The other smiled, his eyes lighting. "Not for me," he said. "Anything I could do for her wouldn't be half enough. Ann's the finest woman in the world. It was mighty hard for her to leave friends and relatives and the home we fixed up."

"Humph!" McCuen stared out of the window and far away toward that purple line of the Sangre del Salvadors and the V-shaped cleft of Canyon Pass. At length he asked:

"What's your name?"

"Carnegan. Bill Carnegan."

"Well, Carnegan, there's just one job I know of." The super drummed on his desk. "I doubt if that job would interest you. A Mex had it last, and he went cuckoo."

"What is it?" the hogger inquired with instant hope. So often he had carried back to Ann a discouraging, "Nothing doing today, sweetheart. But tomorrow I'll find something." There had been a lot of tomorrows.

"Track-walker," McCuen said gruffly, "out on the hump." After a pause he added: "Men don't stay in Canyon Pass long. The solitude gets inside of their skulls and they do queer tricks."

"But I wouldn't be alone," Bill hastened to point out.

"You mean you'd take your wife?"

"Sure. I couldn't leave her here. Where I go, Ann goes. Mountain air is just what she needs to help her get well. And it won't be forever. Things will be picking up after awhile. Then I'll get something better."

"How long you been married, Carnegan?"

"Eight years."

McCuen's eyes softened under shaggy brows. He stroked his chin thoughtfully. Here was a big husky fellow from en-

gine service stepping down from the cab to walk the ties—
and offering no complaint.

The superintendent's mouth twitched a little. Such devotion to a woman was something to think about, in this cock-
eyed age. He wrote a brief note and handed it to Bill.

"Take this to the roadmaster—Mr. Godett. The last office
at the end of the corridor. I guess he'll fix you up."

And so Bill Carnegan went to Canyon Pass. Bill and Ann.

It was spring. The mountains were cool. Traces of snow
lingered in the deeper clefts of the high peaks. They made
a wild, unfriendly world, those Sangre del Salvadors. It took
Ann Carnegan a long time to get used to their untamed
majesty.

The ever-changing vistas—dawns that poured gold over the
high rims, flaming sunsets, the quickly descending curtain
of night, the blasting winds that poured eternally through
the pass—all filled the woman with awe and consternation.

The vastness of this bold, raw country was a far cry from
the friendly life that had been hers back there on Elm Street
in old New England.

Though she fought it with all her might, Ann was terribly
homesick. But she never let Bill know. Nights when the
dread wind trumpeted through the canyons, her pillow would
be wet with tears. And then when morning came she would
be ashamed.

Life and health were here. After all, she could do no less
than match the gallantry, deed for deed, of the man who had
given up much for her. And so Bill saw only a brave, smiling
face.

Never once did the man hint of his own tragedy. But Ann
sensed the hunger that haunted his eyes when the trains went
roaring by. She knew that Bill missed sitting at the throttle
with drivers pounding under him. By comparison it was a
dull existence, this walking the ties with a wrench and a
maul.

And yet Canyon Division had never had a track-walker as faithful and untiring as Bill Carnegan. It seemed, having been at the throttle himself, he realized the importance of his task. The Sangre del Salvadors were filled with constant menace. Slides, falling rocks, washouts—all went to make the place a railroad man's nightmare.

Summer came, the season of torrential rains. And when Frowsy Head and Thunder Mountain wore trailing veils of black, they gave ominous hint of cloudbursts. The Big Stormy, dry at other times, would become a swollen torrent, rolling down boulders and debris.

Bill was anxious about the trestle over the canyon. And when thunderstorms sounded their booming war drums at night, he would dress, take his lantern and go out to make sure that all was well at the gorge.

And always when he returned, chilled and wet, Ann would be up and have a fire going and a pot of coffee on. That light gleaming in the window stirred strange emotions in his heart. He would slip an arm around Ann's waist, saying, "You're a grand sweetheart," and kiss her.

"I have to be," she'd answer, "to keep up with you, Bill."

Crews reported to Del Rosa that Carnegan's lantern was always there to greet them when the weather was bad. Its twinkling assurance lifted the burden of responsibility for those whose business it was to see that the trains went through safely. McCuen and Godett spoke of it more than once.

Too, the men on the trains came to watch for the slender form of the woman in the door of the little shanty at Milepost 104. She was as much a part of Canyon Pass as Carnegan himself.

And when the section foreman's wife was sick, Ann went to the section house at Paraje to be of such service as she could. When a freight went off the iron in the Narrows, Ann attended to the injuries of the fireman and a brakeman, and made coffee for the crew while they waited for the wrecker.

Now and then a hungry 'bo was fed, or the coat of a Mexican gandy dancer was patched. Or they were expecting a new arrival at Pedro's house, and Ann would make a baby dress. So they began to call her the Angel of Canyon Pass.

The young lady from New England found plenty to occupy her time, and busy hands helped her forget. From a shanty beside the tracks she lent her magic touch to the making of a home. Curtains framed the windows. A flower garden took shape. Stones were set in a neat border and whitewashed. The garden was bright and vivid, for Ann loved gay colors—especially red.

The section boss and his men always had a little spare time for landscaping when they were in the vicinity, and it was a good excuse to visit the friendly Mrs. Carnegan.

Vines climbed the drab sides of the little yellow building. A red rose unfolded its petals on a bit of trellis. Geraniums added color. There were hollyhocks and wild verbenas. Passengers on the trains looked from Pullman windows and marvelled that a workman's hut could be so lovely.

The general superintendent said it only showed what could be done, and advocated that stations along the line follow the example set for them by the track-walker and his wife in Canyon Pass.

McCuen, coming in from a tour of inspection, spoke to Roadmaster Godett, suggesting that a small addition to the one-room structure at Milepost 104 would add materially to the comfort and convenience of the Carnegans.

"That bridge gang at Wagon Tire are tearing down a couple of shanties," said the roadmaster. "There's the material, and we've got a work train going to Rag River the first of the week. It wouldn't be much of a job, and Mrs. Carnegan ought to have a kitchen."

"You're damn right!" McCuen agreed. "Why, that shack out there attracts more attention now than the scenery. They tell me that half the women on the trains complain because they can't stop and look at that garden, and maybe get some slips."

One day an old Indian named Maggie came to Milepost 104. She had been gathering piñon nuts in the vicinity, and decided to visit the white man's home as a possible new trade outlet.

It was Ann's first woman visitor, and she could have offered no warmer welcome to a neighbor dropping in for a call back on Elm Street.

Maggie said, "How!"

And Ann, proud of a little Spanish taught her by the Mexican section hands, replied: *"Como está!"*

The squaw knew Mex, and her stolid face brightened. "Me Maggie," she said. "Indian name Na-va-wi."

"Me Ann. I call you Na-va-wi. I am so glad you called."

And the lady from New England served lunch, just as she would have done for a visitor at home.

Old Maggie dug down into a pocket of her voluminous skirt and produced a number of desert stones—tourmalines, agates and bits of brightly colored petrified wood. Ann's eyes sparkled. She loved these jewels of the wasteland.

She bought two or three stones, and asked Maggie to come again. Later she sent to Del Rosa and Amargosa for gay pieces of calico and other articles that she felt might find favor with the Indian squaw. It was lots of fun sitting out there on the stoop and bartering with Maggie.

Ann Carnegan's health improved. There was a healing tonic in the rarefied air of these desolate mountains. Slowly she was rebuilding—winning her fight to live.

A great weight lifted from Bill's heart. He went whistling about his work. Life was good after all. A track-walker's job was better than the best run in the world—so long as he just had Ann.

Too, the roadmaster had hinted there was a better position in store for him. Ann had heard a great deal about the old

Indian pueblo at Nunez, where Maggie lived. In time, circumstances made it possible for her to visit it. When she returned to Canyon Pass she was enthusiastic about the bit of ancient world she had seen. It had been like turning back the pages of an old book, she told Bill.

For a long interval Maggie did not come to Canyon Pass, and Ann missed her. One of the Mexican section hands finally told her that the trader at Paraje said the Indian squaw was sick. So Ann went to Nunez, taking along such homely remedies as were at hand, together with presents for Maggie's grandchildren.

She rode in a caboose to Paraje, and from there was driven to Nunez in a shaky flivver owned by one of the section men. She stayed away from home several days.

When Mrs. Carnegan took her departure, old Maggie, now on the road to recovery, said: "You *bueno!* Good! Padre say Great White Father got um heap fine angel. Show picture. You angel. Na-va-wi never forget."

And old Maggie never did.

In June of the second summer that Bill Carnegan and Ann had been in Canyon Pass, tragedy laid its dread finger on Milepost 104.

Ann caught cold. She told Bill it didn't amount to anything, just a case of sniffles. But suddenly it settled on her chest. That night there were chills and fever. Bill flagged a westbound freight and sent for a doctor. The doctor came from Del Rosa the next morning on No. 2. A nurse was with him.

They fought valiantly to save her, but it just wasn't in the cards for Ann to live. The patient died two days later, her hand in Bill's.

She smiled up into his face, and whispered: "Good-by, Bill. It—it's all—been so wonderful—with you. . . ."

The former hoghead was never the same again. After that first stunning, tearing blow had eased a little, he faced things with a strange, vacant fixedness that made men shake their heads.

They spoke awkwardly of sorrow, of sympathy, while Bill stared at them with eyes that looked beyond, toward that far horizon and a woman smiling at him through the mists.

They asked Carnegan where he wanted Ann buried—in the cemetery at Del Rosa, or back East.

Superintendent McCuen was there, and Roadmaster Godett, and the section boss and others. They awaited his answer, grave, troubled. They saw here a man under strain, moving as one who walked in his sleep. Where did he want her buried?

The lines that creased his face softened at last. "Why, bury her here," he said slowly, as though there could be no other course. "I want her close, because I'll be keeping watch in the pass."

McCuen, grizzled railroad veteran, found a lump in his throat. Godett fumbled for his handkerchief and blew his nose. The section boss swore under his breath.

The husband wanted her buried here! Hardened men of the high desert looked from one to the other.

"Out there on that knoll across the canyon," Bill was saying, "where she can see her garden, and look down to the foothills. . . ."

Thus they laid poor Ann Carnegan to rest at Milepost 104, just west of the Big Stormy.

The section men erected a wooden cross, and bordered the mound with white stones from Ann's garden. And Bill set out a red rose, her favorite color.

The first thing that enginemen on eastbound trains saw as they rounded the long curve at the summit of the Sangre del Salvadors was that white cross on Mrs. Carnegan's grave.

The Angel of Canyon Pass no longer waved from the little house down the track, but the train crews somehow felt that she was still there—watching for them. More than one veteran of the throttle lifted his hand in solemn salute as his engine pounded past.

Bill continued to walk his beat to Milepost 110—out and back each day. He cared for the garden, and smoked his pipe on the stoop in the evening, with the stars looking down.

When thunderstorms crashed off Frowsy Head at night, Bill followed his usual procedure. He dressed, took his lantern and walked to the trestle over the Big Stormy, to be sure that all was well. Before going out he would light the lamp. He liked to see the yellow glow of it when he returned, and would tell himself that *surely* Ann was there waiting for him.

Old Maggie came to Canyon Pass again one day. She brought a beautiful piece of polished chalcedony. The wrinkled old squaw had, in truth, stolen it from the curio store at Paraje. She could have sold it to tourists. But Maggie had not taken the agate for profit, but for love. She put it on the Angel's grave.

Then there was the bottle, dyed a rich purple by long exposure to the sun, that Bill discovered at the foot of the cross. Ann had been very fond of glass thus colored. Also, in the course of time, a cluster of sparkling rock crystals found their way to that mound of earth.

And there was a round piece of grained ruby glass, snuggling in the dirt—a safety reflector, lost from some car or truck down on the highway. Old Maggie had remembered that Ann was fond of red.

One day Bill saw the Indian gathering piñon nuts down beyond the Narrows, and he called to her.

"You still bring Ann pretty stones," he said. *"Gracias! Mucho gracias!"*

"Na-va-wi love white sister," the squaw replied. "She good woman. She good to old Maggie. She wake up from long sleep some time. See presents Indian bring."

"Yes, God bless you, Maggie, she will know. She's watching

all the time." A tender smile lighted Bill's face. "I can feel
her close—walking with me."

A few days afterward, Bill came home late. Clouds were
gathering around Thunder Mountain and Frowsy Head.
Black veils threw their long streamers over the higher peaks
of the Sangre del Salvadors.

All afternoon squalls had been snarling far off on the
desert rim, with lightning playing on the horizon at half a
dozen points. Distant thunder had kept up an almost constant grumble.

The former hogger prepared and ate his supper, and sat
for a time on the stoop. In the fading light he walked up the
track and across the trestle and on to that bit of raised ground
where the grave was. He never missed a night. He knelt beside the cross and breathed a prayer.

Then he lingered for a little, tenderly rearranging the
stones of the border, smoothing the earth. The rose Bill had
put there was unfolding a blossom, a beautiful bud that
had opened to smile at him.

Each of the presents that old Maggie had brought he
picked up, wiped off carefully and returned to their places.

A freight came roaring over the summit from the west.
The whistle moaned under the easy drag of the engineer at
the cord. The fireman and brakeman both crossed the cab to
look from the gangway. Bill waved at them.

Faces in the cab of the pusher and in the caboose saw the
track-walker, and men shook their heads. A strange picture
here in the dusk—a lonely figure, a grave, a cross.

A storm was centering around Frowsy Head. The lightning was sharp and frequent. Thunder boomed through the
mountains with jarring reverberations. A large proportion of
the run-off from the eastern watershed of Frowsy Head spilled
into the Big Stormy.

A new storm moved up from the south toward Thunder

Mountain. Bill stood in the door of the shanty watching. It looked bad.

Thunder Mountain and Jawbone dumped water from their rocky slopes into the Narrows. There was always danger of slides and falling boulders.

Bill donned oilskins and boots. "Guess I'd better go down to the Narrows," he told himself.

He lighted the lamp on the table near the window. Ann's picture was near the lamp. It showed her waving her hand and smiling.

The track-walker took his lantern and went out. On the threshold he paused to look back. His eye went to every familiar object that she had touched—and again to the picture.

"Good-by, Ann!" he said. "I'll be back in a little while."

He went out to the trestle over the Big Stormy. There was very little water in the canyon. It seemed that the storm had moved over to the western slope of the divide, there back of Frowsy Head.

Bill started down the track toward the Narrows. It had begun to rain as he reached Milepost 105. A squall was coming off Jawbone.

No. 1, the crack westbound limited, came doubleheading up the grade from Paraje. Her two big Mountain type locomotives roared full-throated in the night. Rain slanted across the headlight of the first engine in gusty sheets. Gray rivulets spewed from the rocky slopes.

The flicker of a lantern near Milepost 106 announced that Carnegan, keeper of the pass, was guarding the rail.

Two brief whistle blasts cracked the salute of No. 1. Blurred faces in the cabs looked down and muffled voices shouted greetings at him. Bill yelled and waved his lantern.

He started back. He had gone perhaps a mile when he detected a new note menacing the night. He stopped for a minute to listen, then went on with a quickened pace.

He had felt so sure that all danger was past, there at the Big Stormy. But now a grim premonition laid hold of him. A quarter of a mile farther on, he paused again.

Faintly a dull roar came to his ears above the noise of wind and rain. It was an ominous sound. He had heard it before. It was not unlike the rumble of an approaching freight train, drifting down the grade.

Bill broke into a run. A cloudburst was coming down Big Stormy Canyon. Frequent squalls had softened the approaches to the trestle. Only the day before some section men had worked there, filling in those little gullies cut by coursing rivulets. It wasn't the structure itself for which trackmen felt concern, but those fills behind the concrete abutments.

The rain was slackening now. And yet the thunder of tumbling water grew louder. There were, too, the crash and grind of trees and boulders against cut-bank canyon walls, gouging brittle earth, as the increasing accumulation of debris was hurled along in the teeth of the mounting flood.

Somewhere sodden clouds had emptied themselves high in the mountains—the last mad caprice of the storm. Even now stars were peeping through around Frowsy Head.

When at last he neared the Big Stormy, Bill was close to exhaustion. He had long since discarded his cumbersome raincoat and boots. His feet were cut and bruised from the rock ballast.

He glanced at the light in the window of his home as he stumbled on past the little building beside the track. It seemed to give him renewed strength. He felt that Ann was close beside him.

As Bill approached the trestle he was met by muddy water. It was coming down the right-of-way ditches, creeping over the ties. A wide sweep of it spread before him, a veritable river, flowing, gurgling about the steelwork.

Minutes were precious. Every second that ticked away was a step toward eternity. If No. 6 were on time, she was already getting close. Not a month before, the schedule to Chicago had been cut two hours, while newspaper and magazine advertisements boasted of this new fast service.

Water poured across the rails like a mill-race. Its power was terrific. It clutched at his legs with devilish ferocity, trying to drag him down. A foot dropped between the unseen ties. Already the earth was crumbling. The fill had started to go.

Bill pitched forward. Something in his leg snapped. Blinding pain stabbed him. He felt himself being swept away. He caught at the submerged rail, now a foot beneath the coursing flood. The lantern and a fusee he had gripped in his left hand were lost.

Death held no dread for Bill Carnegan. Life offered little since Ann had gone. And yet tonight a grim determination filled his heart. It was not himself of whom he thought, but the railroad and the men and women whose lives he guarded.

He was going to cross the Big Stormy, in spite of hell and high water. A fighting Irish heart carried him forward, foot by foot.

Smashed and buffeted by muddy water that tried to drag him down stream, Bill struggled on. Ever in his ears sounded the roar of the torrent.

His right leg dragged uselessly. He advanced on hands and knees. A tree came floating down the gorge, its torn roots writhing, flailing like the menacing arms of an octopus. The trunk swung toward him in the gloom. He sought to get clear, but a jagged limb stub struck him on the head, opening an ugly gash.

In desperation, Bill wedged his knee against the guard rail and clung there for a little, gasping. He fought dizziness, almost utter exhaustion. Then once more he crawled, refusing to surrender.

Gone were lantern and fusee. Every last match had long been soaked past all usefulness. Even if the former hoghead could reach that west bank of the Big Stormy and solid ground, he had no means of attracting the attention of the engineer at the throttle of No. 6. They'd never see him in time.

And yet in the brain of Bill Carnegan there burned one spark that would not die. In his ears, above the din of waters, he thought he heard the low, sweet voice of the girl he'd wooed and won back in old New England.

Now he was going to keep a rendezvous with her—there by that mound, and the cross, ahead. Something carried him on, something that lifted him across those last flood-torn rail-lengths to solid ground across the Big Stormy.

No. 6 was on time. Two engines over the Sangre del Salvadors, and fourteen all-steel cars—mail, express and Pull-mans. Crazy Creek Canyon reverberated to the staccato bark of the exhausts and the drumming of steel on steel.

Light rain was falling, the fringe of the storm that had swung toward Thunder Mountain earlier. Charley Donald-son, a veteran runner of the Canyon Division, was at the throttle. He had been watching the lightning flashes out ahead.

"They been getting hell in Canyon Pass," he called to the fireman.

The latter ceased his labor on the deck for a little and stood beside the engineer.

"Anyhow, it ain't like the old days," he said, "when there was a wooden trestle over the Big Stormy, and the Mex track-walker was more likely than not pounding his ear in the shanty."

"That's right, my boy," the hogger responded fervently. "Carnegan is out there now looking after the track. When we bat 'em over the hump and start rolling down the mountain, we know that everything's O.K."

"It was mighty tough, Carnegan losing his wife the way he did."

Donaldson sighed. "It sure was."

"You know, Charley, that grave kind of gives a man a funny feeling. Don't it you?"

"Why, I dunno. I sort of think of Mrs. Carnegan as being there beside the track," Donaldson said, "just watching over things."

The fireman agreed. "Yeah, that's right. Bill and her. My God, it must be awful lonesome for him."

No. 6 swung at last over the high rim of the Sangre del Salvadors. Lights shone from the windows, warm, inviting. Life on the train flickered past with cinema-like rapidity. A few travelers lingered in the dining cars. Men and women lounged at ease in club car and observation. Porters were busy making up the berths. An old man dozed in a section, a gray-haired woman beside him. A mother smiled down into a baby's face. A honeymoon couple sat holding hands, their heads close.

Charley Donaldson leaned across the padded arm-rest, his keen eyes squinting past the glass weather-wing along the track ahead. Two emerald dots hung like a pendant against a black velvet curtain.

He turned his head toward the left and sang out, "Green eye!"

And the fireman called back, "Green on the block!"

A stubby granite post whipped past. Milepost 103. The beat of the exhausts had quickened to a hurried mutter. Drivers and side-rods were but a clashing blur. Fast-rolling wheels were checking off the miles with a singsong clickety-click that measured the rail-lengths as one counts heartbeats.

Heavy cars cradled with gentle undulations that indicated smooth, swift flight. No. 6 was right on the advertised. Speed the watchword.

The big passenger haulers heeled to the curve west of

Milepost 104. The silver beam of the electric headlight washed the steep slope to the right of the track in swift review.

Juniper and piñon sprang out of the raven blackness, crouching shadows of boulder and gully, sharp-drawn striations in a red bank hewn by erosion.

On swept the far-reaching finger, like a spotlight hunting for figures on a darkened stage. And then, for just an instant, it seemed to pause, as though that which it sought had been found.

A gently swelling knoll, back somewhat from the right-of-way, with a softening background of piñon. There was a cross, in that dim distance, like a tiny ornament hung on the swelling bosom of the mountain. Gleaming white.

Charley Donaldson never failed to watch for it, as his train swept over the rim of the Sangre del Salvadors. His eyes were on it now in narrowed focus. Suddenly he became rigidly intent.

There was something moving close beside the mound. It was uncanny. The distance was yet too great to vision detail.

Then came a sudden flash of red—a dull-glowing crimson eye. It moved back and forth. The gleam of the headlight swept on around the curve, and it was lost.

Cold fingers clutched at the engineer's heart. The thing was weird, spectral.

The hogger lost not one instant in making his decision. He closed the throttle and snapped one short blast from the whistle, signaling the second engine to shut off. Then his fingers closed over the shiny, brass handle of the ET equipment. He swung it full to the right, *the big hole.*

It would take emergency air to stop them. Charley Donaldson sensed that if anything had gone wrong here in Canyon Pass, it was at the Big Stormy. Rain had been pouring hard out on the divide. There was always the possibility of a cloudburst.

The engineer answered the strange smoldering eye of red with two quick blasts.

Bill's heart swelled almost to the bursting point as he heard the acknowledgment. They had seen his signal. No. 6 was stopping.

The track-walker forgot the agony of his tortured body as he saw that parade of fire-rimmed wheels on the curve. His soul soared to undreamed-of heights. He gasped a prayer of thanksgiving.

The Angel, indeed, had walked with him tonight, her spirit buoying him up, carrying him on, when it seemed that the best he gave would not be enough. She was here with him now.

Bill slumped onto the grave. "Ann!" he choked. "My own dear sweetheart! Through the power and the glory—and you —we have saved a trainload of people."

The fireman, peering ahead, yelled: "It's a washout! There's hell to pay in the Big Stormy."

"My God, look at it!" Awe was in Donaldson's voice. "The flood has cut around both abutments."

His headlight revealed the devastation of the foaming torrent. The big engines of No. 6 ranged on past a little. Then, with a last buckling surge, the train came to a stop, not a hundred yards from the Big Stormy and its murky death trap!

Charley Donaldson lighted his torch and swung hurriedly down, the roar of mad water in his ears. A miracle had saved them—a miracle, and Bill Carnegan.

Moisture that was not rain trickled down the hogger's seamed cheeks as he walked back and his flaring torch revealed the figure of Carnegan slumped down beside the cross.

Others came stumbling toward the spot—engineer and fireman from the helper, uniformed trainmen, men to whom the booming roar in the blackness meant that they had been riding into the valley of eternal shadow.

The waving tongue from Donaldson's smoky torch laid its yellow illumination over the scene. Faces were white, strained, as the group of veterans of the rail found themselves witnessing a scene that would linger in their minds on through the years.

Carnegan! That was the name framed by their lips. Carnegan, here beside the grave of the wife he had loved so much.

Charley Donaldson handed his torch to his fireman and dropped down to slip his strong arm about Carnegan's shoulder.

"What happened, Bill?"

The track-walker told them. He spoke with effort, slow-worded phrases that told of the storm and the sudden onslaught that had trapped him there to the east of the Big Stormy. He made small mention of his desperate fight against the turbulent waters of the flood.

"I lost my lantern and fusee," he said. "But I knew I had one chance. Long ago, old Maggie, the Indian woman who came so often to see Ann, brought this—"

He still clutched in his hand the ruby-grained safety reflector, and he held it out.

"This piece of red glass," he went on, "and those other things there. Treasures, they were, tokens of love. God bless her faithful old heart! It wasn't much, this piece of glass. But Maggie knew that Ann loved red, so she put it there. I—I—well, I figured you'd see the red, Charley." He looked at the engineer.

Donaldson slowly shook his head. "I did, clear as a bell." There was a catch in his voice. "I couldn't have missed it."

The Canyon Division wanted to erect a memorial—the Canyon Division, and the passengers who were on No. 6 that night. And so a beautiful white shaft was placed where the cross had been. On it was put a bronze tablet with the name *Carnegan* in bold betters, as a tribute for all to read, to a railroad man and his wife.

And thus they remain today, eternally on guard in the high rims of the Sangre del Salvadors—Bill Carnegan and the Angel of Canyon Pass.

HUEY,
THE ENGINEER

By Jesse Stuart

Jesse Stuart

JESSE STUART was born somewhere near the head of W-Hollow, near Riverton, Kentucky, August 8, 1907, and still lives about "two whoops and a holler," as the saying is in that country, from where he was born.

In 1929 he graduated from Lincoln Memorial University. Thereafter he was a student for a time at Vanderbilt University and did graduate work at George Peabody College for Teachers. Farming and school teaching have been his work in life—he is Superintendent of City Schools at Greenup, Kentucky—but since before 1934, when his first book of poems appeared, his real work in the world has been turning out poems, stories and novels in successful profusion. One of his novels, *Taps for Private Tussie,* was both a selection of the Book-of-the-Month Club and the winner of the Thomas Jefferson Southern Award for the year 1943. Another novel, *Trees of Heaven,* his two books of verse, *Man With a Bull-Tongue Plow* and *Album of Destiny,* his autobiography, *Beyond Dark Hills,* and his collection of stories, *Head o' W-Hollow,* all have attracted favorable attention of critics and readers.

Huey, the Engineer, was a friend of Stuart's. He ran on the Eastern Kentucky Railroad, a short line which met the fate of many such railroads when their usefulness was diminished by the exhaustion of the mineral or timber resources they were built to serve, and whose remaining business went, to a large extent, to other ways of transport. The railroad ran south from Riverton, Kentucky, on the main line of the Chesapeake and Ohio between Ashland and Cincinnati. Even the sharpest eyed passenger riding one of the C & O main line trains through Riverton today can see no more than a weed-grown cinder bed turning south from the siding. Stuart's story brings back to life this abandoned pike, with "the crowds around the depots a-holding their horses and mules," and the "boys who all wanted to be like him," old Huey, and who now "wonder on what silent train and to what silent land our engineer has gone."

HUEY, THE ENGINEER

By Jesse Stuart

CAN'T YOU HEAR THAT WHISTLE STILL—can't you hear it! Can't you hear the tee rails popping and the flat cars lumbering around the curves and the big-bear engine—fat as a bear—huffing and puffing like a tired horse up a hill with an overloaded express—that humpy-dumpy old E-K engine with her pistons screaking and the long line of black smoke laid back from the stack—following the way the wind was blowing—can't you see it all and the long train of seven cars —two for the passengers—two for coal and two for logs and cattle—maybe I don't remember the two rusted streaks of tee rails running south through the Plum Grove hills—two streaks of rust fastened to the decayed and cinder-buried crossties—rotted at the necks where the tee rails kissed the crossties. Maybe my Pa and my Pa's Pa didn't help make the crossties and my Pa's Pa helped lay the big tee rails in them days—rails that three men could lift—yes, they helped to put the thirty-six miles of track over these Kentucky hills back to the coal, crossties, chickens and the ore—maybe I haven't heard about it all my life—maybe I don't remember the first time I saw that train and ran away through the sassafras sprouts like a scared rabbit.

My Pa will tell you. He was taking me to school. I was a big shaver for the years on my head—for the seven springs and six autumns we'd had—for we start to school in Kentucky in July to save a coal bill in the country school—coal all around us, too—coal in the high hills and the low hills under the shaggy tough-butted white oak roots—fire clay there, too, and that's why the E-K ran wild over the hills for thirty-six miles—that's why we saw the big engine pulling seven coaches over the road just a-snorting and a-huffing and a-puffing, and sometimes on this seven-coach train the engineer would reach his hand out and try to shake hands with the conductor who rode in the back coach. Oh, you couldn't quite do it, you know, but he just tried and the people would laugh. Once John Isom saw 'em do that. And John said he did and he said he hollered at 'em among all that noise: "Watch you don't break the train's ribs pulling stuff like that." He said he didn't think they heard him. That was all. Wind a-blowing in the corn along the train—an autumn wind and apples falling from the apple trees. A body could see just loads of them in the Sandy bottoms. God, but fall-time along the E-K— Don't you remember—train huffing and puffing like a bull coming right out of a hole in the hill—eight of them big holes on thirty-six and one-half miles of track.

After I saw the E-K, Pa used to say to me: "Son, what do you want to do when you get to be a man—teach school, run a big store, run a big farm— Son, just what do you want to do?" And I says to Pa: "I want to be a man like Huey—sit up in that engine and pull the throttle and let 'er fly. Pa, that's what I want to do. Want to have white hair like Huey, too, and let it fly to the wind when the engine rocks, and I want my hair to be long and follow the wind like Huey's hair does when he's pulling that engine. I want to be an engineer."

Pa would look at me as if to say: "Engineer—huh—w'y, the train is a ghost against the wind now—the big train—the C & O has come to the big valley and people don't come out to see the E-K pass like they used to come in for miles and watch it before there was another railroad around. The old E-K is a dead duck trying to swim. The old E-K is a goner—w'y, I've worked on the section and don't you think I know a sick track? The E-K track is not only a sick track but it is a dead track." That is what Pa kept trying to say. But Huey stayed right on that track. Huey kept pulling the throttle and don't you know people rode that train. A lot of them said it was dangerous to ride it. But Huey said it was not. People believed Huey. People liked Huey for thirty-six miles—they all knew him and when they heard his whistle moan they would pull out their watches and get the time. One would say: "Here comes Huey. Set your watches. Never over thirty minutes off unless a tunnel fell in, or the cut caved in, or a tree fell across the track—a trestle fell in or a bridge washed out—" No, never, never— Huey at the throttle and that engine always rode the rails—over the two rusty streaks that run to the north to the Ohio River and to the south— Ah— let me see, over the hills—no, under the hills—eight of them, people! And the bridges and trestles—ah, let me see, fifteen miles of them? No, that is not right when there are eight miles under the ground or something near that. That would leave only thirteen miles of easy sailing track. The way you count it you add the holes in the ground plus the bridges and the trestles and subtract that from thirty-six and one-half miles of the old E-K. The Lord knows I can count for I have been to school. When I used to go to school—I used to see Huey every morning. Just one place on the patch to school we saw Huey. We waited for him. Hid in the willows by the track and jumped out and waved our dinner buckets at Huey to surprise him. But he always had his eye on the spot where the willows were so he could wave at us and rare back at the throttle and laugh—don't think I don't remember how we used to quarrel over who was going to be like Huey. Walter Felch used to say he's going to be like Huey when he got to be a man—sit up in a train and ride and have everybody watching him pull at the throttle—never the brake— And I said I was going to be like Huey, too, and then he said only one of us could be like Huey. And I told him that Pa told me that Huey learnt a lot of the men that was out on the main line to pull an engine right on the old E-K. They tried to get Huey to go out and pull an engine there and he just laughed. He wouldn't leave where he'd been for years for no strange track. He wouldn't leave the people and the curves, the tunnels and the stores along the tracks. God, no, he wouldn't leave all this and the bridges. Huey was in many a wreck but he never got a bone broke. He knew where to take it easy and where to take it fast. He'd been over the bumps and the bridges and in and out the holes under the hills enough until he ought to have known what was what along that track.

He knew the patches of sprouts along the track and the barns and the apple orchards. W'y, Huey knew who owned the bulls along the road and who had in this patch of tobacco and that patch of cane. He knew all about the boys along the track. And you can just see honest Abe Johnson over there now in his corn knee-high to a grasshopper—without a shirt on his back plowing in the hot sun. That's the way Abe went most of the time. And he'd stop his mule and rest between the plow handles till Huey went by. He'd wave at Huey and holler and Huey would wave. And the wind would blow down the corn if it was a windy day along the Sandy bottoms. Smoke from the engine would blow back across the fields like a ribbon in the wind when sister Mary is running against the wind. Huey would just wave at everybody. W'y, old Winston Leppor said he believed Huey could be elected President of the United States because he knowed so many people. Thirty-six miles long and God knows how many miles wide, for the people used to come in to see the train—all the people knowed Huey.

Good old days they used to be, said Grandpa, good old days. Not back in the Rebellion. It was a bad time then to ride the train. But later on through the days of Grant, Garfield, and Hayes—w'y, they's more butter and eggs and crates of chickens come in on that train then than you could shake a stick at if you stood and shook a stick all day. Train stopped at every station and loaded on chickens. Everybody raised chickens along the E-K. It was a chicken country. People had to have salt and soda and coffee for their tables I guess. Couldn't very well raise them here in Kentucky. Let the hens pay for them. And calico and percale for dresses and silks and satins. Had to have some of them to go along for the well-dressed people and the girls getting married. Wasn't married at all unless she was married in a silk dress. Let the hens pay for that too. Well—you'd be surprised what a flock of hens can do in the spring and by grabs, they don't do it—up and sell the hens and get you some that will do it. That's what Mom always done. Pa was always for giving the hens the second chance if they didn't do any good one spring. But Mom just give 'em one chance. She said that was enough when there were other hens just waiting for the chance. And she'd up and crate the old hens that perhaps didn't find any gravels for their craws Pa said—well, gravels or no gravels—Mom just up and crated them and we hauled them to the station and waited for Huey.

And Lord how mercy—you ought to have just seen the turkeys that come down that E-K in the fall. Lord how mercy—it was one more sight—it was a plum sight. John Anderson would pass and he'd say: "If Huey don't quit hauling so many turkeys, w'y, people going to call him 'Turkey' Huey." Great loads of turkeys—a whole carload a day all through November and a bunch of wagons and them old fizzling automobiles at the other end of the track to get the loads—them old automobiles that scared the wits out'n the people and made the horses break the tongues out of the wagons. Well, a lot of women had to quit driving the mules and horses after them things come into use. That's just exactly what happened. Who was going to run the risk getting a leg, arm, maybe a neck broke over them infernal automobiles! Big things waiting for the turkeys. Yes—and they'd haul them to the Produce House in Greenupsburg, too—a town that never did grow much—has had about a thousand people since 1816. No place to build and when it did build baby by baby—w'y, they always told me when a baby was born in Greenupsburg two men left the town. That's what I always heard. Pa told me and his Pa told him. But that's where the turkeys went. And a lot of people would just ride the train in to get to see a Darkie. Never had any back in the hills. They all live in town, you know. And they'd drive them automobiles that hauled the turkeys. They all had the prettiest teeth—white as a hen egg laid by a white leghorn and just dropped in the nest. They'd sweat and lift the big crates of turkeys and the white men would just show 'em how to do it. They done the work. Honest to God they did. Smokey-Bill, Abe and Honest Jim and old Uncle Dick and all that bunch of Darkies. And you ought to hear them sing, too. They just sung away and the turkeys would stick their necks out the crates and go "plop—plop—kirt—kirt—kplop—kplop—kirt—kirt," and old Abe would laugh and show his big white set of teeth and say: "You goin' to kplop when the ax am on your neck. That's what you am—turkey!" And he would laugh. Turkeys wanting back to green fields on the Sandy River—back among the hills where it had the big fields to run over—not just crowded in a little crate a-sweating—a-huffing and puffing like the engine that pulled them there.

But let me tell you when the engine is going toward the north—it don't have to do much pulling the last fifteen miles of the way. It goes down hill—just nearly has to lock the wheels and it blows like a blowing viper snake all the time like "sssssssssssssss" and there's just a little stream of smoke that goes up from the stack. And in the winter that train always brought two carloads of coal from the mines in the low hills and they said on the other end of the track it hauled six or seven carloads from the Hammertight mines down to Grayson. Yessir—I've heard it but I never got to t'other end of the E-K, more than twice or three times in my life. Just went there then to ride the train the first time and the next two times to see about some cattle. I know they hauled down to Greenupsburg and there they took it on the *Greyhound*. That big boat that used to run on the river— and he said there's a lot of other boats that hauled from the E-K, too. Huey could tell you. If Huey was here he could tell you a lot that happened in the half a hundred years he was a-hold of that throttle. He could tell you about the cattle, too, they hauled in the fall and in the spring—two carloads of cattle a week—sometimes four and five and they always had four or five crates with bawling calves in them—veal calves shipping them from their mothers and they'd cry for them all the way. Huey said he just made himself get used to it. It bothered him a little at first. That was back in the days when the road was good.

And in the spring it was a sight at the cans of cream and milk that come in on the E-K—and the lumber and the people going to Greenupsburg with baskets on their arms. Going to town with baskets of eggs, baskets of butter done up pretty with a buttermold and a swan on the top of the yellow pounds and some with a horseshoe. All depended on the kind of buttermolds the women wanted. Horseshoe was better luck. Could sell the butter easier in Greenupsburg maybe—good fresh yellow country butter—and they'd have baskets of ducks and duck eggs, turkeys and turkey eggs, geese and goose eggs and guineas and guinea eggs— I tell you the women back in the days of Grant, Garfield and Hayes— w'y, they went loaded on that train to Greenupsburg. After the rebellion you know. Them was good days and Huey pulled long trains. W'y, yes—there was another train on that road in them days—Jonas Black, I believe, let me see wasn't he from Grayson and didn't he run that train? Now, I may have it wrong but I believe he did. He come from the other end of the line—started eight o'clock in the morning and passed Huey at Midway—and Huey started from our end of the road at eight in the morning and passed him at Midway. I believe he beat Huey there because Huey had to go up hill going out and kindly down hill coming back. Well, when they done that we got mail twice a day at the Riverton post office. You see Jonas brought it from the other end of the line and Huey brought it from the other end of the line. Huey took it out from our end of the line and Jonas took it out. That was when we got mail twice a day in them good old days.

Believe me it was a lot better to ride on a train the old people will tell you than it was to ride a mule to death. Just like one end of you had growed in the saddle when you started to get off—just have to heave and pull to get yourself limbered up and to pull your bones in shape and get the stuck end out of the saddle. Old people if they were a-living—people in the days of Grant, Garfield and Hayes will tell you, too, that it was a lot better than listening to the gravel fly against the dashboard of the surrey all day long and see the wheels roll around the flanks of the oak-covered hills. Better than to hear the wheezing of the axles and the horses getting their wind and seeing the foam fall from their flanks. Better to listen to the chug-chugging of the train any time and to see the white and black clouds of smoke roll out over the green hills—better to see it roll with the wind over the winter barren hills—honest it was— And boy, them excursions back in the old days. Ask the men about them. Ask me, too, boy—I remember them and I'm of the new generation— I'm of the third. I remember them. I'll let the old tell you first about what they saw and I'll tell you what I saw. W'y, in the days of Grant, Garfield and Hayes—they'd have some of the awfulest baseball games down at Greenupsburg and people would come with the team. The other end of the line would play our end of the line. Grayson would play Greenupsburg and the train would pull seven coaches—all the coaches they had, and they'd put on box-cars sometimes to hold the people. They'd be on top the engine and Huey'd go out and say: "Boys, don't care where you get so you get down low when we pass through them tunnels. If you get your heads knocked off it is your own risk. Get me, boys." "Yes, Huey, we got you. We'll watch our heads for they are our own." And they would laugh. And they'd follow the boys to the game. All of the people. Some said there's where the E-K used to make their wheelbarrow loads of money was on them excursion ball games. W'y, everybody saved for a week to get to come to the ball game on Sunday. Girls all trigged up and the boys, too, and they'd come and hold hands—drink that red pop from the stands and lots of times the boys would be drinking something else for red pop can't make them stagger—and they'd holler and whoop. I wish I could just tell you about it the way it was. I wish you could have just seen one of the games. They'd holler "batter UP!" And they'd dust the plate with a broom and they'd start the thing. The people would get on their own sides and start hollering. When the score got close men would go to meeting one another between the sides and they'd start fighting. More men would go out to get them out of the fight and they'd get into it. And the fight would start. And the baseball bats would start. People would go to hauling guns and the Sheriff would go out with his deputies and he'd deputize more men to help him break up the fight. If they was on our end of the line we just fined their men. If we was on their end of the line they just fined our men. So we just about broke even.

Huey would be there. He'd just sit there and look on. Huey was a young man in them days. They'd try to get Huey to root for this side and that side. Of course I'll always believe Huey felt for our side for he was from this end of the line. We'll never know. But Huey would say: "Boys, I can't be for neither side. I haul all of you. I live among all of you.

I'll just watch the game." And Huey didn't ever get on neither side. He sat back off on the old E-K railroad bed where the fielders always got—right about where the center fielder stood. He said he could see it better from there. And Huey couldn't a-taken sides, for if he had the people wouldn't have ridden on the train. It would have hurt the company if Huey had got on one side or t'other side. So Huey just set there between the two sides out where the pizen vine was on that old diamond at Greenupsburg.

And after the game the boys would get on the train—sweaty and tired and a lot of them with their lips busted and noses smashed—and they'd get their bats and balls and water jugs and go home. They'd holler smart things at us and lick out their tongues and we'd holler smart things at them and lick out our tongues. I guess we had the right to lick out our tongues at them if they had the right to lick out their tongues at us. We'd nearly all the time win the game when they come and played us and we'd nearly always lose when we played them. You know you can play better ball and fight harder on your own territory. Look at Gettysburg back yander in the Rebellion won't you. Fit on Yank territory and they winned that battle. First big one for them to win. They ought to a-fit on their own territory and they'd a-fit harder. That's the way it is in a ball game. I know it used to be that way with us here.

Well, I remember the last hanging we had here and the scaffold out in the open for people to see. Had to put on a lot of box-cars that day and then couldn't haul 'em all. It was a sight at the people that went out on that train—went to the hanging. W'y, after you got there you couldn't get to see anything for so many people. You couldn't get near the scaffold to see him hang and you couldn't get near enough to hear his confession. Too much hollering and going on. People having a good time and there with smiles on their faces—glad to see the man hang for what he had done to a woman. It was a awful day and the people all got worked up there that day and bloodthirsty and started a lot of fights. Two trains on the track that day. They run two excursions—one from our end of the track and one from the other end of the track. Hanging took place in an old orchard not far from Midway. Dinners on the ground that day to feed the people. They was warned to bring their own grub and they brought it and spread it on the ground. People had a good time that day all but the few fights on the ground, and they can always be expected when a crowd of strange people get together at a hanging.

And in the spring the E-K always hauled the people to the big Baptis' Association—that was always held on the upper end of the line. That's where all the Baptis' live—back up yander! And they had their big Association and big revils and preachings that lasted a week where every Baptis' preacher had a chance to preach. Some went four hours long. That's the one that got most of the yaller pullets to eat I always tell my wife. She's a Baptis' and I kindly tease her a little bit. And they'd preach of a night and wash their feet of a day. Lord, what times they used to have back there in them groves by Little Sandy. That old river could sure tell some tales and that train can, too. Come right off the train a-preaching and a-singing—that old E-K Huey could tell you about it. It was back in the days of Grant, Garfield and Hayes —and God Almighty it comes right on up from that. That's when it started—w'y, just a short time ago they had enough for a train load—they had to have an excursion. People just wanted to go along the track and they demanded it. Just told Huey they wanted an excursion and they got it. Tramped the weeds down under them groves till it looked like where General Morgan's men used to camp back yander in that Rebellion when them old Abolitionists use to swarm through here.

I tell you the train didn't haul so much in the early nine-

ties. It just hauled big loads of money—carloads of money
for the hills. You talk about awful times. We had them back
then. God, I remember taking bushels of money home and
putting it under the bed when Grover Cleveland was President of the United States. We paid off in corn—in seed corn
and lassies. A bushel of seed corn for a day's work—seed corn
or bread corn—either one you wanted to call it. I remember
Pap bringing corn home and putting it under the bed.
Wouldn't let us kids have any to parch in grease on the
griddle. Huey was pulling them train loads of corn back
then—train loads of money. Couldn't sell a turkey, couldn't
sell a chicken without you got paid in lassies or corn. Two
gallons of lassies for a day's work under Cleveland. Talk
about hard times. And people saying we's going to have another Rebellion—going to have a big war. And people got
scared afraid the world was coming to an end. But we pulled
out of that without a war. The war come later though. Just
to think the people among the hills couldn't take lassies and
corn for their chickens, ducks, turkeys, butter, cream, milk—
they already had lassies and corn. They had all the money
and it's just as bad to have all the money on your hands than
it is not to have any. So—they couldn't trade it in at the
stores. Banks wouldn't hold corn and lassies. And the girls
couldn't be married in silks and satins. Lots of people
couldn't ride the train. They couldn't give Huey a peck of
corn to ride over the two streaks of rust that run to the north
and to the south. God, no, they couldn't do it when they
didn't have a place to put it, Huey's Conductor Bill couldn't
put it in his pocket. No, sir, he couldn't.

Well, the war did come. It come with Spain. Huey took
many a man down to Greenupsburg to enlist for the Stars
and Stripes. Band was a-playing and the boys coming up to
march away. They rode from the hills over the two streaks
of rust—and Huey's hair was getting gray then. He was behind the throttle pulling them someplace. He pulled them

down past where they used to break bottles and bats at the ball games but they didn't stop there to fight. They went on to fight with Teddy. They can tell you about it.

Yes—I remember when they took one train off, said they couldn't get the money they used to get. Coal leaving the hills around Hammertight and not as much ore as the people thought. Ore playing out. Train wasn't near as big as it used to be—dwindling down. People thought first Little Sandy would be a rival to the E-K and get a lot of the trade. Well, the Little Sandy couldn't float big barges of pig iron from the old furnaces. They tried it and one couldn't get over the Riffles. It went to the bottom. People say that load of ore is right over from the old Scott place in the Little Sandy River now. They say it's buried in the sand at the bottom of the river. Little Sandy couldn't haul pig iron and ore like the E-K and Huey at the throttle. His gray hair in the wind and the men on the section stepping aside—four men to twelve miles of track—stepping aside and the bossman that worked with them made five. "Hello, Huey," they would say, "look at old Huey pulling her won't you—a load this time— watch them cars weave in and out."

Seems like I remember—as the ghosts of leaves in autumn remember and as the smoke from the stack remembers—the days that used to be: days when there were two trains on the E-K when we got mail twice a day and now with one train Huey brings us mail once a day when the tunnel don't fall in and a bridge ain't washed out—a cut's not slipped in—and a tree's not across the tracks—yes—yes—I remember as the ghosts of leaves remember—that was long ago—you remember Grant, Garfield and Hayes—you remember the two streaks of rust over the sand-filled yellow blooming between the rotted crossties—you remember the corn by the tracks and the apple trees loaded with apples—you remember the corn and the wheat— And you remember the four men on the twelve-mile section—section one, two, three, or four—do

you remember how the bosses worked, four bosses worked
with their men to get the Thanksgiving turkey— Do you
remember—seems like I hear the songs they used to sing:
"I'd Knocked the Devil or I'd a-Got My Joe," "Corena,
Corena, Where Did You Stay Last Night?— Come in this
morning and your clothes don't fit you right—" Yes, it seems
like I remember seeing one look at the sun and then at his
watch. I remember hearing him say: "It's about time for
Huey to be getting in here." And the way the wind blew—
the dead leaves—yes, as the smoke goes to the thin air—yes,
I remember—and the click of the shovel and the pick—the
hammer against the tee rail and the shovels against the cinders—I remember—as the ghosts of dead leaves flying in the
wind remember—

One train a day—and we would run to see Huey. We
would come from the Hollow. We would run to the willows. We had heard the dreams of yesterday—only one train
now. It was Huey: "Kept Huey on the old E-K to pull that
train—the old Eastern Kentucky—yes, sir. Will be missed if
she ever leaves these hills." And we saw the crowds around
the depots a-holding their horses and mules. 1909, 1910, 1911,
1912—and the years go by. The tee rails gather more rust
and the crossties get more rotten around the necks. Sections
been cut down. Three men and the boss and they work for
the turkey—sections one, two, three and four. And Huey's
hair is getting white—white to the wind—a white mourning
streak in the wind as the train goes out over the red streaks
through the weeds. And we go to the tracks and pick wild
strawberries by a place in the track. Walter Felch says it's a
cattle guard. I don't know but it cuts our feet and we can
walk on the cinders with our feet. I don't guess the cattle
could get over it. And there's a little place hollowed out
under the ties and a fence comes down to the place, a fence
all painted white—it's right in front of the first tunnel—
maybe it's to keep cows out of the tunnel. And we argue

whether a cow can wreck the train or not. We put little cinders on the track and that big engine Huey pulls crushes the cinders. We hide in the weeds to see. We don't let Huey see us. We can see Huey from the weed patch. And one would say: "God, how I would love to be Huey and set up there in that engine and ride—never have to look at a book all day or go home, get in the wood, get up the water and slop the hogs."

1913, 1914, 1915, 1916, '17—and believe you—another war —believe it or not—no more good big ball games when old left-handed John give them the slow drop and fanned them fast as they stepped up—only the Darkies could hit "Mighty John." They stepped up on the slow ball before it started that slow drop. They hit "Mighty John." Knocked him clean over the haystacks. That's what they done. But no more good ball games. Boys left the hills again for to cross the waters. "I've seen it happen," said Huey, "before, I've pulled the men from the hills right down this line." And Huey smoked his pipe. His white hair flying to the wind and the white smoke, the gray smoke, the black clouds of smoke going out over the fields into the thin air. Lord, them dark days. I was there when they loaded the boys on the train. So many of them so drunk they didn't know where they's a-going. I was there when they put Kim on the train. He never sobered up until he was wearing Uncle Sam's uniform—and that boy of Amos Allbright's—just a strip of a boy fifteen or sixteen—was there to see the boys off. Some crying and some laughing— some singing and some preaching and some cussing— I remember it—and when the train started Owl Allbright swung on the car and says I'm going too—and he went right along. No keeping him back. He went to France. Got in some way. You know Uncle Sam was wanting men in them days—begging them to work and making some of them fight. Didn't have to make the E-K boys fight—of course we missed them at the ball games and we missed them at the church—two

years was awful long and the girls around just a-going with
little strips of boys. Courting right up a limb. I'll tell you
single men were scarce as hen's teeth here among the hills.
And people would be at the post-offices along the track back
in them days. They'd come and say: "Hello, Huey, what's
the news today?" And Huey would say: "Heard we got a lot
more Germans today—all the papers filled with it." And
they'd jump up and down and laugh. Don't think I don't
remember it all and how they run to the post office and ask
for a letter from Kim, Gaylord, Owl, Frank, John, Henry,
Joe, Martin, Dan, Silas—yes—I remember how Huey would
talk from the engine to the boys along the station and tell
them the news he'd heard in Greenupsburg and how the people would say: "Wouldn't be so afraid if that fighting was on
our own land. A dog can't fight near so good when it is away
from home among strange people. You know that."

Two years away from home's a long time. You know that.
And them building roads back into the hills. Cars going out
now and hauling chickens, lassies—barrels of them and the
turkeys and eggs. Times changing. Amos Allbright said:
"Them automobiles will never last. Make too much noise.
Smell too bad. Scare too many horses on the road. People
won't stand for it. Ought to elect a Representative and send
to Frankfort agin 'em." But Amos was wrong. They did last.
And they started to beating Huey. W'y, people what's more
even rode to town in them holding baskets of eggs, butter and
chickens on their laps—the good women even done it—their
dresses flying up over their heads when they stood up behind
in the truck and rode—right out in public—women that brazen. Lord how mercy—no wonder the younger children's so
hard to do anything with—old people acting like that—and
the old E-K—is it just a rattletrap against the wind—

God, a uniform in 1917— W'y, it was the hunkey-dory thing
—now look at it. No one didn't care for the boys in their
pretty uniforms like they did when they come back to the

hills on furloughs and told about what they's going to do to the Germans. And Huey would listen and laugh: "Going to to do the same things to the Germans old Teddy's boys done to the Spaniards, are you? Going right after 'em. Need old Teddy over there. I'd feel better satisfied." "Yes—we're going to pour the hot lead right in 'em. I hope they got good guns. One a body can shoot good with—heavy and easy to hold. One of these like them old rifle with six sides—" But now: "That damn war. What the hell did we ever get mixed up in that thing for. German people good people. I liked the Germans. Englishmen think they're something on a stick, Huey." "Is that right, boys? And we're about all English—" "Can't help that. That's right." "Well, get on the old boy and I'll haul you back where you belong," Huey would say. And the soldier going home would say: "How's Pa and Ma, Huey?" And Huey would say: "Saw them at the post-office yesterday. Come up at Hopewell when I stopped there. And I talked to them a good little bit. Your Pa's got a bad cough. Nothing don't ail your Ma. She's well and hearty for her years. Yes—starting to farm a lot out there. Got in all that horse-shoe bottom this year. Going right after it."

1920, 1921, 1922. And did you hear about it? Well, they plan to take the old E-K away. Yes—that is right. I'm wondering what old Huey will do now. Getting so they can't make it pay. W'y, it's not safe to ride on any more they tell me. They tell me the crowd has been condemned. You see they've cut the sections down to two men and the boss. Yes, that is what has happened you see.

Is that the E-K just coming in? Look at my watch. Nine o'clock at night. Huey's due in here at three o'clock in the afternoon. Guess a tunnel's fell in. Have been having a time here lately. Three wrecks in one week. Three too many. Used to be a feller had to go to the station to catch the train. But I can stand out there with my basket anytime and flag the train and go from anyplace along the track. Say, did you hear what old Huey had a fellar to pull on him the other day? He was some fellar standing by the track and a right smart dressed fellar you know. He flagged Huey and Huey stopped. He got on the train and rode over to the station. And when Conductor Bill started to get his fare— W'y, he just got off and said: "Gentlemen, I just wanted to be neighborly and ride with you. I didn't know you had to pay." And the fellar said he didn't have no money. Huey just let it go. Well, there wasn't anything he could do about it but let it go. We've been a-laughing about Huey's neighbor ever since. And since that time Huey don't pick up no more strangers unless they look good. Huey's liable to lose his job you know.

When the boys went out to the pond to frog, w'y, Huey stopped the train and put them off at the right place. You know up there at that Reeves pond. A bunch of good fellars and Huey he knows 'em all you know. I tell you Huey's been on that road a long time, boys. Ever since I can remember. W'y, he knows everybody in the country. They just come and ride the train to say they've been on Huey's train. W'y, they say they're really afraid to ride the train but they can stand one trip of what Huey has stood a lifetime of. Just the other night when the train pulled in late—w'y, the tunnel fell in when the train was going through it. Murt Hensley said she heard a lumbering in the coach and when they come out on the other side to where the daylight was there was a rock big enough for twenty yoke of cattle to pull—laying right in the coach beside her and the whole top of the coach caved in where it had come through from the top of the tunnel. W'y, Huey puts that train over nothing but two streaks of rust and the wind. And Huey is right there pulling that train every day. Don't pull much anymore. Just two and three people sometimes. But the old E-K keeps going on two streaks of rust—red streaks through the ragweed tops and the dewberry briers and the sankfield.

The other day when Huey was taking a crowd of big hunters out to Anglin—w'y, they had the dogs tied in the coaches and when they come to Hilltop—w'y, one of the boys saw a covey of birds and Huey stopped. They unfastened the dogs and got out and got ever last one of the birds and got back on the train and went on to Anglin. I tell you a lot of engineers wouldn't let you do that. But it's just as Huey says. If he says we can bird-hunt I guess we can bird-hunt and he don't have so awful much to haul anyway. Hauls out an awful bunch of baseball players and froggers to the ponds and hunters to the hills. But they say the old road is just ready to play out.

1923, 1924, 1925, 1926, 1927, 1928—The old E-K goes on. Huey is at the throttle. His hair is white as clean sheep wool and he has a big head of hair. The years pass. Men come and go from the track. Some go to better jobs on the C & O. "I'll stay with my throttle, boys," says Huey, "been here a long time. And I know everybody. Know this country like a book. Schoolboys all come to the track out through the hills and watch me—holler at me. Want to be like me. I want them to be like me. The things they don't know. I've lived so I can die— I've pulled my train as near on time as my track would let me. And I've loved it. Never had trouble with my men in my life. They've never had trouble with me. Say what they will—I've been an engineer that's kept my eye on my rails. Never had an accident in my half-a-hundred years. I'm still pulling my train."

Can it be the truth? Is the old E-K a ghost that has come to stay—no one rides the train. And people come to look at it. It goes on. People come to the post-offices along the track and get the mail and wave at Huey. His white hair in the wind. Maybe it is the ghosts of yesterday—one man and the section foreman to a section now and no more Thanksgiving turkeys. Maybe it is the ghosts of the days of Grant, Garfield and Hayes—who knows and who remembers—maybe Huey

remembers the boys by the tracks and the paw-paws on the
hills—the gold and light gold leaves in autumn and the haw
trees with their iron-colored leaves and their red and dark
red berries—maybe Huey remembers the old cornfields, the
apple orchards, the old houses, the bridges and the trestles
and the cattle guards. The cattle guards are gone now and
the sankfield and dewberry briers have covered up the crossties. The crows fly overhead and caw-caw at two men straining at the tee rails. But two men by doing a little spiking
handle them all right. Maybe as the thin smoke to the wind
and Huey's white hair to the wind—maybe they are the
ghosts that remember—what about the dead leaves in the
wind and August heat from the streaks of rust. All right—
they bear the train twice a day. Huey pulls that train and it
is 1930. Huey's hair is white as cotton. His eyes are a little
dimmed. But he can see a man or a cow on the track. Guess
he can; when he sees a cow on the track, w'y, he gets out of
the engine and shoos the cow off. And if Martha Higgins is
close, w'y, Huey will say: "Better keep that cow off the track
here, Martha, or you'll get her killed. Your Grandpa used to
have a roughish cow that come nigh as a pea getting bumped
off here a couple of times." And Huey will get back in his
engine and start pulling the throttle.

Well, it was in the fall all right. Fall time—yes—I remember
the corn in the shock and the briers with brown leaves on
them—just the color of the rusted rails—and I remember the
boys going along and just pulling out a few spikes and lifting the rails up. Took Huey's Old Faithful to the other end
of the line. Left Huey on this end of the line where he lives.
I remember we'd heard so many times they's going to tear up
the tracks and they didn't do it—w'y, we just didn't believe
them. But this time the train didn't whistle for Three Mile
and we went to see. Sure enough they were taking up the
rails. Had a bunch of boys working and they were eating
apples and throwing the cores at one another. Had one old

sour-faced fellar on there and I says to myself: "Hit that bird with an apple core and you'll have him to fight." And there was the devilish boy of Mort Anderson's on there. Call him Possum and I just ups and says to myself, "They'll be a fight on this work car before the day is over."

When I passed by Riverton I saw Hester Anderson. He had a pistol and he said: "I'm looking for that sour-faced dough-bellied fellar that hit my brother Possum over hitting him with an apple core. He mashed my brother Possum's face—Possum just sixteen years old and one hundred and fifty pounds—that fellow two hundred and forty pounds and thirty years old. But I got the difference and I want to see him." And there were no trains that day.

That was the day the engineer fell asleep. He fell asleep not to wake up for a long time—perhaps in another morning —not just to get off at eight o'clock and to pull the throttle over the rusted rails. But no more trains and Huey—he passed on. We heard about it. "Huey is dead." W'y, the schoolboys all cried. They wanted to be like Huey. Pulling a train over two rusted streaks of steel—through the spring, summer, autumn, winter—unafraid of track and weather—he pulled his train. It was his train—he knew every bolt and every piece of steel. It had been faithful to him and to us. We knew them, too.

There wasn't any train to pull us to his funeral. It would have been a big excursion. And if we had just had Huey to have pulled us there. Of course he got a little tottery toward the last but a lot of people said it was the track that Huey was going over that made him scoot all over his cab— If he had just been here to have pulled us to his own funeral. There were enough there for a big excursion—the biggest funeral that has ever been in these parts. It would have taken both trains to have pulled them all to Huey's funeral.

We saw Huey there. He was quiet. He was dressed up a little bit now— Didn't have the glasses up on his forehead and the red bandanna around his neck like we used to see him wear. But his eyes were the same and his lips were the same. He had his eyes set on the rails—half a hundred years and not an accident. And in his face were the dreams that we remembered and soon would not be remembered—the great crowds at the ball games and the trainloads of boys and girls —the boys that rode for Teddy and the boys that crossed the waters. Some were not hauled back alive—and the noise at the ball games—the section men a-singing and the click of the shovel, spade, mattock, hammer, hoe. The click of steel battering steel and the wind a-whining through the dewberry briers—and Huey with his hand on the throttle and the scream of the whistle—and us down behind the willows waiting to wave at Huey—all wanted to be like him. But now— the silent hands—the steady quiet eye and we stand and shed our tears unashamed of tears for our engineer that once pulled the train where no track now is—nothing but the wind and dents in the earth and cinders ground down and old bridges—but we remember—we'll always remember—and Huey—our engineer—we wonder on what silent train and to what silent land our engineer has gone.

THE BERTH OF HOPE

HOPE

By Octavus Roy Cohen

Octavus Roy Cohen

Epic Peters is the Paul Bunyan or the John Henry of Pullman porters—which is to say that there never was and never could be such a porter as Peters. The Pullman porter, in real life, is not a character in black-face. He is, with rarely an exception, a responsible and competent workman in his job of adding to the public comfort and convenience. But the literary convention of the Pullman porter is something else entirely—and Octavus Roy Cohen's creation represents the literary convention raised to the chuckling point.

Cohen was born in Charleston, South Carolina, on June 26, 1891. His first job was as a civil engineer for the Tennessee Coal, Iron and Railroad Company in 1909. Later he drifted into journalism as a reporter or in editorial work for newspapers in Birmingham, Alabama, Charleston, South Carolina, Bayonne and Newark, New Jersey. Not content with engineering and journalism, he set out to be a lawyer. In 1913 he was admitted to the South Carolina bar and he took up the practice for two years. By 1915 Cohen decided to write; and, if a long string of books, several plays, and about thirty motion pictures are any criterion of success, it was a wise decision. He has enjoyed cumulative popularity as an author, especially a writer who excels in Negro and mystery stories. Among some of his well-known titles are: *Polished Ebony, Come Seven, Highly Colored, Lilies of the Alley,* and *Romance in Crimson.* His railroad book is, of course, *Epic Peters, Pullman Porter.*

The Berth of Hope is a clever story of a Pullman porter running between Birmingham and New York on the Southern Railway. Anyone who recalls the schedule of those trains as they ran in the middle 1920's from Birmingham through Atlanta and Spartanburg and Charlotte and Greensboro and Danville, not to mention Washington and Philadelphia, will recognize the author's fidelity in matters of railroad operations.

THE BERTH OF HOPE

By Octavus Roy Cohen

THE HUGE, CAVERNOUS SHED of the Birmingham Terminal Station was no more dark and gloomy than Mr. Epic Peters. That gentleman deposited an elderly maiden lady in Section 9, plastered a professional smile upon his ebony countenance and shuffled unhappily down the aisle of the Pullman. In the geometric center of his tremendous palm lay something cold and round and hard. Once again on the platform, he opened his fingers and gazed with supreme and pessimistic disdain upon the financial offering of the spinster traveler.

"One dime!" commented Epic bitterly. "One single measly dawg-gone terrible thin dime! An' mebbe one mo' dime when she gits off. The porterin' business suttingly ain't what it used to be."

He flicked a speck of dust from the silver service stripe which decorated the sleeve of his blue uniform jacket and meandered sadly down the platform to where sat the fat little porter in charge of the car for Atlanta passengers.

"How's tips, Joe?"

The pudgy face beamed.

"Pretty fair. One man give me a dollar. How they is with you?"

"Terrible! Folks ain't so loose with their change as they once was. Seems like when they goes to New Yawk they don't make no 'lowance a-tall fo' tips. I has got two dimes, one two-bit piece and one half dollar, an' leavin' time ain't so

225

long off." Epic propped his elongated frame against the side
of the Pullman. "Tell you the troof, Joe, Ise thinkin' of ap-
plicatin' myself into another distric'—Chicago or mebbe Los
Angeles."

Joe sighed enviously. Seemed to him that successful men
never were contented. Here was Epic Peters with one of the
star through runs, and he was talking about transferring his
efficient and engaging personality to other parts of the country. Two passengers appeared and Epic lurched slue-footedly
away, leaving Joe staring raptly after him. Joe worshiped Mr.
Peters. He knew that Epic was one of the star porters on the
Southern system—a man with eight years of seniority behind
him.

"Anyways," breathed Joe, "does porters like him get dis-
allisfry, then mebbe some day I gits me a chance to remove
myse'f off this pikin' li'l Bumminham-to-Atlanta run."

As Epic approached the two men who now stood gazing
uncertainly at the silent Pullmans his eye lighted on the purple check which one of them held and a flash of interest
crossed his features. Drawing-room, eh? Two men! The combination usually proved interesting financially. His face
beamed as he approached them.

"What space you gemmun got?"

"Drawing-room to New York."

"Right this way, cap'ns; right this way. Gimme them
grips."

They followed him down the aisle of the car. He flung
open the drawing-room door and deposited their suitcases
within.

Then he ostentatiously busied himself with rearranging
the soap and towels in the lavatory and in dusting the windows. One of the gentlemen appeared to comprehend that
he was being hinted at. He thrust a dollar bill into the un-
reluctant hand of Mr. Peters. That colored gentleman bowed
profusely.

"Thanky, cap'n. Does you gemmun want anythin', just press the button an' Ise with you soon as the echo comes. 'Tain't fo' nothin' they calls me Hop Sure."

The men glanced at each other and smiled. One of them was very tall and rather thin, but with a pair of cold gray eyes which contained little of softness. The other was short and stout; but, too, there was something about the set of his jaw and the hunch of his rather broad shoulders which informed Epic that neither he nor his companion was a traveling man.

Hop Sure returned to the platform. Somehow, with the crinkle of the dollar bill still tickling his palm, the train shed seemed less empty and gloomy. His lips expanded and he hummed a few lines of a little song that was always more or less in evidence when he was not unpleased with the world:

> "I plays my cards against my chest,
>   I nusses all my chips;
>   I never joke an' Ise never broke,
>   'Cause Ise hell on gettin' tips."

A gentleman and his wife boarded the car and Hop Sure was enriched by another half dollar. The events of the past few moments had caused his spirits to soar considerably. No longer was he contemplating an immediate transfer to another Pullman district. That was Epic's way—he was an extremist, inevitably either thrilled to the zenith of beatitude or wallowing in the nethermost depths of dank despair.

After all, the portering profession had been rather unlucrative recently, even on this choice run between Birmingham and New York. Travel had been light and parsimonious, and Epic's wages of sixty-six dollars a month were highly insufficient to his needs. Faithful and efficient on the road, he was yet considerable social pumpkins in Birmingham, and he required cash and plenty of it to maintain his position and dignity.

The huge engine which was to haul them on the first lap of their long journey backed under the shed and bumped gently against the waiting train. And just as it did so the two gentlemen of the drawing-room descended to the platform, lighted cigarettes and stood regarding Epic with an interest which was more than merely casual.

Returning their scrutiny, Epic Peters became more forcibly impressed with his original conclusion that they were a trifle different from the usual run of travelers. He felt an uncomfortable desire to shiver. Yet they were decidedly friendly in their manner to him and memory of the dollar tip was still fresh in his mind. Too, he received the impression that they were discussing him. The tall, cold, gray gentleman flashed a fishy glance in his direction and nodded briefly; the smaller and stouter man bobbed his head in agreement; and then, as though prompted by the idlest sort of curiosity, they drifted into the vicinity of the porter and dropped into casual conversation.

"How long before we pull out?"

Epic consulted his watch.

"Eighteen minutes, cap'n. We leaves at 'leven-fifty."

They glanced at each other.

"Eighteen minutes? M'm!— Where do we get breakfast?"

"Leavin' Atlanta, suh. We gits there at six-fifteen Central Time an' leaves at nine o'clock Eastern."

"Do you make the run straight through to New York?"

"Yassuh. Ise the th'ooest-runnin' porter on the line."

"I see—I see." The taller of the two men closed his eyes slightly and Epic felt that he was being X-rayed. "What is your name?"

"Epic Peters, suh. They calls me Hop Sure."

"Hop Sure? On the job, eh?"

"Yassuh. You suttinly said it that time, cap'n."

Again the searching scrutiny.

"Wonder if you could do us a little favor, Hop Sure?"

"Doin' favors fo' gemmun is the fondes' thing I is of."

The tall thin man cast a swift glance about the big shed. Then from an overcoat pocket he produced a package. This he held tight against him, as though to conceal it from the gaze of passers-by. But there was no mistaking the keen and proprietary interest with which it was regarded by the shorter man.

"This is a pretty valuable package," vouchsafed the spokesman. "Very valuable. We're afraid to leave it laying around the drawing-room. I wonder if you would take care of it for us until we get to New York."

Hop Sure eyed the packet. It was about twelve inches long, perhaps half that width and not more than an inch in thickness.

It was a very innocuous-appearing thing, wrapped in brown paper and tied with twine. At least it was not sufficiently bulky to contain liquor. Liquor was Epic's chiefest fear: there was entirely too much investigating going on along the road to suit him.

"I always aims to please . . ." he started uncertainly when the smaller man produced a wallet. From it he took a crisp new five-dollar bill, which he thrust into the not unwilling hand of the gangling porter.

"That's to pay for your trouble," he suggested softly.

Hop Sure's decision was instantaneous. Five-dollar tips were few and far between.

"Gimme," he commanded.

"Be careful," counseled the taller man. "It is quite valuable."

"Boss man, you don't have to warn Hop Sure none. This heah thing goes in my linen closet an' it don't come out until you-all gemmun gives the word. Takin' care of things like this is the bestest thing I does."

He climbed aboard the Pullman, packet in hand. The five dollars surcharged his soul with elation, although he was not unconscious of the appraising glance which bored into his back as he left them. He selected the key to the linen compartment, opened the door, made a nest for the package on the very top shelf, and then carefully placed towels over it. Then, as he locked the door, he found himself face to face with the two owners.

"It's safe there?"

" 'Tain't nothin' else."

"Good!" There appeared to be considerable relief on the faces of the two men. Then the taller one introduced himself. "I'm Mr. Carson," he said. "This"—designating his friend—"is Mr. Garrison."

"Yassuh," beamed Epic. "I know."

A startled glance flashed between them.

"How do you know?"

"Seen the names on yo' bags," explained the colored man. "Always likes to know my passengers pussonal."

They strolled into the drawing-room while Epic returned to the platform to await the inevitable late comers.

The Pullman conductor arrived; the big engine at the head of the train was puffing and snorting impatiently; and, less than five minutes later, the welcome "All abo-o-oard!" reverberated through the shed; the train quivered into action and nosed out into the chill night air. Epic closed the vestibule of his car and strolled inside. All twelve sections were made down and he gazed the length of green-curtained canyon, experiencing anew the thrill which had been his on the occasion of his maiden run.

Epic was fond of portering; he had all the instincts of a railroad man; the thrum-thrumming of wheels on steel rails was sweet symphony to him, and even the insistent ringing of the porter's call bell was not at all times unwelcome.

Too, for the first time in his life Epic had found opportunity to gratify the wanderlust. He was a traveled gentleman, was Epic, and a personage along Eighteenth Street in

Birmingham, where he swelled about in a suit of screaming civilian clothes and spoke with well-studied casualness of "Well, when I was in New Yawk the other day I was walkin' down Fifth Avenue, an'—" They gave him rapt attention when he spoke of New York, and he conversed with equal glibness of other towns along this prize run of his—of Atlanta and Spartanburg and Charlotte and Greensboro and Danville, not to mention Washington and Philadelphia.

He was well liked by the conductors with whom he worked. On more than a score of occasions he had received mention in the roll of honor published in the national publication which deals with the activities of Pullman porters, each of these honorable mentions having been earned by unsolicited letters written to the company by patrons who had cause to be unduly grateful for special services rendered by the somewhat slab-sided, but always genial, Hop Sure Peters.

Epic was prideful in his job, but he was thoroughly a businessman. He gave perfect service to those who were frugal in tips; and if to those who tipped him generously the service rendered was superperfect, that was no business of anybody save Epic. Now his eyes were turned affectionately upon the door of Drawing-Room A, where slumbered the elongated and rather saturnine Mr. Carson and the pudgy and somewhat athletic Mr. Garrison. Six dollars was an unusual sum, even for a porter of Epic's experience, and he was determined that they should get value received in service.

As to that brown-paper parcel: Shuh! He was always glad to take care of things fo' the white folks. Wa'n't nothin' gwine happen to no package they tu'ned over to him; nossuh.

"Fo' six dollars," he announced to himself, "I'd nuss a baby."

Three gentlemen occupied the smoking room until the train backed under the shed at Anniston two hours after leaving Birmingham, but between there and Atlanta the smoker was vacant and Epic curled up on the seat for a well-earned snooze. Outside he could see the silhouette of pine-studded hills against the face of a full moon; the train rocked and swayed as it pitched through the night on a roadbed which had been constructed in the days when railroad engineers believed it was cheaper to go around a hill than to grade through it. But Epic Peters was content; he never grew travel-weary. He hummed as he dozed off:

> "Ise a terrible care-free cullud boy,
>   An' I lives all over the earth;
> I takes my fun like a sonovagun,
>   Ise a houn' on fixin' a berth.
> Ise got me a gal, a good-lookin' gal,
>   A-waitin' fo' me to git back;
> She's boun' to be true, I ordered her to,
>   When I hit her that las' awful crack.
> She listens at me—"

And then Epic Peters dozed off to wake by instinct three hours later, splash cold water into his face and prepare for the arrival in Atlanta.

Outside, the first cold finger of November dawn was puncturing the chill of night. Epic shivered. He worked the stiffness from his joints and glanced at his watch, longingly counting the minutes against the time when he'd be under the shed in the Atlanta station and able to get his morning cup of coffee.

"Coffee! Yum! Tha's one thing which is sho'ly fond of me."

He busied himself making up the berths which had been unoccupied during the night. Then, marked by a faint curl of smoke here and there, and the gaunt, unimaginative outlines of occasional factories, the city of Atlanta appeared in the background.

The nearly two hours in Atlanta were busy ones for Epic. There was first the all-important item of breakfast, then the tidying of his car and the switching back and forth in the yards, as the train was taken to pieces and made up anew for the journey northward. At a few minutes before eight o'clock some one stopped beside him on the station platform and he looked into the friendly yet forbidding eyes of the stout Mr. Garrison. Epic touched his cap.

"Mawnin', Cap'n Garrison."

"Good morning, porter." The man smiled a hard, dry smile. "You have a wonderful memory for names and faces."

"Yassuh, sho'ly has, cap'n. Tha's one of the mostest things I has got."

Mr. Garrison sighted the length of the train.

"Diner open yet?"

"Yassuh. 'Tain't nothin' else. Secon' car for'ard."

The white gentleman started off.

"See you later, Hop Sure."

"You suttingly ain't goin' to miss me, cap'n. Ise gwine stay in seein' distance all day."

The train pulled out of the terminal station. Epic, swapping blue blouse for white jacket, bent himself with the job of awakening late sleepers. This included an insistent buzzing at the door of Drawing-Room A, with an eventual sleepy response from the attenuated Mr. Carson.

"Las' call fo' breakfast comin' th'oo, suh. Better git up right smart."

But evidently Mr. Carson did not get up right smart, for it was very considerably later that he emerged, in fresh linen and with a new close shave. He was without a hat, and Epic gazed with overt approval upon the single streak of gray which stood out in the very center of his black hair.

"A mos' distinction gemmun," commented Hop Sure to himself. "He's a houn' on han'someness."

Mr. Carson nodded briefly to Hop Sure as he moved toward the diner. That dignitary followed him down the aisle and almost collided with the bulky Mr. Garrison, who was just returning from his enjoyment of matutinal nourishment. Epic would have stepped aside, but Mr. Garrison stopped him, and he stopped him in a very peculiar and mysterious manner. He glanced first up and down the aisle of the car, then lowered his voice:

"Hop Sure?"

"Ise he."

"You remember that package we gave you last night?"

"Hot dam! Reckon I couldn't never forget that."

A still lower tone—"I want it."

"Now?"

"Yes. Bring it to me in the drawing-room right away."

Epic beamed.

"Yassuh, cap'n, suttingly will. You says it an' I does it."

Garrison moved on into the sanctuary of the drawing-room. Hop Sure ricocheted the length of the car, opened the linen closet and unostentatiously removed the brown-paper parcel from the top shelf, tucked it in the voluminous pocket of his white jacket and journeyed back to the other end of the Pullman, where he entered the drawing-room after a brief warning buzz.

"Got it?"

"I has."

The packet was extended. Immediately the Garrison hand disappeared in the Garrison pocket to show up a moment later with a bank note. Epic's eyes seemed about to pop from their sockets. Another tip—another bill. "These is the loosest gemmun with their money! I reckon I c'n be terrible useful with it."

Mr. Garrison accepted the packet. Hop Sure took the tip. Then a faint frown corrugated his Stygian brow.

"Boss man, if 'tain't too pussonal a request, would you min' changin' this two fo' two ones?"

Again that cold smile of impersonal amusement on the white man's face.

"Why? Two-dollar bill bad luck?"

"We-e-ell, not back luck ezac'ly, but 'tain't good luck, neither—specially to cullud folks."

The exchange was made and Epic escaped. Outside he paused to shake his head in worriment.

"Two-dollar bill—huh! That ain't the craziest thing I is about. Never did like no two-dollar bills."

The train slowed down. It came to a protesting halt at Peachtree, Atlanta's suburban station for through trains. Epic leaped to the platform and assisted with a considerable number of suitcases which had been wheeled down the platform on a truck. In order to be doubly efficient, he mounted the truck for a moment at the request of a prosperous-looking gentleman in a fur overcoat who gave promise of lavish tips. And from his perch on the truck Hop Sure was enabled to command a view of the interior of Drawing-Room A, his car. What he saw there impressed itself vividly on his subconscious mind. It was, as a matter of fact, nothing to excite particular comment. Nor was it so usual as to be without effect.

Mr. Garrison was standing in the middle of the drawing-room, his broad back toward the double windows. He was bending over and it was patent that he was working intensively. It took Epic just a small portion of a split second to see what his passenger was doing, and the very nature of the act aroused the porter's interest.

Mr. Garrison was engaged in the act of sliding the seat of the couch out from the wall. Peculiar! But more peculiar still was the fact that, once having exposed the storage space beneath the seat of the couch, he proceeded to take from his coat pocket the brown-paper parcel which had been the source of so many lavish tips and to conceal that parcel very carefully. Immediately thereafter Mr. Garrison replaced the mohair cushion, arranged overcoats with studied carelessness upon it and settled in a corner with his Atlanta *Constitution*.

Shortly after leaving Peachtree, Mr. Carson returned from the diner. Epic Peters was standing in the vestibule of his Pullman, staring out at the rolling North Georgia country and listening satisfiedly to the drumming of the wheels and the shrill blast of the locomotive whistle. Carson stopped, lighted a cigar and leaned against the steel wall opposite the porter.

"Nice morning," he commented.

"Yassuh. Suttinly is that."

Carson's thin lips compressed into a pinkish white line which was somehow quite hard.

"When is our next stop?"

He had a habit of clipping his words, making his manner of speech crisp, incisive, and not particularly soothing; it was as though he was not in the habit of having persons disagree with him.

" 'Bout an hour fum now."

"Where?"

"Gainesville, suh."

"For how long?"

Once, many years before, Epic had been star witness in a big damage suit. The plaintiff's attorney had grilled him severely; and now, chatting thus idly with Mr. Carson, Hop Sure was reminded of that miserable hour on the stand.

"We ain't on'y s'posed to stop but fo' two-th'ee minutes, but we ginrally stays there about ten."

Carson's fingers quested slowly toward his pants pocket. Epic watched those fingers fascinatedly; they were long and slender and gave the impression of steely strength. But when they emerged the porter no longer found them the focus of his interest. They held a five-dollar bill. Five! Epic's eyes opened wide under the severe stare which Carson bent upon him.

"See this, Hop Sure?"

"Does I? Boss man, I reckon I ain't never gwine be so blin'

I couldn't see somethin' like that. Or was I, I could tell it by the smell."

"Want it?"

"Aw, cap'n—"

"If you don't—"

"You talks foolishment with yo' mouf, cap'n—beggin' yo' pardon. Money is the mostest thing I always wants."

"H'm!" Mr. Carson puffed reflectively upon his cigar. "Remember that packet we gave you last night?"

Epic nodded. With himself he held puzzled communion— "Hot dawg! Somethin' is sho' happenin' to me, but I don't know what it is."

"I want you to get that packet for me, Hop Sure."

It was on the tip of Epic's tongue to inform Mr. Carson that Mr. Garrison already had the package. But the five-dollar bill, waving slowly and insinuatingly before his nose, stayed his tongue. There came vividly to mind remembrance of the scene which he had observed through the window at Peachtree Station—of the stocky Mr. Garrison meticulously hiding the packet under the lounge in the drawing-room. And, after all, the packet belonged to the pair of them, had been entrusted to him by both acting as one, and it was no business of his what they wanted with it or why this wealth was thus showered upon him.

"Can you get it for me while we're at Gainesville?"

Nothing could have better suited the plans of the long-legged porter.

"Yassuh, sho'ly can."

"I'll get my friend to walk up and down outside with me." Carson inspected Epic very closely. "I want it handed to me personally. Understand what that means?"

"You yo'se'f alone?"

"Alone!"

"Boss, I has got so much understandin' my head aches."

The five-dollar bill changed hands and Carson disappeared

into the car. He seemed so sure of himself—even sure of foot on the swaying floor. He walked without a lurch.

"Somehow," reflected Hop Sure sagely, "I wouldn't be awful happy was that gemmun to git real mad at me."

At Gainesville the two travelers strolled up and down the platform. Epic, selecting his time with great care, boarded the train and flung into the drawing-room. He was nervous, to say the least. This was something new to him. As a matter of fact, he was considerably at sea about the whole affair; but five dollars was five dollars, and if a man demanded his package that was no business of his.

The task of rescuing the parcel from beneath the lounge took but a moment. Even less time than that was required to conceal it in a capacious pocket. Five minutes after leaving Gainesville, Carson joined him in the vestibule.

"Got it?" The packet was passed over. Carson's eyes narrowed. "Remember, this is between you and me."

"Us an' not anybody else a-tall."

"That's it. And be sure you don't forget."

"Boss, I never does nothin' that even soun's like forgettin'."

Travel was not heavy, nor were Epic's duties on this trip unduly arduous. The particular *bêtes noires* of a porter's existence were conspicuously absent from his car—babies, invalids and normally healthy persons who are unable to withstand the quakings of railroad travel.

Epic dropped into Section 8, which was happily empty. He stretched his long, loose-jointed figure and stared out at the swelling Piedmont; the far-flung foothills merging into a background of blue mountains; the acres and acres of plowed fields which a few months since had been snowy with stalwart cotton and now were bare and brown, with here and there a touch of white where the staple had remained unpicked; long vistas of cornstalks, brittle and sapless and broken by the first ravages of genuinely cold weather; pine trees by the mile; little false-fronted towns flaunting themselves to travel-ers' stares; and everywhere dust-streaking flivvers catapulting along the more-or-less good sandy-clay roads.

Once in a while the buzzer would sound at the end of the car and Hop Sure would galvanize into action—a pillow here, a hat bag there. "Porter, are we on time?" "Yassum, we sho'ly is." At 11:30 he made his way into the diner, where, feeling wealthy, he ordered profusely and ate with gusto—soup and fish and fried eggplant and candied sweet potatoes and ice cream and cake. Even at the half rates allowed porters in the dining car, he was somewhat appalled by the size of his check, but paid it without a murmur and determined grimly that he would also commit the extravagance of eating a second meal there when the dinner hour should come.

The porter on the Atlanta-to-New York car left the diner with him. The waiters were scurrying around straightening the dining car against the forthcoming invasion of white passengers. In the vestibule the two colored men conversed briefly.

"How's tricks, Hop Sure?"

"Tol'able, brother, tol'able."

"Prosp'rous trip?"

"Uh-huh. Kinda affluent."

The Atlanta porter grimaced.

"I got th'ee ten-cent passengers on my car. I hates a ten-center. Rather I gits me nothin' a-tall than ten cents."

Hop Sure shrugged sympathetically.

"I never fools with nothin' less'n two bits. Ten centses I th'ows out of the westibule. They ain't even no good fo' slot machines."

The Atlanta porter drifted on. Hop Sure inspected his call board to make sure that there had been no summons for him, then once again he lounged in Section 8. The inner man had been placated and Epic Peters was at peace with the universe.

Georgia merged into South Carolina; the route bent gently northward and swung closer and closer to the alluring foothills of the Blue Ridge Mountains—the bewitching Sapphire Country. And then Mr. Epic Peters became uncomfortably conscious of the fact that a pair of eyes were boring into his head, that he was receiving a telegraphic command to come hither.

As he looked up and saw that it was the pudgy Mr. Garrison who was silently struggling to attract his attention from the passageway to the right of Drawing-Room A, a premonition smote Epic immediately beneath his belt buckle. Nor was that to be wondered at, for a thundercloudish look rested upon the countenance of the glassy-eyed Mr. Garrison, and it was immediately apparent that something had occurred which did not fill that gentleman with any wild surge of elation.

"Somethin' infohms me," postulated Hop Sure as he reluctantly hoisted himself to his feet, "that I is about to heah some more questions 'bout that package."

Immediately, as Garrison saw that the porter was answering his summons, he turned on his heel and proceeded to the vestibule. As Epic joined him, he flung around with a few well-chosen words which were uttered in a manner entirely dissimilar to his erstwhile good-humored indifference.

"Porter, that package has gone!"

Epic disguised sudden and profound agitation with a disingenuous expression; his brain raced back to the five-dollar transaction at Gainesville, by which Mr. Carson had come into possession of the parcel.

"No!" he gasped with cleverly simulated amazement.

"It has!" rasped Mr. Garrison. "Gone!"

Instinct told Hop Sure that he had better hold his peace. What, a few hours before, had appeared to be a logical and simple business transaction, now assumed an aspect which he neither understood nor liked. He rolled his head to one corner of his long neck and voiced a question.

"Where?"

"Where?" Garrison's eyes blazed. "How do I know?"

"That suttinly is right, cap'n. How does you know?" Epic liked the sound of his own voice, it gave him a little more confidence. "Was you to know where yo' package was at you would go remove it away fum there an' put it somewheres else, an' then it wouldn't be gone no more; now would it, Mistuh Garrison?"

"I've got to find that package."

"Yassuh, you suttinly has. An' that ain't no lie. You sho'ly has got to recover that thing back. Does you reckon somebody abstracted it away fum where you put it at?"

"Yes"—grimly. "I reckon just exactly that."

"No! Cain't be!"

"It is. Now listen to me, porter! Recover that packet and there's ten dollars in it for you."

"Ten dol—"

"Yes, ten."

"Wigglin' tripe! Cap'n, you can consider that thing has done been got."

Garrison shook his head skeptically.

"I certainly hope so. Let me know the minute you think you know where it is."

"Ise gwine do that ve'y thing, boss."

Garrison moved slowly into the car, an obviously worried gentleman. Epic took stock of the situation.

"They's on'y two things I understan's about this heah mix-up," he ruminated, "an' I don't know what neither of them means."

The engine sirened hoarsely for a railroad crossing and a moment thereafter flashed by a big gaunt cotton mill; then another and another. Mechanically Hop Sure produced a rag from his hip pocket and dusted the vestibule rail.

"Greenville," he mumbled to himself. "Dawg-gone if we ain't got to this heah town in a terrible hurry."

They reached Greenville, the western gateway of the rich South Carolina Piedmont section. The station hummed with metropolitan activity; only one passenger at Greenville for Epic's car. The porter was amazed to find himself taking more than a cursory glance at the newcomer.

This passenger carried a New York ticket calling for Section 12 in its entirety, but that alone was not what attracted him to Epic's attention. It was rather that, in some subtle and entirely different way, he was remindful of Carson and Garrison, separate and collective owners of the package which already had brought to Epic much money and harassment.

There was no reason why the newcomer should have reminded Epic of either Carson or Garrison; he was as different from either as they were from each other. Yet there was a reminiscent confident set to his broad shoulders; the same inquisitive, distrustful, steely light in the eyes; an identical manner of studied disinterestedness.

But, whereas Carson and Garrison were immaculately tailored and exquisitely haberdashed, this man wore ill-fitting ready-made clothes, a cheap if stalwart shirt and a polka-dotted necktie. His shoes were unduly large and strikingly square-toed.

The stranger boarded the train. Epic deposited him and his bag in Section 12 and returned to the platform. Immediately something happened.

The figure of Mr. Carson detached itself from the shadows of a baggage truck which was piled high with suitcases and descended upon Hop Sure. Mr. Carson seemed more than a little excited, and his cameo face bore an expression of considerable annoyance. It was quite plain to the porter that his white gentleman friend was making vast efforts to control a surplus of emotion.

Carson's lengthy figure pressed close against the porter's

side and into Hop Sure's hand was thrust a packet which long since had become strikingly familiar. Within Epic's heart there sounded a paean of triumph.

"Li'l package," he exulted to himself, "you has come home to papa."

Nor was that all. As he, scenting the need for caution, slipped the parcel in the pocket of his jacket, he heard Carson's voice, low and chill. He glanced at Carson's face and was amazed to see it guileless and expressionless. The man was talking without moving his lips.

"Put that thing back in your linen closet. Keep it hidden."

"Yas—"

"Shut your mouth! Just do as I tell you." The slender fingers disappeared, then reappeared. "Here!"

It was a bill; a nice, new, crisp bill.

"Hot diggity dawg!" enthused Epic silently. "It never rains, but it gits wet."

Carson moved unostentatiously away. The all aboard was sounded; Epic hoisted himself to the platform. And then he stared popeyed at this latest crinkling bit of booty.

"Ten dollars! Great Gawdness Miss Agnes! Fust it's a heap an' then it's twice as much."

Epic stood alone on the platform and tried to think. He had done entirely too much thinking during the day and the sustained and unnatural effort left him weak and headachy. Aside from other gleanings, the two gentlemen in Drawing-Room A had netted him twenty-three dollars and he possessed a profound hunch that the end was not yet.

There was, for instance, the matter of the ten-dollar reward offered him by the portly Mr. Garrison for the return of the lost package. That package was now in Epic's pocket and the ten dollars was in the pants of Mr. Garrison. It was obviously a howling shame that the transfer should not be effected.

The ethics of the situation troubled Hop Sure not in the

slightest degree. By their own mutual admission the package was the joint property of the two men; neither claimed sole ownership or disputed any claim which the other might make. Epic did not see his way clear to disobey the orders of either concerning it, and certainly, since that was the case, it would be the height of absurdity to do other than collect a maximum of profit.

They departed Greenville at precisely two minutes before one o'clock in the afternoon. Epic watched and saw Garrison and Carson disappear into the diner. Then, after a few additional moments of thought, he attained his own decision.

The train was approaching Spartanburg when they returned from their midday repast. Hop Sure, strategically stationed in the passageway, caught Garrison's eye and flashed him a signal wink. The rather-too-large head gave the briefest indication of a nod and less than five minutes later he joined the porter. Without a word, Epic shoved the packet into the huge pink paw of the white man. Garrison's eyes glowed eagerly as he shoved the package from view in his coat pocket.

"Where did you find it?"

Hop Sure's answer came in the nature of a comment.

"Seems like to me, cap'n, you must of dropped that thing behind the lounge in you-all's drawin'-room." Ten dollars was transferred to Epic. "I sho' ain't got nothin' but gratitude, cap'n."

"You've earned it."

"Jus' the same, Ise the gratitudinest man what is. I always has said that cash money is the fondes' thing I is of."

They separated. Garrison was vastly contented with himself and with the situation. He strolled happily up the aisle of the Pullman, believing that the world was a very comfortable place indeed. He favored his fellow travelers with benign glances of warm friendship, and then a sudden hot flush mounted to the very tips of his ears and he unconsciously quickened his pace to disappear on the farthest platform. Once there he mopped a freely perspiring forehead with a lavender-bordered silk handkerchief.

"Phew!" he gasped. "That bird in Section 12! I wonder—"

Mr. Garrison felt weak and all gone inside. There had been a peculiar speculative quality in the stare of the heavy-set passenger in Section 12 which Mr. Garrison did not relish; it was as though the ill-clad gentleman knew a great many things and was intent upon adding to the sum of his knowledge. And then, whereas a moment before the brown-paper-wrapped parcel had suffused Mr. Garrison with a warm glow, it now scorched like molten metal and Mr. Garrison felt the urge to divorce himself from its possession until a more propitious moment.

He was nothing if not a man of action. Whistling with a fine, if nervous, insouciance, he retraced his steps down the aisle of the car, rejoined Hop Sure on the back platform and slipped into the astonished hand of that bewildered colored gentleman the wandering package.

"Hide it!" he sibilated. "And keep it hidden until we get to New York!"

The hand dived into Mr. Garrison's pocket, and when the relieved white gentleman disappeared a half minute later Hop Sure was richer by an additional five dollars. He held it close to his eyes while a single horrid thought smote him— "Cullud boy, you had better pray that these heah moneys ain't counterfeit."

He arrayed his cash before him and compared minutely the Garrison-Carson money with bills which he knew to be genuine. Then he sighed relievedly; obviously it was legitimate. So much then for that; the chiefest of Epic's worries was removed.

The afternoon dragged uneventfully. Messrs. Carson and Garrison remained in the seclusion of their drawing-room and the heavy-footed stranger sat stolidly in Section 12, earnestly perusing the pages of a magazine; only the thirty-eight dollars which Epic had collected from the mysterious travelers gave testimony to the fact that, whatever the situation might be, it was certainly unusual—and highly desirable.

At 4:05 in the afternoon they pulled into Charlotte, North Carolina, and ten minutes later departed. Between there and Salisbury, Hop Sure inhaled a noble meal which he ordered with reckless disregard for expense. It had been a red-letter day for Mr. Peters and he felt it only his due that the inner Epic be fortified against any further excitement. He even thrust a two-bit tip into the palm of an astonished waiter.

In prompt answer to the first general call for dinner, Garrison and Carson left their drawing-room and proceeded to the diner. They studiously avoided the solemn and interested eye of the man in Section 12, although it was plain to the observant Hop Sure that they were far from indifferent to his presence. As they disappeared, the stranger beckoned to the porter.

"Call the conductor," he ordered peremptorily, and Hop Sure leaped to obey.

Somehow, the man's voice and manner impressed upon him the absolute necessity for unquestioning, efficient and prompt obedience. But even so, he couldn't help thinking that perhaps—

The conductor seemed to be expecting the summons, for he came wordlessly. Then for five minutes the blue-uniformed Pullman official and the man with the ill-fitting suit talked with low-toned earnestness. Hop Sure watched, feeling vaguely that he was not entirely an outsider. Nor did he have long to wait before learning that his instinct was correct. The two men arose, glanced quickly around the car and disappeared in Drawing-Room A. They closed the door behind them and Hop Sure could have sworn that he heard the click of the thumb latch. He sank heavily into a seat.

"Fo' eight yeahs," he reflected, "I has been porterin' on this road, but never befo'—nossuh, not even ever—did I see any sech fumadiddles. 'Tain't nachel"—his fingers touched the crisp greenbacks which reposed in his pocket—" 'tain't nachel—but it suttinly is highly financial."

Epic was aroused by the insistent sounding of his call-board buzzer. Drawing-Room A. Timidly he responded to the summons. The conductor and his flat-footed acquaintance turned to glare at the porter, who, in turn, stared with stern disapproval at the confusion into which the two men had thrown the drawing-room. Even to Epic's none-too-fast-moving mind it was immediately apparent that a search had been conducted and it was equally apparent from their expressions that it had been bitterly unsuccessful.

The conductor's greeting was brief and to the point. He nodded toward the stranger.

"Do what this gentleman orders, Hop Sure."

"Yassuh, cap'n."

An order came crisply from the other man:

"Open that upper berth."

Hop Sure produced his key, inserted it in the berth and lowered it. Immediately the stranger swung himself into the berth. And then, article by article, each thing the berth contained was carefully opened, shaken out and thrown on the floor, where, under the conductor's orders, Epic re-folded it.

Hop Sure labored silently. He had the disquieting hunch that the brown-paper parcel was the object of this particular search. So far as he was concerned, he couldn't understand all the interest or excitement, and with the money in his pocket he felt more like a participant in the drama than a mere spectator thereof.

The man lowered himself to the floor and bade Hop Sure set the room to rights—quickly. He turned to the conductor.

"Not here," he commented crisply.

The conductor answered with equal terseness, "Evidently not."

Then the stranger to the porter: "Not a word of this, understand?"

His hand extended a dollar bill. Hop Sure nodded eager agreement.

"I understan's absolute, suh."

"Good!"

The trio left the drawing-room. Fifteen minutes later the other pair returned from the dining car and secluded themselves. As they passed Section 12 Hop Sure fancied that he discerned glances of interest bestowed by them upon the heavy-set stranger, but that gentleman paid no heed.

At nine o'clock—half-way between Danville and Lynchburg—Hop Sure was summoned to the drawing-room and ordered to make down the berths. He was immensely relieved to note the complete absence of suspicion in the manner of his two benefactors. It was plain that they were unaware not only of the drawing-room's having been searched, but also of the freedom with which Hop Sure had acted as clearing house.

His task completed, Hop Sure returned to the main car, where for the ensuing hour he was kept excruciatingly busy making down berths for tired travelers. By ten o'clock the car was composed for the night; but in Section 12 the stranger sat stolidly reading. Epic grew nervous: a task unfinished preyed upon his mind. He knew that sooner or later that section had to be made and he preferred to do it now. At length he approached the white gentleman and touched his cap.

"Shall I make up yo' berth, boss?"

The other man answered rather peculiarly—"You may bring me a table."

Wonderingly, Hop Sure obeyed. The man produced a deck of cards and plunged promptly into the absorbing intricacies of Canfield. Hop Sure hovered uncertainly in the aisle.

"Any time you craves to sleep," he suggested hopefully, "jes' press that button yonder."

The man answered without looking up, "I will."

Two men occupied the smoking compartment, the platform was chilly. Hop Sure perched himself upon his little stool at the lower end of the car where he commanded a view of the drawing-room door. He could see that at eleven o'clock the game of Canfield was still enthusiastically in progress. Less than five minutes later he saw something else.

The drawing-room door swung slowly back; the gray streak of hair which marked Mr. Carson appeared briefly in the aperture. It was evident that Mr. Carson saw the man in Section 12 and equally evident that he was not pleased thereby, for the door closed abruptly. A half-hour later the performance was repeated. Hop Sure shook his head sadly.

"Ise dawg-goned if I understan's all I knows about this."

Shortly before midnight his buzzer sounded; the call-box indicated a summons from Drawing-Room A. Epic started down the car. As he reached Section 12 a steely hand fastened on his arm.

"Call from the drawing-room, porter?"

"Yassuh."

Two one-dollar bills passed from the man to the porter.

"You didn't hear it," suggested the other. "As a matter of fact, you are not going to hear any rings from the drawing-room tonight—understand?"

"B-b-but, cap'n—"

"No buts. The conductor told you to obey my orders. And in case that doesn't satisfy you—"

Heavy spatulate fingers flashed to the coat lapel and flung it back. Hop Sure found himself gazing horrifiedly at the glittering surface of a silver star.

"Oh, gosh!" he moaned, remembering vividly his partici-pation in the comings and goings of the brown-paper parcel. "I might of knowed you was a detective!"

"Why?"

" 'Cause wa'n't you tryin' to detect somethin' in that drawin'-room a while back? Wa'n't you, cap'n?"

"Perhaps."

"Cap'n"—Hop Sure lowered his voice—"them two gem-mun ain't done nothin' wrong, has they?"

The detective frowned.

"Go back and disconnect the buzzer signal from the draw-ing-room—and keep your mouth shut."

"Oh, gosh! Tha's the one thing I ain't gwine do nothin' else but."

Hop Sure staggered to the end of the car, disconnected the buzzer and sat depressedly on his stool. His mind groped heavily with the events of the past twenty-four hours: the constant influx of money, the peregrinations of the brown-paper parcel, the presence of the detective—

Somehow, Epic Peters felt that he was an unwitting but dangerously incriminated participant in the evildoings which were coming to a head on this eventful journey. He didn't know what it was all about, but he did possess an overpow-ering hunch that he would not relish a general comparison of notes by the parties most vitally concerned.

He repressed without considerable difficulty an impulse to tell the detective what he knew concerning the package. The proposition seemed too fraught with the menace of the un-known. After all, the contents of that parcel were none of his affair; he had been asked to keep it in his linen closet until their arrival in New York, and he couldn't very well see why he should do anything else, particularly since it was liable to get him more deeply involved in a situation which already had creased his forehead with horizontal furrows of intensive worry.

And so through the long night, across the state of Virginia, during the long wait in Washington and on the trip northward from there over the Pennsylvania system, the peculiar vigil continued: the detective immersed in his game of Canfield, Hop Sure wide eyed and nervous on his stool at the end of the car, the occupants of the drawing-room occasionally poking their heads through a crack in the door.

The train reached and passed North Philadelphia. Hop Sure, weary of brain and foot, waked his passengers and busied himself half-heartedly with the task of putting the car shipshape. The detective's Canfield went incessantly on. Once Hop Sure approached the silver-star man.

"Shall I go make up the drawin'-room, boss? We is reproachin' New Yawk."

The other answered without looking up.

"No!" he said.

At Elizabeth the drawing-room door was flung violently open. Mr. Carson, heavy of eye and haggard of face, boldly summoned Hop Sure by gesture. And as that dignitary started toward him, something else strange and unexpected occurred—the detective rose, smiled and edged his way into the drawing-room.

It was plain from the expression on the face of Mr. Carson that the visit was not relished. The door closed softly and Hop Sure stood swaying in the aisle. His brain was traveling like a racehorse now. The journey was nearing its end; the brown-paper parcel reposed in the linen compartment; it was obvious that Hop Sure would have no opportunity to return it to its owners—unless—

Hop Sure reached a difficult decision and drew a deep breath. Between his satanic majesty and the blue depths of the sea there was apparently nothing for him to do but follow out the letter of his instructions. He hunched that all was not well, and that it was shortly to become even less so;

but more than he feared the results of wrong actions he dreaded the consequences of no action at all.

With heart pounding in his bosom, he opened his linen closet, took the brown-paper parcel from the top shelf, dropped it in the depths of his jacket pocket and made his way uncertainly toward the drawing-room. No matter what happened, the period of inaction was at an end; that much in itself was relieving. As to what the results would be—he dared not think. Sufficient unto the hour was the evil thereof. He was well content that the future held worries of its own.

He sounded the buzzer and immediately the door was flung back. Hop Sure met the level eyes of the detective. Behind the broad back of that official, Epic found himself staring at a graphic and expressive pantomime. Plainly as words, the gestures of the two gentlemen in the drawing-room carried the message to vamoose. Hop Sure paid them absolutely no heed.

"What do you want?" It was the detective speaking.

"I has got somethin' belongin' to these gemmun," blurted Epic, "somethin' I was to give back to them when us arrove in New Yawk."

He plainly discerned the expressions of consternation which crossed their countenances; he fancied vaguely that they were regretting the lavish tips which they had thrust upon him. A big and dark hand came from his jacket pocket clutching the brown-paper parcel.

"Heah 'tis, gemmum," he announced with forced geniality. "I suttinly did take pretickeler care of it fo' you-all."

There was a general clashing of glances, a scrutinizing, speculative look in the eyes of the detective. Both Carson and Garrison were visibly annoyed, the former indicating his perturbation by pallor, the latter by a display of beetlike redness.

"What I has done played," reflected Hop Sure, "is hell; but they ain't no backin' out now." He took one step forward

and held out the packet toward the long, thin **Mr. Carson.**
"Heah you is, cap'n."

And then Epic Peters received the ultimate shock of an
amazing journey, for Mr. Carson stared at him gravely, shook
his head with studied and admirable calm and spoke in a
cool, even voice:

"I never saw that package before."

"Good Gawdness—"

"And I've never seen it, either," interrupted Garrison.

Hop Sure stared amazedly from one to the other; a sen-
sation of hot indignation suffused his bosom. This reeked
strongly of a conspiracy to put him in a demoralizingly false
light.

"Does you-all gemmun mean to stan' up there on yo' own
two foots an' say you di'n't gimme this heah package to take
care of fo' you ontil we arrove in New Yawk? Does you-all
mean to say you di'n't tell me I was to keep it hid in the
linen closet? Does you-all two inten' to stultifry that you
di'n't infohm me—"

There was glacierlike chill in Carson's tones.

"I mean to say all of that and a great deal more. I mean
to say that you are presumptuous and impertinent and I
don't care to hear any more from you. We know nothing
whatever about that packet; never saw it before and"—with
sharp irony—"never expect to see it again."

Epic Peters collapsed limply on the lounge. He stared with
helpless appeal into the amused face of the detective, who
had been a silent but interested spectator.

"Will you listen at them gemmun, cap'n?" pleaded Hop
Sure. "They gimme that packet in Bumminham with they
ve'y own han's an' they said to me, they said, 'Po'ter, we
craves you should take care of this—' "

The detective shook his head slowly.

"But they claim they never saw this package before."

"Oh, lawsy—"

"And you certainly wouldn't dispute the word of two gentlemen, would you, porter?"

"Nossuh! I wouldn't 'spute no gemmun no time nohow. An' I ain't claimin' that they is falsifryin', neither. But I does claim one thing, cap'n—I claims one thing an' I claims passionate—I claims that these two gemmun is awful forgetful."

Gently the detective removed the package from Hop Sure's grasp. He faced the other white men.

"You are quite sure this isn't yours?" he asked.

"Positive," came the chorused answer.

"You never saw it before?"

"Never!"

"You didn't entrust any package of any sort to this porter's keeping?"

"No!"

"Golly Moses, boss man, them gemmun ain't got no mem'ry a'tall!"

The detective smiled.

"Suppose we see what's in it," he observed, as though speaking to himself.

He produced a pocketknife with which he cut the string; he removed three layers of brown paper, disclosing to view a handsome leather case. With his eyes focused on the two other white men, he flipped the lid back.

"Oh-h-h!" came Hop Sure's hoarse voice. "Jools!"

They filled the room with glorious color: the collar of diamonds and emeralds glittered and sparkled and gleamed, fairly dazzling the popping eyes of Mr. Epic Peters, in whose charge this treasure had been for most of the journey from Birmingham. As from a great distance he heard the monotone of the detective, speaking as though to himself.

"Peculiar situation," the detective was saying. "Worth tens of thousands—and nobody to claim it. Funny thing, too: they told me over long-distance in Greenville that this had been

stolen in Birmingham the previous day and that it was supposed to be on this train. Police authorities in Alabama figured the men who took it wouldn't have had time to split
up the loot and separate." He looked up friendlily at Carson
and Garrison. "You're quite sure you never saw this before?"

"Positive," asserted Mr. Carson somewhat sickly.

"Never!" echoed Mr. Garrison.

"Then," smiled the detective, "there's nothing for me to
do but turn this over to the proper authorities as valuable
and unclaimed property."

It seemed to Hop Sure that Garrison and Carson were relieved—and then he noticed that the train was jerking to a
stop.

"Manhattan Transfer!" he exclaimed, leaping for the door.
"I has to git out an' do some porterin'."

Thirty minutes later they reached the Pennsylvania Station in New York City. Messrs. Garrison and Carson were
the first two passengers out of Epic's car. The glares which
they bestowed upon him were not unduly friendly, and Hop
Sure was excessively pleased to note the celerity with which
they ascended the exit stairway. Last out of the car was the
detective. He seemed vastly contented. Hop Sure was positive that the grim-visaged man was smiling.

He halted at Epic's side and turned his bag over to a
redcap.

"You were of quite some assistance, porter," he commented.

"Yassuh, cap'n, thanky, suh. They calls me Hop Sure an'
Ise the servinest porter runnin' south to nawth. Any time
you craves my 'sistance—"

Still smiling, the detective produced a wallet. Then, before the staring and amazed eyes of the porter, he counted
off two gold-backed twenty-dollar bills and a pair of crisp
fives.

"Fifty dollars," he announced. "That's for you, porter."

The detective walked swiftly off, leaving Epic staring in dumfounded amazement at this new and colossal accession of wealth. The events of the past thirty-six hours flashed kaleidoscopically through his brain. He shook his head in utter and happy bewilderment.

"Fifty dollars!" he murmured to himself ecstatically. "Fifty dollars cash money in hand!"

He withdrew from his pocket the thirty-eight dollars given him by Garrison and Carson. He gazed first at the fifty and then at the thirty-eight. The faintest semblance of a sneer appeared on his lips.

"Thutty-eight dollars!" he breathed disdainfully. "Shuh! What them two fellers don't know about tippin' is nothin'!"

MRS. UNION
STATION
By Doug Welch

Doug Welch

DOUG WELCH, as a really good newspaper reporter should, can write about all sorts of subjects. He describes social life among the police in *We Go Fast* (*Saturday Evening Post*); the ordeals of a young married couple in *Rolling Stones* (*American Magazine*); a back-stage domestic squabble in *Brand New Woman* (*American Magazine*); the antics of two camera "fiends" in *Photo Finish* (*Saturday Evening Post*); and the salvaging of a short-line railroad in *Pop Pops Off* (*Saturday Evening Post*). But about no subject does he write with more conviction than about railroads —perhaps because he is "an old time-table reader from way back."

He was born in Boston, June 21, 1906, and graduated from the University of Washington where he majored in English. Always identified with newspapers, Welch has successively been a reporter for the Tacoma *News Tribune,* Cleveland *Plain Dealer,* Seattle *Times* and Seattle *Post-Intelligencer.* He resides in Seattle.

To the O. Henry touch both in its telling and in its denouement, *Mrs. Union Station* adds flawless railroad detail, whether in standard gauge or O gauge. The story first appeared in the *Saturday Evening Post* in 1937.

MRS. UNION STATION

By Doug Welch

WITH HIS WATCH IN HAND, and with an expression of vast displeasure on his usually placid face, John H. Alston, superintendent of the Lonely Valley Division of the Chicago, Omaha, Salt Lake & Pacific Railway, watched the locomotive and ten sleek cars of No. 6, eastbound, otherwise the Hurricane, slowly thread their way into the Grand River station.

"Twenty-seven and a half minutes late," he informed Conductor A. L. Benson and the world in general. "What the hell do you think you're running? A street-car?"

"We had trouble up the line," said Conductor Benson softly, with the prim satisfaction of a man who has a perfectly valid excuse.

"What kind of trouble?"

"A woman passenger pulled the air on us."

"I don't believe it," said Superintendent Alston flatly. "I don't believe there is a woman anywhere in the world who knows how to pull the air on a train."

"That's what I thought," said Conductor Benson. "But I found out."

"If she was here," said Superintendent Alston, brightening at the thought, "I would punch her right square in the nose."

"Oh, no, you wouldn't," said Conductor Benson dreamily. "Not this little pretty, you wouldn't!"

"Here we spend a million bucks to cut the running time over our division by twenty-one minutes," said Superintendent Alston, "and then some Jane with a two-dollar ticket

pulls the air on us because she forgot to turn off the gas
heater or leave a note for the milkman, I suppose."

"It's a very sad story," said Conductor Benson, "and it will
take me some time to tell it."

"Well, we missed our connections here with the Dixie
Mail," said Superintendent Alston, "so you can just come
into my office and dictate your story to my stenographer, and
I will let you do the explaining to the general manager's office
instead of me."

A young woman passenger (dictated Conductor Benson)
pulled the air on us at Junction at 12:19 P.M. today, and
pretty near stood the train on end. She got on at Salsburg
only about nine minutes before. We have a slow order over
the P. B. & T. crossover at Junction, and we were approaching this crossover at greatly reduced speed—I would say not
faster than eight miles an hour—when this young pretty
makes an emergency application from the rear parlor car.
We stop with a hard jolt, but we don't pull any drawbars
and we don't slide the wheels much. Engineer John Hadley
claims he finds a flat on one of his drivers as big as a dot,
and he comes back and says he is going to spank this passenger personally, right now. He even starts toward one of
the Pullmans to borrow a hairbrush, but the passenger begins to cry, so he doesn't. I wouldn't have let him anyway,
on account of our slogan, "The Passenger Is Always Right,
Except When He Doesn't Have His Fare." We are delayed
twenty-four minutes at Junction while we look the train
over. A couple of passengers took headers in the aisle, but
nobody was really hurt.

The young pretty who makes this emergency application
is a Mrs. Steven Applebee, of 4531 Wandon Drive, Salsburg,
and although she wants to get off the train at Junction, I
make her stay aboard until we reach Central City. We don't
usually make Central City on this run, but after I hear the
little lady's story, I figure it will be all right with the com-

pany if we let her off, so she can grab No. 11 back to Salsburg. She is a very fetching little package, and she is practically up to her ears in trouble if she don't catch No. 11.

I ask this pretty how she knows where the emergency air valve is located on the parlor car, and she says her husband is a model-railway fan, and she knows where everything is, including the patch on the fireman's jumper.

"But, madam," I say, "don't you know that when you make an emergency application from the back of a train, you are liable to break that train right in half, and also maybe flatten every wheel?"

"Certainly I know," she replies, "but I wanted to get off."

There is a fellow in the car who tries to break into the conversation a couple of times, and she says to him, "Go away. I don't ever want to see you again. You are hateful."

"But, Helene," he protests, "what have I done?"

"You are a wolf in sheep's clothing."

This surprises me greatly, because he is only wearing a double-breasted blue serge suit. Well, the passenger begins to cry again, so I take her into an unoccupied compartment in the Chicago sleeper, and she tells me the whole story. This is a very sad story, and I practically have my handkerchief out a couple of times, and I will not omit any of the details, because I think it will help explain the frame of mind of a pretty who makes an emergency application on a fine train like No. 6.

"Have I mentioned that she is a very classy-looking little doll?" asked Conductor Benson.

"You haven't been talking about anything else," said Superintendent Alston. "Go on!"

Well, this Mrs. Applebee (continued Conductor Benson) is not what you call the thinking type, but she is certainly a choice piece of scenery, equal to anything we have got on the Mountain or Coast divisions. She is a cuddly little pretty with great big eyes, and she is very innocent and trusting.

"I am going to tell you everything," she says, "because you have a kind face. And if you don't let me off this train pretty soon, the line will be responsible for breaking up a family, and I know it doesn't want to be pointed out as a home wrecker."

"I should say not," I reply, "because we always advertise as 'The Family Line.'"

Well, it seems like this Mrs. Applebee has been married about a year, and her husband is a salesman. He is also a model-railway fan, but she never suspected it until after they were engaged. She says love must have made her blind. She says being married to a model-railway fan is a very terrible thing, and there isn't anything you can do for it except take an occasional headache tablet.

It seems like before they are married, her husband—his name is Steve—drives her every evening to a spot on Ransom Hill where there is a first-rate view of the Salsburg depot and the lower yards, and also the city dump. At first she thinks he only goes there because it is a quiet place to park. But it seems like very often, right in the middle of a pretty speech, he pulls out his watch and says, "It's just about time for the 7:23." And even while he is holding her hand he counts the cars on the 7:23, and if there is an extra diner or a private car, he can't talk about anything else the rest of the night.

She says he also takes her to all the moving pictures which have trains in them. And after the show, maybe she says, "I don't think that girl is much of an actress." But he says, "Yes, but did you see that big articulated 2-8-8-4 Northern Pacific freight locomotive?" And once she has to sit through a double bill twice, so he can get a second look at the inside of a Wabash signal tower.

Well, before the wedding he spends two solid weeks reading time-tables. They are going to New York City on their honeymoon. And on the afternoon of the wedding, the best man says to him, "Now there isn't anything to be nervous about." And Steve says, "I'm worried about those connections in Chicago. Maybe I ought to have taken the B. & O."

Well, the ceremony is over, and they get aboard our train, and they are pulling out of Salsburg. Mrs. Applebee reaches over and pats his hand. "And now I belong to you, Steve, dear," she says. "I am your own little Helene."

But he is looking out the window at a switch engine, and he says, "I can tell one of those a mile away."

"One of what, dear?"

"That goat," he says. "That yard hog. It's a rebuilt job. Used to be a road engine once. You can tell by the big boiler and the firebox. They've put small drivers under her, but she still has a road engine's lines."

"Well, that's very nice, dear, I am sure," she says.

"He must have seen old 768," commented Superintendent Alston. "She's a fine old engine. Yes, sir, a fine engine."

"Yes," said Conductor Benson, "but listen."

It takes them about four days to get to New York City (said Conductor Benson) because they don't stay on one road more than a couple of hours or so. I can hardly believe it, but Mrs. Applebee tells me they use our line to Chicago, and then go to New York by way of the New York Central, the Pennsylvania, the Nickel Plate and the Lackawanna. She thinks they are also on the Erie, too, but it is late at night. Anyway, they get on and off trains so many times that she begins to feel like they are being followed by someone.

"Are you sure, Steve, dear," she asks, "that we aren't running away from something?"

"No, lovey dovey," he says, "as long as I am in this part of the country, I want to see as much as possible of the railroads and their equipment."

And another day, when they have two hours to wait for a connection, she suggests they take a bus.

"Good heavens," he says. "Do you think I want it to get back to the Salsburg Model-Railway Club that I rode on a bus!"

When they finally get to New York, the very first night he takes her down to the Grand Central Terminal to listen to the train announcing. And the next morning while he is shaving in their hotel room, which overlooks the Pennsylvania Station, he calls out all the stations between New York and Boston on the New York, New Haven & Hartford's shore line, and all the stations between New York and Washington, D. C., on the Pennsylvania.

By this time, of course, any other woman would either call in the house physician or a lawyer, but, like I said before, this Mrs. Applebee is a sweet little thing just trying to get along, and she doesn't realize that coming events cast their shadows before. She tries to get into the spirit of things. She shrieks with girlish glee, she tells me, when Steve takes her up into New England and upper New York State to ride on the Central Vermont and the Rutland. He likes the Central Vermont all right, but he is somewhat disappointed in the Rutland because the brakeman wants to talk baseball instead of block signals.

In New York City, of course, they ride all the subways. Sometimes they wait a half hour at Times Square until a train comes along which has a front window and a vacant seat. Steve sits in this seat and peers into the tunnel ahead, and he don't say much except, "We are coming up on that red block pretty fast," or, "It doesn't seem to me they allow enough headway between trains." He tries to involve a motorman at the Coney Island station in an argument as to which is best, straight air or automatic air. But the motorman doesn't seem to care whether he has to stop his train with straight air or automatic air, or by dragging his feet.

"That bum ought to be driving a milk wagon," Steve says. "I bet he don't know a brake shoe from a pair of kid's rubbers."

Mrs. Applebee makes a big hit with her husband one morning by imitating a news butcher.

"Cigars, cigarettes, tobacco, candy, fresh fruit and souvenir post cards," she says.

"Honey," he tells her, "you're wonderful."

"It sounds like a great honeymoon," commented Superintendent Alston.

"Wait until you hear what happened when they got home," said Conductor Benson. "This is where it really gets sad."

Well, they no sooner arrive in Salsburg (continued Conductor Benson) and settle down in their new house than he invites her to a meeting of the model-railway club. Of course, he has talked almost constantly about the club ever since he met her, but she hasn't any clear idea of it. She thinks maybe they all get down on their hands and knees and pull choo-choos around. To tell the truth, whenever he starts talking about locomotives and drawbars and valve gears and 3 per cent grades, she just sits and looks at him with awe, and thinks how handsome he is, and how nice and kind his eyes are, and what a lucky, lucky girl she is to be married to such a splendid creature.

"I have asked some of the other fellows to invite their wives, too," he says. "I don't see why we can't all work and enjoy the system together. I think you girls will get as much fun out of it as we do. Of course, you won't be able to run trains right away. You will have to start by operating some of our manual switches and crossing gates, but after a while you can work your way up into an occasional local freight."

From what Mrs. Applebee tells me, the club has an

O-gauge system in the basement of the Johnson home. You know, Johnson, the Salsburg banker. Each man has contributed something like a locomotive or a string of box cars or maybe a couple of Pullmans. The track and the equipment—even the stations, crossing gates, bridges and signal towers—are built strictly according to scale, about a fourth of an inch to a foot in real life. They call this railroad the Chicago, Alton & West Coast, and it has about five hundred feet of track arranged in loops. One of these loops runs out of the basement and circles through the Johnson rock garden.

Mrs. Applebee says the club meets three times a week. One man sits at a table and acts as dispatcher, writing up train orders. Another makes up passenger and freight trains in the Chicago yards, and each of the others has a division, and is responsible for the trains that run over it.

The locomotives are powered with electric motors and they pick up their juice from a third rail. The idea is never to touch a train with your hands if you can help it.

Well, the Applebees hurry through dinner this night because it is a terrible thing to be late and delay the trains. In fact, Mrs. Applebee says the only reason her friends, the Browns, are hardly speaking to one another is because Mrs. Brown had to go and have her baby on the very night that Mr. Brown was supposed to sit in as relief dispatcher.

When the Applebees arrive at the Johnson home, she finds the crowd down in the basement, the ladies gathered politely off in one corner, pretty breathless about the whole business. Mrs. Applebee says her first reaction to what she sees is that Mrs. Johnson must be a very patient woman to let her husband and his friends muss her basement up that way. Mrs. Applebee says Mrs. Johnson's laundress is probably a contortionist. There are tracks at various levels all around the walls, across the floor, and even suspended from the ceiling. It doesn't make much sense to Mrs. Applebee.

Steve walks over to this banker, who is sitting at the table, and he says: "Let's have the order for No. 17."

"No. 17," says the banker, "meets No. 16 at Alton and No. 402 at East Kansas City. You've also got a slow order over two sections east of Alton on account of track repairs."

Well, Steve walks over to the Chicago depot and yards, which is on top of the Johnson workbench, and he stands beside a locomotive and seven Pullmans.

"Train No. 17!" he calls out. "The Continental Limited! Now leaving on Track 4 for Pontiac, Atlanta, Springfield, Alton, Kansas City, Denver, Salt Lake City, San Francisco, and all points west! All a-b-o-a-r-d!"

"I think you're making some of this up," protested Superintendent Alston.

"No, I'm not," replied Conductor Benson. "I'm telling it just like she did, only I'm not so bitter about it."

Steve throws a switch (continued Conductor Benson) and the train starts moving. Mrs. Applebee notices that all the men have their watches out. It seems like the running time is figured in seconds, and any member who turns a train over to another division late has to have a pretty good reason. Like, for instance, the night the Johnson Airedale tried to take a bite out of the observation-lounge car of No. 15, the Kansas City Flyer, when it was swinging around his kennel at a good seventy-mile clip. They keep the Airedale chained up during the club meetings now.

The Continental Limited races around the wall behind the furnace, speeds toward the washtubs and disappears into a tunnel in the wall of the fruit closet. It comes out again at a higher level and stops at a small, lighted station.

"No. 17 arriving at Alton on time!" says Steve. And, according to Mrs. Applebee, his face is glowing like the night he proposed.

The ladies follow this train over the other divisions all the way to San Francisco, which is at the foot of the garden, and they utter glad little cries over the locomotive's headlight and the way the light shines out of the car windows. And pretty soon some of the ladies are assigned to various duties. Mrs. Applebee gets a manual switch in the Chicago yards.

She doesn't understand the operation of this switch very well, and she gives it a yank while a freight train is passing through. It seems like seven cars are derailed.

"For goodness' sakes," she laughs. "I guess I am not much of a switchman, am I?"

And she picks up one of the cars and starts to put it back on the track.

"Don't touch those cars!" her husband shouts.

She says her husband is acting like he just caught her making eyes at the iceman. His tone is quite sharp.

"The only way we can get those reefers back on the rails," he says, "is with the wrecker."

Well, they bring the wrecking train down from Alton, and the other men gather around, shaking their heads and saying, "Tch, tch, tch!" It appears that what Mrs. Applebee has done is a very terrible thing indeed. It is the first derailment on the Chicago, Alton and West Coast Railway in three weeks, they tell her. They spend a solid hour getting those cars back on the track without using their hands.

"Oh, let's have something to drink," one of the ladies suggests.

"I should say not," says Johnson. "Didn't you ever hear of Rule G?"

"Why, no," says the lady.

"Well, Rule G is the no-drinking rule on every railway in the country," says the banker, "and we don't drink while we are on duty. Not on the C., A. & W. C., we don't!"

"No," explains the banker's wife, "not since old Judge

Semple got liquored up one night and staged a head-on collision in Tunnel 5. He was expelled!"

When the Applebees are leaving that night, it is this same Mrs. Johnson who gives Mrs. Applebee a warm, sympathetic little squeeze of the hand.

"Poor dear," she whispers. "You'll learn to be a railroad man's wife one of these days, but the period of learning is terrible. When I was getting accustomed to it I used to have hideous dreams. I was always being chased by a time-table. And don't think that I don't have to be constantly on guard, even now. For three years I have been fighting to keep Mr. Johnson from building a trestle right across the goldfish pond. The goldfish pond is Great Salt Lake."

"Of course, I don't blame you, dear," says Steve, on the way home, "but did you ever see anyone turn a switch on a regular railroad while a train was passing over it?"

"I guess not," she says.

"All right, then," he says. "Why did you do it?"

"I don't know, Steve," she replies, "and let's not discuss the matter any more."

The next time the club meets she pleads a headache, and she is not surprised when Steve later reports that all the other wives seem to have headaches too.

It isn't long after this that the club decides to change over from a third-rail to a two-rail system, which involves a good deal of rewiring and some track relaying. Steve is busy at the Johnsons' every weekday night, and all day Sunday he spends his time at his own kitchen table, putting together a New York Central Hudson-type locomotive. The parts for this cost him fifty-eight dollars, and it means that Mrs. Applebee has to struggle along another month without drapes for the living room.

Mrs. Applebee says she sometimes wishes Steve would be attracted to another woman, because she would know what to do about that. She would get herself some snappy new

clothes and try doing her hair differently. But she says there
is nothing a woman can do whose husband is suddenly that
way about a New York Central Hudson-type locomotive
with a feed-water heater, a Baker valve gear, alligator cross-
heads and a booster on the trailer truck.

"Yes," commented Superintendent Alston, profoundly
stirred, "you take these Hudson-type engines—they're pretty,
all right, but one of our 5200 Mallets can outpull two of
them."

"Yes," agreed Conductor Benson, "but I never yet heard
of anyone going nuts over a Mallet."

Well, anyway (said Conductor Benson), Mrs. Applebee
wants to go upstate to attend the university home-coming,
but Steve is just putting the paint job on his new engine, and
he can't possibly leave it. So Mrs. Applebee drives up with a
girl friend. And it is there she meets this Tommy Germaine.
From what I gather, this Tommy Germaine is Mrs. Applebee's sugar pie when she is in college. He spots her at the
alumni dance the night before the big game, and he prances
right over.

"Well, if it isn't the lovely lady again," he says. "I swear,
you grow more beautiful every day!"

"Oh, Tommy!" she says. "The same old Tommy! Even the
same old line."

"You're married!" he pouts. "I read about it in the papers.
I sulked for weeks. Wouldn't eat anything but a little barley
broth. People tell me I almost faded away."

"Oh, Tommy," she laughs. He sweeps her out on the dance
floor.

"By the way," he says, "what does your lord and master do,
besides hurry home every night to his sweet little wife?"

"He's assistant to the vice president of the Chicago, Alton
& West Coast Railway," she says.

"I never heard of it," he says.

"It's a model railway," she explains. "He's really district sales manager for International Small Appliances Company, but the model railway is his life's work."

"I should think," says this Tommy Germaine, "that you would be his life's work."

"Oh, hush up," she giggles.

Well, he takes her to the game next day, and that evening they go with two other couples to a little roadhouse to dance. Mrs. Applebee says that it's just like a month at the beach. She feels young and attractive and appreciated again.

"I'm going to see more of you, I hope," this Tommy says. "My company has assigned me to the Salsburg office, and I move next week. I'd like to meet your husband."

"You'll love Steve," she tells him. "And if you want to make a real hit with him, bring along a couple of time-tables or the picture of a caboose."

She has such a good time at the home-coming that she feels almost guilty when she returns home. She tells Steve everything.

He listens to her kind of impatiently and says, "Well, that's fine. I wish I could have gone up there myself. Do you know what Johnson said about my engine?"

"No," she says. "What?"

"He claims the paint is too black. He says it ought to be more of a gun-metal shade. What do you think?"

"The first coat looked perfectly all right to me," she assures him.

"I'm glad you say that," Steve says, very pleased.

This Tommy Germaine doesn't lose any time. He isn't in Salsburg two days before he telephones.

"It's me," he says. "And hungering for a real old-fashioned home-cooked meal, if I may be so suggestive."

"You may be, Tommy," she says, "and you may come right out tonight, if you don't mind corned beef and cabbage."

Steve and this Tommy hit it off from the start.

"I hear you're interested in railroads," says Tommy. "An uncle of mine works in the passenger department of the Santa Fe."

"Is that so?" comments Steve with great interest. "That's a mighty good road, the Santa Fe. They put out a very readable time-table."

Steve has Tommy out to the model-railway club as his guest a couple of times, and gets him admitted to the Forward Salsburg and Wide Awake Luncheon clubs. It is not long before this Tommy is practically a member of the family, and he thinks nothing of dropping in unannounced. Mrs. Applebee also sees a good deal of this Tommy at country-club dances and on the golf course. From what I gather, Steve is not only busy with the model-railway gang but his company has also extended his sales territory and he has to spend considerable time away from home. So he begins to rely more and more on this Tommy to keep his social end up.

No matter what the neighbors and the old boys and girls on the clubhouse porch say, however, Mrs. Applebee is not too pleased with the arrangement. She doesn't mind Steve's trips out of town, but she is certainly reaching what she calls "the saturation point" concerning locomotives and railroad trains. The big blowoff comes the night of the country-club formal.

Mrs. Applebee goes to some trouble and expense to get her hair done differently, but all Steve says is: "What's the matter? You look kind of funny tonight." He dances with her a couple of times, then turns her over to this Tommy. Steve ducks away to the bar, where the model-railway club is having a special meeting. It seems like one of the boys wants to introduce a streamlined engine into the system like the Milwaukee uses on the Hiawatha on the Twin City run out of Chicago. The rest of the boys are thumbs down. What is the sense, they are asking, of building a beautiful model engine, then covering it with a piece of painted tin which hides all the working parts?

"I don't know," says Steve, stepping into the argument. "If all the other lines are going into streamlining, I don't think the Chicago, Alton and West Coast can afford to hold off. Don't forget we are running through highly competitive territory. I think it will be all right to have one streamline job, and maybe call it the Albatross."

"Who ever heard," one of the boys says, "of naming a train after a bird?"

"All right, smart guy," says Steve. "Didn't you ever hear of the famous Flying Crow on the Kansas City Southern? Or the Gull on the Boston and Maine?"

"You've got me there," the guy admits.

"While he was listing trains which are named after birds," said Superintendent Alston, "why didn't he mention the Flamingo on the Louisville and Nashville, and the Southern Pacific's Lark and the New Haven's Owl?"

"I guess he didn't think about them," apologized Conductor Benson.

While Steve is all wrapped up in this discussion (continued Conductor Benson), Mrs. Applebee is dancing with Tommy and getting madder every minute. Finally she sends Tommy to get Steve.

"Steve," she says sharply, "I want to go home!"

'What's the matter?" he asks.

'Never mind," she says. "I want to go home."

In the automobile he details all this streamlining argument, but she makes no comment. When he puts the car away and comes into the house, he finds her standing in the middle of the living-room floor, looking pretty grim.

"Steve," she says, "sit down!"

"Why, what's the matter, honey?" he asks.

"Steve," she says, "you and I are going to have a talk."

"Have I done something?" he asks, getting alarmed.

"Steve," she says, "we have been married eleven months. Am I still as pretty as you used to say I was?"

"Why, of course, honey," he replies, puzzled.

"And I keep a nice, clean, comfortable house for you, too, don't I?"

"Why, sure," he replies. "Look, if I've done something that—"

"And I'm economical and helpful and sympathetic and encouraging, am I not, Steve?"

"Sure you are, honey," he says. "I don't understand—"

"All right," she says. "Then why don't you pay more attention to me? Don't you love me any more?"

"Oh, I see what you mean," he says. "I guess you're sore about tonight. I did disappear for quite a long time. We got to talking about that new train, whether we ought to have a beaver-tail end or a conventional open-end observation car."

"It isn't just tonight, Steve," she says. "It's every day and every night."

"Why, gosh, Helene," he says, "I had no idea that—"

"That's all you talk about from breakfast until bedtime. I sometimes feel as if I were married to a union station."

"But, Helene," he says, "I had no idea—"

"And I try to be patient and understanding," she says, "but now I have reached the point where I will throw my things into a suitcase and walk right out of this house if I ever hear you speak of a locomotive and coal car again."

"Not coal car, Helene," he says gently. "Call it a tender. Coal cars are called hoppers and have nothing to do with a locomotive."

"You see?" she says, and she bursts into tears.

Well, he puts his arm around her.

"Gosh, Helene, I never realized. I won't ever look at another train again. I will even turn my head when we drive by the depot."

"No, I don't want that," she says. "I just want you to love me a little more."

So for a couple of weeks they have a regular love nest. Of course, every so often he will speak of something crude like a seventy-ton Lehigh Valley hopper or a New York, Ontario & Western caboose, but she realizes this is purely force of habit. She isn't too severe with him. As long as he is in a flowers-and-candy mood 90 per cent of the time, she is not going to begrudge him the other 10 per cent. She knows that some men are solitary drinkers, she says, and that some men chase after other women, and that some men spill cigar ashes down the front of their vests, and that there are no absolutely perfect husbands on the market.

In fact, Steve is so nice to her that she feels maybe she has been almost cruel; she catches him one night, sitting on a soap box in the garage, reading a new issue of the Missouri Pacific time-table. He folds it up quick with a guilty expression, like she had caught him smoking corn silk.

"I was just wondering what time the Scenic Limited runs out of St. Louis," he says.

"You poor, dear and abused man," she says. "I didn't mean that you couldn't read time-tables in the house if you want to. And, as a matter of fact, I see no reason why you shouldn't attend the regular meetings of the club."

She is feeling, she tells me, perhaps too generous at the moment, because you can't taper off a model-railway fan like you can a drug addict. Show him an eccentric rod and he's off again. You've got to keep him away from machinery and the sound of locomotive whistles, and put him on a soft diet.

Well, they coast along happily until today, which is their wedding anniversary. Mrs. Applebee says they are figuring on driving up to Reflection Lake for the day. It's about a hundred miles, and they plan to start at nine o'clock this morning. Well, they are just locking up the house when the phone rings. He answers it.

"Helene," he shouts. "Barkerville is in town!"

"Who is Barkerville?" she asks, with a sinking feeling.

"He's the owner of the famous Sunrise Valley Model Railway in California," Steve says, "and that's the line that the movies use for all their trick shots of railway wrecks. He's at the Johnsons', looking our system over, and the boys want me to come over."

"Oh, Steve," she says, very sadly.

"I'll just be a minute," he promises. "I only want to shake hands with him."

"Steve," she says, "today is our wedding anniversary."

"Don't you worry, honey," he says. "I'll be back in no time. You wait in the house until I honk the horn."

Well, this is nine o'clock. At ten o'clock she telephones the Johnson house and Mrs. Johnson says the whole crowd has gone down to the Talbot home to look at a tin-plater Talbot is converting into a scale job. She calls the Talbot home, and Mrs. Talbot says yes, they were there, but they have gone somewhere else, and she doesn't care where they have gone, and she doesn't care if they never come back, because Barkerville woke up the baby by imitating the way the Western Pacific sounds in the Feather River Canyon.

At eleven o'clock Mrs. Applebee is fighting mad. And then the doorbell rings. It isn't Steve. It's this Tommy Germaine.

"Oh, Tommy," she sobs. Well, she tells him the whole story, and he sits there looking like he has just found out that Steve spends his evenings going around peeping into windows.

"This is no way to treat a sensitive, pretty and high-spirited woman like yourself," Tommy Germaine says. "This is ghastly."

"I am going away," she says, "to teach him a lesson. He can't do this to me."

"I think you are right," says this Tommy.

She writes Steve a note and props it up on the living-room table.

"Where are you going?" Tommy asks her while she is packing a few clothes.

"I'm going to Grand River, to Mother," she says.

"It's not far," Tommy says. "I will accompany you a little way. You need a friend along at a time like this."

"Good old Tommy," she says. "You are a real friend, aren't you?"

When he is getting their tickets at the depot, he says: "I hate trains. Stuffy old cars and green plush seats. Smoke and cinders and jolting and bumping."

"It's not quite so bad as that," she assures him. "In fact, this is a new train we're going on. Aluminum alloy and air-conditioned."

And when we get under way, she looks out the window and spots this same yard hog.

"It used to be a road engine," she says idly. "You can tell by the firebox and the big boiler."

"Helene," he says, not hearing her, "there is something I want to tell you. I couldn't have told you before. Perhaps I ought not to tell you now. But I've always had a certain feeling about you, and that feeling lately has grown into something pretty important."

"Please, Tommy," she says.

"Helene," he says, "for the past few weeks I haven't been able to think of anything else but how nice it would be to settle down in the country, in a sweet little house—"

"Tommy," she says, "you mustn't say such things. Not now anyway. Later perhaps. You are very sweet, Tommy, and I like you very much."

"And just settle down," he continued dreamily, "with a sweet wife and my workbench, and—"

"Your workbench?" she echoes. "What do you do with a workbench?"

"I make model ships," he says.

"You make what?" she demands, half rising in her seat.

"Model ships," he replies. "I've got over fifty already. Some of them have been exhibited in the greatest—"

"Why, you heel!" she storms. "You insufferable heel!"

And she runs back in the car and pulls the air on us. She says she realizes then that all men are nuts in one way or another, and Steve is no worse than average.

"Why, you fathead!" roared Superintendent Alston. "Why didn't you let her off at Junction? You left her in a pretty mess. Her husband probably got that note she left!"

"Don't get so hot!" shouted Conductor Benson. "That's why I stopped at Central City. She went into the station to telephone a neighbor to get the key under the back-door mat and take the letter off the living-room table."

"Did the neighbor get it?" demanded Superintendent Alston.

"Certainly," said Conductor Benson. "I held the train until she came out of the station to tell me. And I told the agent to flag down No. 11 and put her on board. She was home again in only an hour."

"Well, that's better," said Superintendent Alston. "We railroad men have got to stick together."

"But the funny thing to me," said Conductor Benson, "is the idea of all these grown men playing with model trains. It amused me so much that the next time I am in Salsburg, I'm going to run over to the Johnson house to see what they've got."

"You and me both," said Superintendent Alston. "We may be able to give them some pointers."

REMARKS: NONE
By William Wister Haines

William Wister Haines

A NEW IMPETUS along the right of way sometimes brings a fresh start along the road of literature. When the Pennsylvania Railroad started eletrification on a grand scale it gave a job to one William Wister Haines, lineman, and Haines in turn gave to America its only novel on trunk line electrification. The tense pages of the novel, *High Tension*, show that romance in railroading has not gone with the elimination of the link and pin, nor has it departed with the passing of the Johnson bar.

William Wister Haines was born in Des Moines, September 17, 1908, and lived in Iowa until his eighteenth year. He was graduated from the University of Pennsylvania in 1931. Young Haines worked at a number of trades but his true metier seems to have been, first, line work for power and light, mining companies and finally, the Pennsylvania, and, after that, writing.

In his writing he reversed the usual order of successful authorship. He did not start with the "pulps" but sold his first story, *Just Plain Nuts*, to the *Atlantic* in 1934. In the same year he completed his first novel, *Slim*, the story of a youthful lineman on power projects and railroad electrification.

Remarks: None has its setting on the electrified portion of the Pennsylvania, and develops its theme atop a wire train, not many inches away from lines that are "hot" with 11,000 volts of alternating current.

REMARKS: NONE

By William Wister Haines

I

I WAS SORRY FOR REGAN. He was a good lineman when that woman left him alone. He wasn't the best I ever seen. He was too young and he hadn't been around enough. But at that he was good enough to rate a job in a good wire train. And if he could of had a decent chancet at breaking in he would of been hard to beat. But he didn't, and he ain't likely to get it now until they electrify hell.

I needed another lineman and I was just about to tell the Man to send me out one when Scarfe got me to put Regan on. We'd cleared up one morning and the men was hanging up their tools and taking off their overalls in the shop car. The night's work was all done and I was writing it up on the swindle sheet when Scarfe come up to the drafting table.

"I got a friend I want to get a job for, Jig. What's the chance of getting him into this train?"

"Is he a good lineman?"

"He's as good as I am on transmission work."

"That'd be good enough for me if this was transmission work, Scarfe. But it ain't. How is he on catenary?"

"I don't think he ever worked none on railroad electrifyin'."

"Then why don't he get him another job at tower building or wire stringing? They's plenty of that going on."

Scarfe looks kind of funny. "Well, Jig, I think it's his wife.

All the transmission work's out in the sticks. I think she kind of likes to live near the bright lights, so he wants to get a job here."

I was surprised to hear nonsense like that out of Scarfe. He's got right good sense. So I arced at him a little.

"I suppose if this guy's wife taken a notion she wanted to see the West Coast, I'd have to take this wire train out there and electrify some of them redwood trees, wouldn't I?"

"Lay off it, Jig. This guy's a friend of mine and needs a job bad."

"Sounds to me like what he needs is a divorce or a club to beat some sense into that woman. The whole rig's bum, Scarfe. You say yourself this guy's never been in a wire train. What good would he be to us out here rebuilding this inter-locking at night while he was wondering which of them bright lights was shining down on his woman? You know what this job's like. You can't afford to have a guy on it that's seeing blue eyes where he ought to be seeing red lights. Don't look so huffy: I meant signal lights."

"He's a good man, Jig. I could carry him a few nights, and after he caught on he'd cut it fine."

"He might. But I can get men that'll cut it fine the first night."

"Jig, I'd like it mighty well to . . ."

"Sorry, Scarfe. But as long as I can get men that know the difference between a cross-track feeder and a rivet gun, it's only fair to the company to do it. Sorry, but it's no dice."

Just then the engineer come in for me to sign the release slip for the engine, and the other linemen scrambled out to ride it back to the transfer. Scarfe he didn't go with 'em, though. He waited till they was all gone and him and me was the only ones left in the train. Then he come over to me again.

"Jig, I rigged this wrong. I should of knowed better and

I'm sorry. Now I want to tell you the truth about this Regan guy."

"All right, Scarfe, let her rip."

"Me and Regan was buddies for years. Clumb buddies on half a dozen big transmission jobs. He was as good a lineman as ever wore a belt, considering he was young. Then he met up with a broad out there in the sticks where some guy had ditched her. He fell for her something awful. She seen he was making good money, so she marries him. He'd been shooting craps and he had a roll you could of used to guy a gin pole with. So she got him to quit his job and go to town to spend it. He done it. Then when his dough was gone and he wanted to look up another job and make some more she wouldn't leave town. He went off alone finally and come out to the job where I was at. He was useless; like to fell out of every tower he clumb. All the time he was worryin' about that woman. The Man finally canned him. But he goes down to the pool hall and knocks off another little roll with them dice. And then he goes back to his wife and they spend it. That's been going on now about three years. The reason he don't get a transmission job is he's blackballed with every company in this part of the country. I've got him into jobs before; he done fine with 'em till that woman got to bothering him and then it's the same old story. I figured she'd quit him and so the best thing was just to let it drift till she did. But she ain't going to quit him. She ain't getting any younger or fancier and she knows how good them dice can treat him when they take the notion."

"And he puts up with it?"

"Laps it up. He thinks the sun just comes out to light up them gold teeth of hers."

"Somebody ought to lay her out real careful on a pile of broken bottles and run a steam roller over her a few times."

"I'd like to burn her heart out with a steel torch, but I

doubt if a torch'd cut into where it's at. That wouldn't do
Regan no good, noway. He's still nuts about her and always
will be till he gets over it by hisself. You can't say nothin' to
him. I tried when he was first fixing to marry her. All that
come of it was him pulling his pliers on me. Yes, he did—and
him and me good friends, too. I taken his pliers away and
throwed 'em out a window and told him to wise up. But he
wouldn't wise up then, and he ain't since. And now he's in a
bad way. His belt and tools is in hock, and unless you'll give
him a chancet they might as well stay there. I don't think he
never worked at nothing but line work, and he wouldn't want
to, noway."

"You say he's a good lineman."

"Yes. He'll catch on to railroad work fast. I think he might
come out of it and get shut of this broad if he could get back
on a good job again. I hate to pester you about it, but it's
serious. I kind of feel like it might be the last chancet he'd
ever get. I wasn't never going to say nothing about this, Jig,
but I wouldn't be here talking to you if it wasn't for him. He
done me about the same kind of favor I done you last winter
and . . ."

"O.K., Scarfe. I didn't know it was that serious with you."

Scarfe had done me what he called a favor. It was on a
breakdown. He'd clumb about forty yards through a mess of
broke and burning wire a asbestos squirrel couldn't of crossed
to where I was hanging in my belt so cold I didn't even know
my overalls was on fire. He beat out the fire and carried me
over to a body beam, walking and crawling all the way along
wire I wouldn't of hung a lunch bucket on. Him and me had
beds side by side in the hospital for almost a month, but I
never did learn the whole story till the day they come in to
give him the medal.

"Bring him out tonight, then. But remember, I ain't prom-
ising to keep him unless he can cut it. I'd like to do you both

a favor, now I know all about it, but this work's too risky to
fool with a man that ain't on his toes."

"Much obliged. Jig. I'll carry him till he gets going."

2

Regan come in with Scarfe that night about ten-thirty. He
was a nice-looking guy, not big like Scarfe, but not no runt.
He looked soft like he hadn't been working for a while, but
he had a kind of a good-natured face and good steady eyes.
And he had a way about him I liked, not nervous or jerky,
but quick and easy-moving. You could see he was a lineman
right off; he walked like one and he talked like one.

"I guess Scarfe told you," he says to me, "I ain't never been
in no wire train before."

"Yeah. Ever use steel skates?"

"No. I never clumb no steel pole in my life. I've used
wood hooks a bit, though, and clumb some towers."

"Well, don't try no steel skates at night. You can practice
on 'em in the mornings after the sun's up till you get used to
'em. In the meantime you just do what work they is to be
done on the decks of the tower cars or off the ladders. I guess
you've worked off ladders, ain't you?"

"Yeah. Plenty in transmission work."

"All right. Working on these decks will be new to you.
Watch out you don't trip on some of the scrap hardware and
spill off the top. It's a long fall down to the tracks when them
towers are pulled up. Have you worked much around hot
wire?"

"I've worked twenty-three and forty-four and sixty-six hundred with rubber gloves. And I've worked clearance rigs on
transmission crossings. What's the voltage here?"

"Fourteen thousand. We work it all on a time-clearance
basis. Most of this railroad yard has to be hot for service all
but a few hours of every night. So don't never go up on deck

till I've told you the wire's dead and you've saw the ground sticks on it. And when me or Beckett, the straw boss, says, 'Everybody down!' that's what it means. If you fool around on deck after hearing that, you'll find yourself about half cooked before you ever get to hell. And remember, even when we got the power out on one section of wire, all the other wire in the yard will most likely be hot. You keep close to Scarfe. He knows every kilowatt in this yard by its front name and he'll keep you away from them."

"Yes, sir."

Regan was all right. He was green at catenary, but you can't expect a man to come right off transmission work and savvy a railroad job the first night. It's too different. In transmission work you just got towers to build or wire to string out over open country. You can start out in the morning and work till your tail drags with nothing to bother you. In railroad work you always got to wait till you can get the use of the track. And in a hot yard you got to wait till track and power clearance synchronize. And then you got to get your train moved in to where you want it, your towers pulled up to the right level, your deck lights set, and your men to work. And you got to do it fast. And you got to keep your work in hand so that you can tie it up quick and get your train out faster than you taken it in if the signal tower suddenly needs your track to handle traffic on.

Regan wasn't used to rawhiding the work for short shots and then having nothing to do, but he caught on fast and he was smart about planning his work so he wouldn't never foul us if we had to move sudden. And he was a good lineman. He could handle a rope or walk wire or steel or hang off a ladder with anyone. He clumb nice, too—quick, light-footed, and easy-moving. He wasn't used to working at night with only flood lights for light, but he never said nothing about it, and in a couple of nights he was running around in the dark like a mole.

And if he was green on catenary he made up for it by hard work. He was always the first guy to follow me and Beckett on deck when the train stopped at a new place. He'd be the first guy to grab a hook ladder when I put the spotlight upon some work that couldn't be reached from the deck. He was handy about stretching out the blocks when we was getting ready to tension. And he was quick to help swing out a outrigger when we had to lay on one track and do our work out over the next one. He never batted a eye about working on that outrigger. The first time he seen us use one, it wasn't no more than locked in its stirrups when he walks out on it. I calls to him.

"Regan, hook your belt on that messenger wire. You're just about six foot above the smokestack of any freight that wants to go under you there. If it taken a notion to puff just right, it'd knock you and that outrigger, too, three foot in the air."

"I figured if one come under me I'd just step clear of the outrigger and stand on the wire till it went by."

"That's right. But keep your belt hooked over the wire. That's what you're wearing it for."

"Yes, sir."

A freight did take a blast at him that same night and knocked him off the wire, but his belt held him all right. And when it was over he just went back to work, not paying no more attention to it than he done to the way the other guys kidded him.

Scarfe helped him a lot. Them two was real buddies. Before Regan come along, Scarfe he'd always been a loner. He was as good a lineman as I ever seen, but he mostly worked alone and he didn't hang out none with the other guys offen the job. I figured he might of been born that way or he might of had him a buddy got killed. But when Regan come to work and I seen them two together I knowed why Scarfe hadn't never paired up with no one else. Him and Regan worked together all the time and they was a sweet pair. What

Regan didn't know about catenary Scarfe did, and he learnt
Regan fast. They'd arc at each other all the time.

"All right, Mr. Scarfe, if you stand there much longer your
feet'll grow roots right down through the deck!"

"Well, just as quick as you get your hand out of the company's pocket and get up that ladder I'll hand you these
blocks!"

Regan was good about the hot wire, too. Anybody's apt to
be nervous around hot wire. And they was many a night's
work in that yard we done with the gang just eighteen inches
from a look at the Holy Ghost. But Regan didn't mind it,
and he wasn't careless, neither. He'd look it all over in that
calm way he had and then he'd get in good position and go
right to work on the cold side of a set of insulators just as
steady as if he'd never heard of a lineman burning up. He
watched close how we put the ground sticks on to protect us,
and when he come up on deck after us he taken Scarfe aside.

"This wire running right across the deck here is the one
we seen the ground sticks put on, ain't it?"

"Yeah. It's dead. You noticed how Jig put his hand on it
when we first come up, didn't you?"

"Yeah. But how about them insulators down there by the
end of the deck behind Beckett?"

"That's a air break—cold on this side, hot on the other.
That's what Beckett's standing there for, so no one won't
forget and reach or walk past them insulators."

"I wouldn't put my hands acrost no insulators in this yard
if I seen a bolt bag full of gold pieces hanging on the other
side!"

I noticed when we holed up in a siding after that first shot
Regan he borrows a blueprint off me and, instead of spend-
ing the slack time drinking coffee and throwing water and
rough-housing like the other guys done, he got Scarfe to
explain a air break to him and to learn him off the prints
about sectionalizing circuits. In the morning after we'd

cleared up and the other guys had went home, Regan takes a pair of skates out of the shop car and puts in about a hour of his own time practicing climbing a pole with 'em. In a few days he could run up and down a steel pole like a shadow.

3

In short, Regan caught hold good, and after a few nights Scarfe come around to see me again.

"Well, what do you think of my boy, Regan?"

"He's still here, ain't he?"

"Yeah. I knowed you wouldn't fire him when you seen how good he is."

"You was right about him. He's a lineman and he's going to be a good catenary lineman. How's his home life coming?"

"He's still living with that woman. And he won't say no more about it than he ever would, so I guess she's got him down as bad as ever. But that don't bother you, does it?"

"Hell, no. It ain't my business, just so he comes in here sober at night. As long as his work lasts like this, he's O.K. with me."

It lasted till the night after he drawed his first pay. If him and his woman was fighting before that, they wasn't no sign of it on the job and that was all I give a damn about. Pay night was a Saturday. It was a good one, too. We'd had some overtime and they must of been right close to a hundred bucks in the linemen's envelopes. When I give Regan his, he taken a look at the amount where it's wrote on the outside and grins.

"Thanks, Jig."

"Nothing to thank me for, Regan. You earned it. And if you keep on like you been doing, you'll earn a lot more like it."

As luck would have it, the railroad was running a lot of Sunday excursions to the seashore that morning, and after about three-ten we couldn't get no track at all. I had the engineer run us up on a siding and I hung the train up for the night. I put the boys to work cleaning up tools, inspecting and reeving blocks, and generally overhauling our equipment. But they wasn't a night's work in that, and a little after five o'clock we was done. Beckett he takes out his pay and looks at it.

"That either ain't enough or it's too much! Shoot a fiver, Joe!"

"Wait a minute," I says. "If you guys want to shoot craps in here, I'll go over to the office. Keep a good lookout, though."

I'd signed the engine off, so I didn't go back to the train till about seven. All but Scarfe had rode the engine in.

"Well, who done the winning?"

"Beckett and Paul Renford. The rest of us lost our shirts."

"Somebody's got to if anyone wins. Regan lose, too?"

"Yeah. They dry-cleaned him."

"Good. He don't never squawk over losing. His woman will, though. She'll holler till her teeth get hot."

I don't know how much hollering she done, but that night Regan come in to the train with a black eye. It wasn't one of them real good ones that come free with a quart of whisky and a loose tongue, but it was black, all right. His hands wasn't cut or bruised none, neither, so I just about knowed where that black eye come from. They ain't many men around could of give Regan a black eye and kept from bruising his hands, too. I didn't say nothing about it, but of course the other guys kidded him. He didn't seem to mind it none; he just taken it with a kind of a foolish grin until Joe Mitchell made that wisecrack.

"How did you say you got it now, Regan? You've told us so many ways I've forgot which of 'em you meant."

Regan grins so no one wouldn't take it serious and says, "Oh, I got it off a swinging door."

Joe he looks at it real close: "Looks to me more like it was a swinging whore!"

And then Joe was picking hisself up off the floor and it looked mean till I got between 'em.

"If you guys want to fight, just wait till I write out your time!"

Joe he spits out a tooth and some blood and I guess he would of went for Regan if he hadn't saw I had my pliers out.

"I ain't looking for no fight, but it's a hell of a note when you can't make a good-natured crack without a guy getting sore and busting your teeth out!"

"Just one tooth!" I says. "Regan, are you through fighting or do you want me to fire you so you can spend the whole night at it?"

"Naw," says Regan. "I don't want to fight no more. But if any of the rest of you guys want to pop off at me about this lamp, make sure it's me you're kidding."

Joe he was a pretty decent guy. "If I'd knowed it was a broad give it to you, Regan, I wouldn't of said that. If you want to fight some more, I'll meet you anywhere you say, but if you don't, it suits me."

"Forget it, Joe. I'm sorry I got so hot. I should of knowed you didn't mean nothing by it."

So that was that, and them two didn't fight no more.

4

But they was more wrong with Regan than that eye. I found it out directly we went out to work. About one-twelve the special-duty man come in and says we can have one of the new tracks all night and a twenty-five-minute shot on another right off. I told him to take us out and uncouple so we could leave one tower car and half the gang with the all-night job and then I'd take the engine and the other tower car and the rest of the outfit and cruise around the yard working when and where we could.

I left Beckett with some of the guys where they was a lot of work could be done in one place. I left Joe Mitchell with him. And I taken the other half of the outfit and Regan with me. It don't never do no harm to keep two guys that just been fighting from working too close to each other till you're sure they really are made up.

Regan he wasn't worth his weight in broke insulators. He fouled up the blocks every time we went to use 'em. He cut a piece of auxiliary wire before I even had time to mark it, so it was just the grace of God we didn't have to run in a new piece two hundred yards long. He put a pair of pull-off bars on upside down so they would of tore the smokestack off a locomotive, let alone the pantograph off a electric, and he just generally fouled the whole job.

If we'd been working on stuff that was new to him I wouldn't of said nothing. But this was just the same kind of work we'd been doing all week and he should of knowed better. I told him so, too, and he just nods kind of listless-like and says he's sorry.

About four o'clock we got a few minutes in the clear and I sent the men down into the shop car to eat. That is, all but Regan. He was just finishing wire-locking a crossover when I had to move the train, so I left him out on it, and as soon as we got the track again I run the train back in under him and picked him up. Then I sent him down to eat. In a minute I went down to the shop car to get a blueprint and there set Regan drinking coffee but not eating nothing.

"You better eat your dinner, son. We're going to work right through till seven-fifty-six this morning."

"I ain't got it with me, Jig. I'll make out all right with just some coffee."

"How come you ain't got it with you? If it's over in

Beckett's half, go after it. You can walk over there in a few minutes and no one wants to work on a empty gut."

"No. It ain't over there. I didn't bring it out with me. I ain't so hungry tonight."

I starts to ask him why he'd come out without a dinner, and then I remembered. His woman had been too busy blacking his eye to make him up a dinner. So I says to him, "They's a couple of extra sandwiches in mine I ain't going to eat. Help yourself to 'em."

I almost had to force him to take 'em. But when he did he forgot about not being hungry and eat 'em like he hadn't saw no food for a week.

Eating didn't help him none, though. All the rest of that night he was dopy. If we'd been working real close to anything hot I'd of sent him down off the deck till we got it done. But we wasn't. Down on them new tracks where we was you could get a lot of clearance all around you. And what with having a fight in the train, and it being the night after pay, I told the special-duty man to keep us there all night. It ain't always you can work like that. Mostly you got to expect your gang to be just as good one night as the next or fire them that ain't. But this was a long job and we was working seven nights a week on it. And when you're running a show like that it pays you to use your head about timing the work to suit the men as much as you can. Regan and Joe wasn't neither of them soreheads and I figured that by the next night the whole outfit would be steadied down all right.

5

They was, too, all but Regan. He was just as useless as he'd been the night before. He just set around when we was cleared up like he was sulking to hisself. It wasn't over Joe, neither. Him and Joe spoke to each other civil when they come in that night and they buddied about carrying some rolls of guy wire over to the train before we went to work.

When we got out to work, Regan was the first guy to follow me and Beckett on deck, but up there he didn't seem to do no good. And that night we was out where it was hot all around us. We was working on Four, which wasn't hot, of course. Out in mid-span we had about eleven foot clearance from Three and Five, which was hot as the devil's fork. But they was places at the cross spans, and where a couple of crossovers run through Four, that wasn't eighteen inches from the kilowatts. And that's no place for a man that ain't got his whole mind on the work.

I watched Regan close to see if he'd snap out of it. He didn't do nothing wrong I could put my finger on, but he didn't snap out of it, neither, so I says:

"Boys, I want all but Scarfe and Paul and Beckett to lay back when we come to these spans and crossover breaks. Three men's enough to do all we got to do there, and it's too close to the hot to have a bunch hanging around. You other guys do the work out in the mid-spans."

That suited everyone and it give Regan less chance of hurting hisself or someone else. But at that he like to kilt us all.

Out in one of the spans of Four they was a crossover dead end running diagonal acrost the span and about ten foot above deck level. It was red hot and we couldn't get power clearance on it. We had to go in under it to work, but before I run the train in there I says to the gang:

"Boys, they's a hot one crossing over above us in here. We got plenty of clearance to keep under it if we take it easy and work low. But remember: it's right up there all the time even if the lights don't show it. I don't want no one to climb up on the messenger or even to pick a ladder up off the deck. And anyone waves a hanger rod or tie wire over his head might just as well be waving to the undertaker to come get him. We're going in now: watch the move!"

The engineer run us in under there nice and easy and we went to work. For a few minutes the gang done fine. We was putting on hangers and the men kept them copper rods down low till the tops of them was tight to the messenger and couldn't get up to kiss the kilowatts above us. And they was good about handling the tie wire in rolls instead of cutting it off in lengths. We got the span tailored in good shape and I goes down to the end of the deck to sight it. The hangers mostly fit nice. In all but one place that riding wire was flat enough to of rode a pantograph a hundred miles an hour. One hanger was about a half inch short, though. The men was stationed along the length of the deck standing back from the wire so I could see it to sight it. They was out of the light and I couldn't see who was nearest the short hanger, so I says:

"Somebody take that fourth hanger off. Put a longer one on there and tie it till I can sight it and tell you where to cut it."

Regan was nearest to it. Instead of taking the old hanger down first, he stoops over to the deck and grabs a long section of new hanger rod. As he come up with it he swings it way up over his head. I couldn't do nothing. I would of throwed my pliers at him, but I was fifty foot down the deck, and even if I hit him square on the head it probably wouldn't stop the lifting motion of that hanger in time. So I hollers, "Flash!" and throwed myself face down on the deck. It wouldn't help Regan none if I got my eyes burnt out watching it. The other boys had all saw it and I heard them hitting the deck as I did. I closed my eyes and wondered if they was a scrap of tie wire or a drop cord touching me, but I knowed better than to look.

Then they was a hell of a crash up the deck, but no flash or stink, and no crack like a breaker switch makes when a hot

one bites something. I looks up and there was Regan sprawled
out on deck with the hanger still in his hand and Scarfe on
top of him. The other men begun to look up and wipe the
sweat off their faces, and Scarfe he gets up off Regan kind of
slow, like he was tired, and wipes his face.

"Scarfe, how far did you have to jump to get to Regan?"

"I don't know. I didn't stop to figure."

"He was standing right by me," says Beckett. "I thought of
jumping and figured they wasn't time."

We figured it up, and Scarfe he'd jumped about seven
foot. He'd started that jump just when the rest of us figured
it was hopeless and ducked to save ourselves. And he hadn't
knowed for the whole of them seven feet that them kilowatts
wasn't coming to meet him, let alone be there waiting for
him if he was late. I doubt if they was six inches between the
end of that hanger and the hot crossover when he hit Regan
and knocked him and the hanger down. Regan he'd cut his
cheek a little when they hit the deck, and the way the blood
stood out on the white of his face was a sight.

"Scarfe," he says, "I'm much obliged to you."

"All right," says Scarfe.

I couldn't let it go that easy, though. It was too close.

"Regan, go down to the shop car and iodine that cut. And
then you can wait there till I come down."

"Yes, sir."

"Boys, I ain't got much to say about what just happened.
You all seen it and you know as well as I do how close it
was. And you know where most of us'd be if it wasn't for
Scarfe. Let's not have no next time. Now, a couple of you get
a hanger on there and let's get this span done."

Some of the guys put a hanger on, and Scarfe he followed
me down the deck to where I was sighting it.

"Let Beckett sight that, Jig. I want to talk to you a second."

"Sight this, Beckett, and then move the train down under
the beam and start the outfit riveting."

Beckett nods, and Scarfe and me slip off to a corner of the deck out of the way of the work.

"Jig, I want you to give Regan another chancet."

"I figured you would. That's how come me not to fire him right where he done it. But it's a serious business, Scarfe. If it hadn't been for what you done, our shop-car boy and the grunts would still be clearing the burnt meat off the deck. I don't want to can Regan, but you can't have stuff like that going on."

"You ain't going to have it going on. He's got good sense. He seen what happened and he'll be all the better for being that close to a burning. It takes something strong to make a impression on a guy with a woman like that on his mind. He's had it, and he'll do all right now."

"I ain't thinking so much about him as about the rest of the gang. If he was the only one he could hurt, it wouldn't matter. But he ain't. They's at least three good women I know of come within six inches of being widows tonight just over Regan having his mind on that broad of his. You know that ain't right."

"I know it. And you got a right to can him if you want. But if you'll give him one more chancet I'll see he either snaps out of it—or quits before he does hurt someone."

"Well, I'll have a talk with him. I've give him some time to be thinking this over and maybe he'll be ready to talk sense."

"I'm right obliged to you, Jig."

I went down and had a talk with him. I didn't cuss him, but I talked to him stiff. And he taken it good. He was sorry and he knowed I had a right to can him. I told him I didn't want to can him, but I'd have to unless he come out of it and done better. I told him he was a good enough lineman to know this ain't a job for a man that can't keep his mind on it. He nods and then he looks at me kind of funny.

"Jig, was you ever married?"

"Hell, no. And I never fell off no real high pole, neither. But if I did I'd try not to hit the guys under me as I come down."

He caught right on. He didn't say nothing for a minute or two, and then he nods.

"I see what you mean. I'll try to do better."

"You'll have to do better if you're going to stay here. I got no kick on your work when you keep your mind on it; it's good. But you either got to get shut of whatever's worrying you or get shut of the job."

"I been worrying about private affairs, Jig. If it come to what you say, I'd have to get shut of the job. But if you'll give me another chancet I think I can run 'em both all right."

"One more, then. And I want to see you make out with it."

He thanked me so hard I hated to hear it. And for a while after that he done fine. He'd caught on a lot to railroad work now, and him and Scarfe was as good a pair as I ever worked. They wasn't no crap game in the train the night after the next pay, neither. I don't never mind a gang shooting craps if they ain't no work to be done. But I seen what come of that last game and I told the boys they'd have to do their crap shooting off the job. And so that week Regan taken his money home. At least I judge he taken it home, because the next night he had a good dinner with him and no black eye. And he kept his mind on his work.

6

The week after that we had a hell of a funny accident. It was the only one I ever knowed that was funny, but it was, though it like to scared us to death.

It must of been about four-ten in the morning. We had the train laying right under a beam and was changing some messenger suspensions. Everything was dead and grounded in the section where we was. The nearest hot wire to us was the hot side of a air break down under the signal bridge about a hundred yards away.

Well, about four-ten we heard a ruckus down near the signal bridge and some of them stray dogs that hang out by the slaughterhouse acrost the yard begun to bark like hell. I couldn't figure it for a minute and then I caught on all of a sudden.

"Get away from that wire, boys! Them dogs have chased a hobo up that signal bridge. If he fouls that break, it might throw something back this way!"

The boys throwed theirselves down on the deck, and one or two that was up the ladder clumb up onto the beam and laid out on that where they'd be out of the way if a wire burnt through. I throwed the spotlight on the signal bridge, but it was so far I couldn't see the hobo at all. If it hadn't been the signal bridge I wouldn't of knowed what it was, 'cause a hobo don't go around carrying steel skates so he can get up a pole when dogs chase him. But on the signal bridge they was ladder steps all the way up from the ground, and a kid could of clumb it. They was hot wire all over that bridge, too—jumper loops offen the signal circuit, and feeder taps and short air breaks and any amount of other junk. It would of been a bum place for a lineman that knowed his stuff to be fooling around in the dark.

"They's fourteen thousand volts of juice all over that signal bridge, hobo! Stand still till I come down there with a light and run them dogs off, and I'll show you how to get down alive!"

He didn't answer, but them dogs barked worse than ever. Beckett he speaks up.

"He thinks you're a railroad dick and if he answers he's jail bait."

"He's hearse bait if he fools around that bridge. And this train's got to move out of here in three minutes. Renford, get that ladder down and then move the train back to the siding. And keep the men away from that wire. Beckett, you and Scarfe come with me and we'll see if we can get this tramp down before he kills hisself!"

We run most of the way. I got no special use for hoboes, but they ain't no sense in letting a guy burn hisself up just because he thinks you're the law and is scared to come down out of a death trap like that. But we was too late. We was still about thirty yards from the bridge when a breaker switch lets go like a load of dynamite. We couldn't see the hobo in the flash and we didn't hear his body hit the ground, though we knowed the surge must of knocked it loose of the contact or the breaker would of blowed again. But the wind was blowing our way, and the first whiff that got to us after that breaker blowed settled it. You don't forget that smell.

Well, we got to the bridge and looked all around under it, but we couldn't find no body. The dogs had run off when the breaker blowed. I put my light on the bridge, but I couldn't see nothing up there, so I clumb up and looked at every lead on it. I found where the flash had been, all right. They was a broke bell in a set of flash-scarred insulators. But they wasn't no sign of a body nowhere and we couldn't figure that out. Fourteen thousand'll tear a man up something awful if it hits him right, or again you got to look his body over close to find where the contact was. It's freakish stuff, but at that I never heard of it carrying no one off. And it wasn't no kite blowed into that wire, neither. A kite don't smell like that.

I clumb down again and stood there talking to Scarfe about it when Beckett give out a laugh.

"There's your hobo!"

I looks where he's holding his light, and there was the head and shoulders of a cat. That was all they was left of it. The rest of it, I guess, was blowed all over the yard. All the fur was burnt off the part we seen. It was ugly, but it was better to look at than a dead hobo.

We all stood there and laughed at it. We'd been tensioned up tight, thinking it was a man.

"Them dogs run him up there," says Scarfe, "and somehow he slipped acrost them insulators. We'll never know how."

"Who cares how?" asks Beckett. "I don't, and I bet the cat don't, neither. He ain't never going to be hungry again, nor have to scratch around on rainy nights to get food, nor let them tabby cats worry him, neither. His trouble is over, quick and painless."

Scarfe he give a start. He don't say nothing for a second, and then he says kind of low, like he was talking to hisself, "Yeah. That's one cure for any trouble."

It struck me odd, Scarfe being so serious about a stray old cat, but I didn't have time to think about it before the gang come up bringing a stretcher. They wasn't serious. They laughed like hell when they seen how we was fooled. Beckett he says we ought to fill out a real accident report and send it to the head office—fill it out like it was a lineman named "A. Cat."

"How would you fill in that part where it says 'Remarks'?" asks Scarfe. He wasn't so serious now the other guys had come up and was standing there laughing.

Beckett thought a minute. "That wouldn't have nothing to do with it. Just fill that part in like you generally do it. 'Remarks: None.' "

So we throwed what was left of the cat back in the bushes and went on back to the train.

7

Payday come again, and the night after it Regan come in without no dinner. He had a long scratch on the side of his face, too. When we got our first shot he put his belt on upside down and all the tools fell out around his feet. He wouldn't

even of knowed it if Beckett hadn't arced at him to pick 'em
put and get conscious. Up on deck I watched him like a hawk,
and I didn't have to watch long. We was tensioning, and the
first thing Regan does is put a little set of four-inch blocks
acrost a splice where he knowed damned well he was going
to have a pulling load of about five thousand pounds. Scarfe
seen him do it and tried to get them blocks off before I seen
it. But when he seen I seen it, he just turns away and shakes
his head.

"Regan, you go down to the shop car and help the shop-
car boy make up them pull-off straps tonight."

"Yes, sir."

Scarfe taken me aside after Regan had gone.

"I'm right obliged to you for not just firing him right up
here where everyone could hear it."

"I hate it, Scarfe. I like that boy and I'd like to keep him.
But you seen that last stunt yourself; I'll just have to give
him his time in the morning. It ain't fair to him nor to the
others to keep him. It could only end one way."

"Yeah," says Scarfe. "Only one way."

He stood there for a while after that, keeping out of the
way of the rest of the gang, and I didn't bother him. He
thought a lot of Regan and he felt bad about it. I did, too. I
guess I felt worse for Scarfe than I did for Regan hisself. But
by and by Scarfe come out of it, and, if he was kind of quiet,
he did put out a good night's work. Then about four o'clock
he comes up to me.

"Jig, you going to make that change at the signal bridge?"

"I was going to, but I ain't sure now, Scarfe. I can't get
power clearance under there for twenty minutes, and I'll
only get a fifteen-minute shot then. If I could spare a couple
of men to get everything rigged and ready in advance, I
could make it. But I'm afraid I'll have to let it go till tomorrow night."

"I'll rig it for you, Jig."

"One man ain't enough, and that's all I can spare."

"Let me take Regan. He's still on the payroll."

"It's too risky. Everything down there's still red hot."

"He'll do all right with me, Jig. I know him, and I can take care of him and rig it right, too."

"Well, I'd like to get that done tonight, Scarfe, but . . ."

"Jig, let me do it. Regan and me are buddies. I know he's done, but he and I seen each other through a lot of tough places and I'd like to see him through one more. This is likely his last job and I'd like to work with him one more time."

"All right. Want a helper to carry your stuff?"

"No. I'd rather it was just him and me. We ain't got so much stuff to carry."

I walks down to the signal bridge with 'em and showed 'em what I wanted done. Regan he still seemed kind of dopy, though he looks at me and paid close attention when I was warning him about the hot wire. And he clumb all right.

I watched 'em till they'd got up onto the bridge and pulled their ladder up. And then I hollered to 'em to watch the hot stuff all the time, and I starts back over to the train to see if Beckett had the tensioning done. I was just wondering if I done right to trust Regan at all when I heard the breaker switch blow. . . .

As I run, all I could think of was if I'd fired Regan right off the deck in the first place Scarfe would be still alive. But when I got there Scarfe was still alive. He'd clumb down off the bridge and picked up Regan from where he fell and carried him over to the side of the track. When I come up he was just standing there looking at him.

I put my flashlight on Regan, and then I shut it off and taken off my overall jumper and throwed it over his face. I put my light on Scarfe, and then I taken it off him, too. He was all right. His overalls was singed and his eyebrows and lashes was burned off, but it was more than that made me take my light off him. It was something in his face. He didn't say nothing and neither did I. We could hear the other guys coming and see their lights bobbing as they run. And then Scarfe give a kind of a cry.

"I got to tell you, Jig. I got to tell you the truth . . ."

I cracks him hard acrost the face with my open hand.

"Buck up, Scarfe. They ain't nothing to tell. We both seen this poor guy trip and fall acrost that wire. Lots of accidents happen that way. 'Remarks: None.' "

He taken a long breath and kind of shook hisself. And then just before the other guys come up he says, "I guess you're right. Thanks, Jig."

WIDE-OPEN
THROTTLE

By A. W. Somerville

A. W. Somerville

THE SON OF A RAILROADER, A. W. Somerville was brought up on trains, tracks and terminals as some boys are reared on a farm, a river or a baseball diamond. He was born in Ferguson, Missouri, a suburb of St. Louis, on June 9, 1900. His first railroad job was with the Texas and Pacific at Marshall, Texas, as a machinist. He has worked with other roads and in other capacities, and always, whether checking locomotives, inspecting box-cars or working for a railroad contractor, he took in, with Kipling-like thoroughness, details which subsequently were incorporated in his remarkable yarns.

Somerville wrote nearly a score of stories, all on railroading, for the *Saturday Evening Post*. Most of these yarns appeared in the late twenties and early thirties. Among the long list of titles are: *Authorized by Time-Table, Comin' Down the Railroad, High Water, Green Rags, Over the Hump, Tale of the Old Main Line,* and *Tin Train,* a story of early streamlining.

Wide-Open Throttle is a story of a time that never was on the railroads. There never were such railroaders as Oil-Can Tommy and High-Wheeled Mike, of course, at least not as late in railroad history as the beginnings of double-track operation and refrigeration. But the story of their rivalry on parallel tracks sheds light, even if it is the light of exaggeration, on the ways of thought in the railroad world before the safety movement was dreamed of.

Counterbalance stems from Somerville's own department of railroading, the shops. In operating railroads there are men who keep up the track, others who keep cars and engines fit, and still others who run them on the rails. They work together—they must —but each sort of railroad man has his own pride of craft and his own opinion of the shortcomings of the others. Between competent description of shop practices and shrewd glimpses of the never-ending rivalry of the crafts in their common work of seeing that the trains run, the story moves merrily to its unexpected ending.

WIDE-OPEN THROTTLE

By A. W. Somerville

"YOU AIN'T NEVER HEARD tell of Oil-Can Tommy Wilkins and High-Wheeled Mike Cassidy?" demanded Johnny Griswold, freight conductor.

"Not yet," I admitted.

"Kid, they was runners!" said Johnny. "What I mean, they'd take the bridle and roll! They ate up bad track like you'd gobble hot beans! An' they hated each other. Ain't I ever told you this yarn?"

"Not yet," I repeated.

Johnny stoked his pipe. We struggled east out of Townley on a four-track artery, tons by the thousand of fresh foodstuffs for the hungry stomachs of the seaboard. Eggs, butter, green stuff, grapes, rolling east to the seaboard. Oranges from the Pacific, melons from the Rio Grande, bananas from the tropics, meat from the Western plains, carload after carload of perishable, Red Ball freight. From North and South and West these reefer cars came rolling into Townley, to be rammed to the cities of the East via the great steel highway through Lucas and Bottle Neck and Washburn.

"This was their stampin' ground," said Johnny, "from Townley east to Lucas an' Bottle Neck an' Washburn. Double track in those days as far's Bottle Neck, an' then single track. Just dirt ballast, paper-weight rails, an' rotten, wormy ties. Lucas was a grade crossing then with the Northern Central, an' it 'uz th' place where Oil-Can an' High-Wheeled fin'ly concluded their arguments an' their races.

"You don't hafta believe it, kid, but those two guys helped put this railroad on the map. They showed th' brass collars sumpin about freight; in fac', you might say they pretty near give 'em a brand-new idea about freight. Th' first Red Ball cards ever printed come from Townley, an' th' first freezers ever carded Red Ball pulled outta here. Nobody believed that a full-tonnage freight train could be kept on a passenger-train schedule until Tom Wilkins an' Mike Cassidy opened up their eyes.

"They was runners, kid. Nobody, before or since, could keep th' butter spread like those boys. Either of 'em coulda handled fifty cars of eggs on a sixty-mile schedule, an' never bust a one! There'd be lots a cold-storage plants starvin' to death today if there was more like 'em!"

The row between Wilkins and Cassidy began the first day they laid eyes on each other. Oil-Can came to the system from a dinky little logging outfit. High-Wheeled came from a standard-gauge railroad, immediately following a difference of opinion with an engine-house boss. They—Oil-Can and High-Wheeled—met in the master mechanic's office at Townley; both applied for jobs as engineers.

Cassidy was first to ask for a job, but Wilkins was shrewder and grabbed an application blank and filled it out. The written record was given precedence over the verbal application, and from that day on, Oil-Can Tommy rated one job ahead of High-Wheeled Mike on the callboard. It galled the Irishman that a scissorbill from the backwoods, a man who had never handled engines other than wood-burning teakettles, should take precedence over a promoted engineer from a man's size railroad.

"You're a wise guy, ain't you?" sneered big Mike Cassidy as the two men left the office. "Come an' shove your application under my nose when I'm askin' for a job! Who ja think you are, you bloody woodchopper?"

"Listen, you!" replied the thick-chested Wilkins. "You quit your last outfit becuz they wouldn't give you seniority, an' this outfit gives a man seniority an' you crab about it. Run along before I rub your nose in the dirt!"

"Whose nose?" inquired Mr. Cassidy.

"Your nose," advised Mr. Wilkins, and socked him on the snozzle.

Mr. Wilkins and Mr. Cassidy tangled violently and enthusiastically. They knotted. They clouted with vigor. They gouged, they scrouged, they pummeled. Mr. Wilkins described a noble parabola complicated by a swan dive, having been on the receiving end of a roundhouse swing to the button.

He lit in a cloud of dust, but rose as a golf ball bounces and met the charging enemy with a haymaker labeled explosion. The aim of the two combatants appeared to be simultaneous extermination.

The master mechanic noted the disagreement from his window, brought a chair out on the office porch, seated himself comfortably, lit a poisonous stogie and proceeded to enjoy the break in the routine. The trainmaster heard the racket, got another chair, lit an equally evil stogie and also proceeded to enjoy the break in the routine. The two officials spoke amiably to each other for the first and last time in the annals of the railroad. The master mechanic bet on Cassidy, the trainmaster bet on Wilkins.

Mr. Wilkins and Mr. Cassidy extended themselves to the utmost, yet neither could accomplish anything really definite in the way of a victory. The immovable object met the irresistible force so many times that the audience became dizzy. It soon became obvious that even a moral victory for either warrior would be a most impossible arrangement. A long-drawn-out conclusion was well on the way.

"We better put a stop to it," said the master mechanic, "as soon as they get tired enough to be handled. I got two engines waitin' on 'em!"

"I've had two trains waitin' all mornin' on you," said the trainmaster unpleasantly and promptly.

"You better start sortin' cars," from the master mechanic unctuously. "I'd hate to stop a good fight just to prove you're still a liar."

The two officials squabbled raucously until an involuntary truce fell between High-Wheeled and Oil-Can. Flesh and blood had been taxed beyond exhaustion, and unconsciousness was about to merge with disintegration. It was a comparatively safe operation to declare an armistice, which the two officials accomplished by sitting on Mr. Wilkins and Mr. Cassidy. The battered pair were informed regretfully that the railroad had to run. The trainmaster had some cars he wanted moved; the master mechanic had two engines ready for service.

Despite overwhelming ocular evidence that both hogheads were in far better shape for a hospital cot than for service on the road, down they went to the engine house. The nose of High-Wheeled Mike was not a feature but a pancake; his whole ensemble was indicative of a head-on collision with a large and animated Chinese dragon. The ears of Oil-Can Tommy flapped when the wind blew; he had more bumps than a horned toad; he was a sight to bring tears to the eyes of a wolf. They finally got their engines, after defying everyone in the roundhouse. To each was assigned a pilot, for neither knew the road. There was also some doubt as to whether either could see the road. The trainmaster, by superhuman effort, only delayed them an hour while he made up the trains. They got their orders, or what were known as orders in those days.

It so happened that Cassidy got away first. He headed out on the south track, as his orders stated.

"We've got forty miles to go to Bottle Neck," the pilot informed the battered engineer. "You'll find the switch against you there."

"Yeah," said Cassidy, not much interested.

"If that man on the north track don't show by then," went on the guide, "we'll run around him. But if he's right on our tail, we'll have to let him go. The north track is the superior track."

"Why didn't they put us on the north track?" Mike asked.

"I dunno," was the answer, "unless that guy back there rates. Was he hired before you was?"

"We jes' talked that over," said Cassidy bitterly, between swollen lips.

The Irishman considered as they rolled along. He'd show this scissorbill, this splinter pusher, this slob of a Wilkins!

He crabbed at the fireman. Steam, announced Mr. Cassidy, was what he wanted. "Put her on the peg, boy, and keep her on the peg! I like to hear her pop," said High-Wheeled, "and I like to watch her roll!"

The tallow pot bailed in the bituminous. Cassidy beat her out of steam, tried to knock the stack off. The tallow stuffed her full. Cassidy took the coal out of the firebox, through the flues and up the stack as you'd pour salt from a shaker. The tallow leaned on his scoop and gave vent to short but highly expressive words.

"Do you wanta break my back, you Irish tramp?" beefed the shoveler.

Mr. Cassidy leaned down from his throne, annexed the loose-mouthed party with a hand like a clamshell bucket.

"Ye'll shut yer yap," High-Wheeled recommended. "I want nothin' outta you but work! Wur-r-rk! Jes' lemme hear one more dribble outta you an' I'll pinch you in half!" Mr. Cassidy shoved his lop-sided, terrifying phiz up against the fireman's mug, bawled: "I'm a little tired right now, stoopid, or I'd unravel you!" He pushed the man back toward the middle of the cab deck. "Warm that scoop, boy!"

The tallow warmed the scoop—warmed it vigorously. They went battering east over the dirt-ballasted track, throttle wide open, rolling from side to side giddily, pitching like a flipped nickel.

"You like to wheel 'em, don't you, brother?" contributed the pilot nervously.

"That's my name," said Mike Cassidy. "High-Wheeled— that's my name, friend."

The tallow bailed in the coal. Mr. Cassidy tried to knock the stack off. The pilot hung on as best he could.

"There's a crossing at Lucas!" finally shouted the guide. "You gotta approach under control, prepared to stop!" To put the matter lightly—very lightly indeed—the pilot was sore. Blankety-blank hoghead, didn't know the track, didn't know the road, didn't know a bloody thing except to widen out and roll. If he didn't break the train in half on a sag, he'd probably leave the rail on a bad joint. Blankety-blank hoghead! "You gotta cross Lucas under control! Ten miles an hour!"

"I'll watch for it," said Cassidy generously.

"You'll cross at ten miles an hour!" commanded the pilot.

"Zatso?" inquired Mike.

"Yeah, zatso!"

Mr. Cassidy annexed the pilot, using the same effective method employed previously on the tallow pot. And Mr. Cassidy regarded the pilot coldly from very close range, using his best eye.

"My delicate friend," quoth Mr. Cassidy, "you're the pilot on this mill, an' it's your job to tell me about the road. But don't start givin' me orders, becuz I don't like orders, an' I might—I don't say I would, ye understand—but I might beat the compound hell out of you. Becuz you don't look wide enough across the seat to be givin' me orders! What I want outta you," said Mr. Cassidy with great emphasis, "is advice!"

The pilot, without any hesitation, let it be known that he preferred giving advice to any other form of endeavor. Was it possible that Mr. Cassidy could have misunderstood him? Mr. Cassidy was laboring under a delusion. Undoubtedly Mr. Cassidy must be laboring under a delusion. Why, the pilot testified, he would no more think of giving orders to such a capable engineer than he would substitute soft coal for his favorite chewing tobacco.

They came roaring down on Lucas Crossover, thirty miles out of Townley, with the engine knocking her frame bolts loose and the butter spread behind them. "I advise," said the pilot carefully, "that you shut off and find out if your brakes will work."

"I'll take your advice," said High-Wheeled agreeably, and shut off and applied the straight air.

"They work," said the pilot, after moments of doubt.

"I figgered they would," said the engineer calmly.

They rumbled over the crossing. High-Wheeled climbed on top the coal bunker and looked behind. Far to the rear he made out the engine of one Oil-Can Tommy, and there was evidence to the effect that Mr. Wilkins' fireman was doing very little resting.

"He's a good stretch back," Cassidy informed his adviser. Mr. Cassidy beamed; he radiated good fellowship.

"Now, as I understand this, if he don't show at Bottle Neck, we bend the rail and run around him."

"That's right," agreed the pilot. "The tower will either give you a highball or a stop signal. It's up to the towerman."

"If I get there in time to clear this guy behind," said the engineer, "I get the board, don't I?"

"Sure," said the pilot.

"Well, watch Mike leave that slob!"

Bottle Neck bound, wide open, the fireman attaining perpetual motion. Bouncing like a pair of dice, wabbling like a drunken bum, ripping off the miles. Mr. Cassidy liked to wheel 'em.

They had a few miles left to go when the pilot screwed up sufficient courage to unclamp himself from a grab iron and look behind. What he saw caused his eyes to bulge; either of his blinkers could have been knocked off with a stick. Little more than a quarter mile behind was the engine of Oil-Can Tommy, smoking like a forest fire, weaving like a wiggle worm, creeping up behind them! The pilot cautiously advised the emperor of the situation. The emperor checked up personally. So did the fireman.

"That guy must like to wheel 'em, too!" said the tallow, grinning a very sweaty grin.

Cassidy boiled over. He raved. He took the spare scoop and did his best to empty the coal bunker.

Wilkins couldn't pass Cassidy, and Cassidy couldn't run around Wilkins. Another draw. High-Wheeled finally slapped on the air with a red board looking him in the eye, and Oil-Can Tommy rocketed past at sixty miles an hour. And as he passed the gentle Mr. Cassidy, Mr. Wilkins had the indelicacy to thumb his nose! Tut, tut! This gesture, strangely enough, upset Mr. Cassidy frightfully.

The feud between Oil-Can and High-Wheeled, instead of subsiding, grew with the years. It was probably the most cumulative feud that ever came down the railroad. Occasionally they had an opportunity to put on a dizzy race between Townley and Bottle Neck, and when this happened half the railroad bet on the outcome. Once in a great while Cassidy, handicapped though he was by having the inferior track, made Bottle Neck in time to get a clear board, swing onto the main line, and run around his enemy. Maybe you think the Cassidy cohorts didn't toss a celebration! Once in a great while, also, Oil-Can would leave his rival tied to a post, would take the lead and hold the lead all the way to Bottle Neck, leaving the Irishman to waste good coal and further insult his overworked fireman. Maybe you think the Wilkins adherents didn't tear up lamp-posts and annoy the peace-loving taxpayers!

Usually, however, when they raced it ended a draw. Just a dizzy race, twin engines, equal tonnage; two freight trains roaring down the double track, side by side, begging for trouble. It was a long-standing, dog-eared chestnut on the railroad that once Cassidy crossed over into the other's cab, that Wilkins knocked him back into his own gangway, that they fought till neither knew what the score was—and that Cassidy brought Wilkins' train in, and Wilkins herded Cassidy's! Chestnuts to the left-hand side, however, it is a fact that Oil-Can and High-Wheeled made the sport of kings about as interesting as a bruising game of bean bag.

Cassidy kept a record of all his runs; every time he crossed the division he would write down his time, his delays, every incident of the trip. In self-defense Wilkins adopted the same scheme, for High-Wheeled was forever bragging of his performances and belittling the runs made by Oil-Can. Competition, so to speak, was razor-edged. Thus, year after year, the records of these two runners accumulated—these two small black books—as much as any other single item, convinced the brass collars that freight could be handled day in and day out, year in and year out, on passenger-train schedules. Once this fact became known and acknowledged, then shipments of perishables began to be sought rather than side-stepped.

Now while Wilkins and Cassidy were conducting their little frolics, marring each other's beauty and running off various heats in their effort to make a bum of Old Man Time, the necessity for providing for the transportation of perishables was slowly seeping into the brains of the railroad brass collars. In these long-ago years, when the Civil War was still fresh in the minds of everyone, such items as fruits and vegetables from afar were luxuries. Lemons, for instance, came all the way from Italy, and only the wealthy could afford them. Oranges, few in number, came by express from Florida to such cities as New York or Boston, and were worth their weight in gold. No perishable was ever shipped more than fifty or one hundred miles. The green stuff the cities consumed came from strictly neighboring truck farms; local slaughterhouses furnished all meats for any given community.

Interesting to note, one of the first commodities to utilize refrigeration in transit was beer. A car would be insulated with hair, the beer loaded in kegs, the ice shoveled over the tops of the kegs, the car locked. Crude, certainly, but a thousand miles meant nothing to a shipment of amber brew. About the time St. Louis beer began to undermine the State of Kansas, strawberries were successfully transported by means of reefer cars in the East. Coincident with the above, someone came to the conclusion that if heat could be kept out in the summertime, a car could be kept warm in the wintertime. Thus, by means of insulated cars, potatoes were brought over mountains and plains in zero weather.

The railroads began to wake up. Perishables, it appeared, could not only be shipped but a great deal of money could be made from the operation. Obviously there were two elements to contend with—proper refrigeration and fast movement. The refrigeration was simply a matter of insulated, well-built cars and facilities for icing. The fast movement of tonnage trains was a problem of operation.

The city of Townley was the focus of a tremendous, fertile valley. Townley Valley could produce a multitude of perishables—grapes, green stuff, dairy products—but there was no market. The cities of the East lay over the mountains.

"Look here," said the traffic department to the operating department, "suppose we make a stab at this perishable business. If it works out we can load the reefers east with grapes and green stuff and dairy products. We may have to haul a lot of empties back, but even at that the revenue on one carload of perishables is equal to two carloads of grain. Who knows, we might some day be making westbound shipments of these fancy lemons, or oranges, or even bananas!"

One day the trainmaster at Townley sought out Wilkins.

"Tom," he said, "I'd like to borrow your little black book. The one you keep your records in."

"Yeah," said Oil-Can. "What for?"

The trainmaster explained. The brass collars had asked that Mr. Wilkins and Mr. Cassidy allow them to see the record of their runs for the past several years. There was talk of shipping grapes from Townley east. Wilkins handed over his book; later that day Cassidy turned his in.

Two weeks later the trainmaster again approached Wilkins.

"Tom," he said, "we're gonna have a crack at this grape business. They're loading eight refrigerator cars now; you get four cars and your Irish sidekick gets four cars. Tonight."

"I been waitin' for this," said Oil-Can Tommy.

Mr. Cassidy and Mr. Wilkins met just prior to leaving time. They had words.

"Keep outta my way, you scissorbill," said High-Wheeled.

"When they see me pass you," sneered Oil-Can, "they'll think you're backin' up."

They were standing beside one of the new reefers, and on the side of this car was a card bearing the legend, Red Ball Fruit Express.

"See that, Mister Woodchopper," said Cassidy, pointing. "Th' idee for that come outta my little book, see? I'm th' guy what showed 'em. Five hours from here to Washburn means twenty hours from here to the big onion. Don't you wish you had th' guts to wheel 'em like me?"

Wilkins laughed in his face.

"You shanty louse," he replied. "I'm th' guy they got th'

dope from, not you! Say, I been waitin' years for this chance
to show you up. Five hours, says you? You'll never smell my
smoke."

They pulled out together on the double, but some ten
miles out Oil-Can pulled ahead, and from there all the way
to Washburn, Cassidy never so much as glimpsed the markers
on the caboose ahead. Oil-Can was a runner; he streaked
across the division in four hours and forty minutes—twenty
minutes less than the best time his rival had ever produced.
High-Wheeled had trouble; he had to stop and set out a car
with a bad brass. He made an astonishing run, however—two
minutes more than a flat five hours.

Three nights later the two rivals faced east on the double
track again with two tonnage trains, and eight cars behind
each engine bore the Red Ball tag. They were three miles
this side of Lucas with honors even, when a flue opened up
on Oil-Can and he couldn't hold the pace. Cassidy ran around
his enemy and burned up the rail all the way to Washburn.
His time that night, according to the train sheet, was four
hours and forty-one minutes. He explained to all who would
listen that he would have clipped another thirty minutes off
had he not stopped to give Wilkins a tow!

The runs made by these two men carved eight hours from
the temporary schedule. A tonnage freight train on a passenger-train schedule! Delivery of perishables guaranteed in
New York the second morning out of Townley! And came
that eventful night when two long drags, solid reefers, solid
Red Ball cars, pointed out of Townley yard toward the eastern mountains.

"Let 'em race," the brass collars passed the word down the
line. "The shippers get a kick out of it. Let 'em race as far
as Bottle Neck, and the first man to the distant signal gets
the main line. Arrange with the Northern Central to clear
Lucas Crossover for us."

The traffic men sold the idea of the race to the brass collars. "Publicity," said the traffic department, "will put this perishable business over like a tent. Cash in on this chance! There isn't a taxpayer in Townley Valley who hasn't heard of Oil-Can Tommy and High-Wheeled Mike. Let the people of the big city in on this; let them know that the grapes, the tomatoes, the green stuff—every perishable out of Townley —was a stake in the greatest race ever staged by man! Twin bolts of smoky lightning! Wide-open throttle! Cash in—cash in!" So they did.

Just before leaving time Wilkins met Cassidy.

"I'm sick of your blab," said Oil-Can. "You've been shootin' off your mouth about me havin' th' north track, an' you've talked once too many times! I'll swap tracks with you, an' I'll throw mud in your eye from here to Bottle Neck!"

"Th' hell you will," said High-Wheeled Mike.

"Th' hell I won't," said Oil-Can Tommy.

They sought out the trainmaster.

"It don't make no diff'rence to me," declared that worthy. when informed of Wilkins' magnanimous offer. "You got about an hour. I don't care what you do."

So they swapped tracks. Oil-Can wanted the world to know just how matters stood.

"He can have th' best track." Mr. Wilkins speaking, very loudly. "Whadda I care for track? I can beat that fathead with no track at all!"

"Aw, shut up!" bawled High-Wheeled from his cab.

Mr. Cassidy was invited to descend and make Mr. Wilkins shut up. Mr. Cassidy descended with that intention foremost in his mind.

"An' were you speakin' to me?" inquired Mike politely.

"I wasn't speakin' to you," corrected Tom, "I was beggin' you."

"Now listen, boys," spoke up the master mechanic indignantly. "There's been enough of this foolishness. Upstairs, both of you!"

"Ye scissorbill," said Mike, closing in slowly, carefully, ponderously, "ye never had nothin' to eat before you come here but pine cones. Ye never knew there was such things as grapes. I'll give ye a lesson in manners."

"You lousy mick!" said Tom, circling, watching for an opening. "I was eatin' grapes before I could walk. I wasn't born in no shanty."

They came together, mauling. The master mechanic narrowly missed being sandwiched; he bawled for succor like a lost calf. Help arrived in the person of the trainmaster and half the population of Townley. It was something of a problem to separate Mr. Wilkins and Mr. Cassidy. They seemed to have an affinity for each other. Quite a few pounds of steam were used, several square yards of hide were mangled, not to mention the loss of a quart or so of blood, before the two warriors were pried apart and subdued.

"Neither of you," said the master mechanic bitterly, tenderly caressing a cracked shin, "has the brains of a jackass! Get on the job or get off the railroad!"

Upstairs went Oil-Can Tommy, shouting pleasant little reminders to his playmate. Upstairs went High-Wheeled Mike, shouting very consistent answers. And three minutes later two whistles screamed, two stacks retched, two trains lunged eastward toward the barrier mountains.

They had equal tonnage, twin engines, and both men were runners. Cassidy had the better track, but Oil-Can didn't give a hoot—a very weak hoot—for rough track. The best way to get over a bad stretch, said Mr. Wilkins, was to get over it fast. Thus were the bumps ironed out.

They left Townley even; five miles out, in open country, they were still neck and neck. Pilots even, gangways even, walking down the double, throttles wide open! Twin bolts of smoky lightning! The greatest race yet staged by man!

Each could see the other plainly in the glare from open fire doors; at times the cab roofs all but scraped as the engines rolled on the rotten track. Cassidy saw Oil-Can pull on the throttle to make sure the cylinders were swallowing every ounce of steam he could cram into them, saw him wrestle the reverse bar back a notch, saw him step down to the deck to swing a scoop in unison with his fireman. Double shovel; let her pop, boy—let her pop! Let her roll, boy—let her roll! Come on, boy, we'll show this slob!

Cassidy yanked on his throttle, set the reverse bar back with one hand, joined his fireman. Double shovel; let her pop, boy—let her pop! Fill her belly and let her roll! Come on, boy, we'll show this scissorbill!

Thirty miles to Lucas Crossover—thirty long, rough miles. Thirty miles in thirty minutes by two battered, broken watches! Thirty minutes, thirty miles; they were on the crossing, rolling like two avalanches; they struck like two mammoth, uncontrolled projectiles!

The trainmaster might have prevented the accident. But he, like the two engine crews, had definite assurance from the Northern Central that the crossing would be clear. How was the trainmaster to guess that a Northern Central freight would pull a drawbar, break in tow, and thus block the eastbound reefers?

Wilkins and Cassidy were on the decks of their respective engines, bailing in coal. Were they afraid of a fast crossing? Not this pair.

Neither looked. Neither of the firemen looked. The trainmaster was five cars back, working his way forward on High-Wheeled's train, fighting a tornado. He saw the box-cars block the crossing, he tried to reach the cab in time. He failed.

The two engines struck simultaneously, tremendously, awesomely. Cassidy's mill clung to the rail, shredding a box car like kindling, breaking timbers like matches. Wilkins' engine ripped through a car, rode up over a four-wheeled truck, slithered as though on skids, smashed into the side of the other engine, bounced crazily, and swapped end for end in mid-air. She was headed due west when she lit, and no less than nine freezers buried her. Cassidy's engine derailed when struck, but her drawbar broke and she rolled clear of the main pile-up. She stripped herself clean as a varnished pole, and the fountain and steam pipes broke in the cab.

The mess the reefers made is indescribable. They were everywhere. Out in open fields, rammed one within the other, smashed beyond recognition or repair. The crossover was ripped up by the roots; the two big pile-ups were at the crossover and at Wilkins' engine.

What few men there were for rescue work—mostly from the Northern Central—found Cassidy first. He was wandering around, dazed, his face wrecked, his clothing in ribbons. Cassidy's fireman had jumped as the engine derailed, and though badly hurt, was judged to be in luck. Cassidy had not jumped, and, though none knew at the time, was most decidedly out of luck.

With crowbars and axes the little gang of men went to work to get Wilkins out. He was alive, somewhere beneath them. They cut and pried, finally got to him. The tank was on his lap; there was no human way to get him out alive without the aid of a wrecker. His fireman was somewhere under the barrel of the engine; they couldn't even get to him. Wilkins had only a few moments of life left, and knew it.

"Hello, Tom," said Mike Cassidy.

"Why, hello, Mike," said Tom Wilkins.

They stared at each other in the gloom.

"I guess I oughtta tell you," said Oil-Can after a moment. "I don't blame you, Mike, for bein' sore about me gettin' hired. I don't blame you for bein' sore." He stopped, summoned his waning strength. "It was a lousy trick. You should 'a' rated me on th' callboard."

"Don't feel that way about it, Tom," croaked Mike dismally. "I was a rotten loser, see. That's all. I knowed all along you really rated me."

Neither spoke for a moment.

"Say, Mike, we've been knowin' each other eight years. We ain't never shook hands yet."

High-Wheeled fumbled about, found the one free hand of his old enemy—a big, knotty hand. They shook.

"I'm sorry." Wilkins' voice was very weak. " 'Twas a dirty Irish trick I played you, Mike."

"Hey?" demanded Mike.

"A shanty-Irish trick," said Oil-Can, and cashed in his chips.

Cassidy made sure that Wilkins was gone, then laboriously climbed out of the wreckage. He was growing weaker; he found it all but impossible to breathe. He stumbled away from the pile-up, lay down in a clear space. The trainmaster found him.

"What's the matter, Mike?"

"They got my number," said Cassidy with difficulty.

"There'll be a relief train here in fifteen minutes," promised the official. "Stick it out."

"I swallered half the steam in the boiler," said High-Wheeled. "I got jammed up agin the fountain. I'm cooked."

The trainmaster knew what live steam does to a man's lungs.

"Anything I can do for you?"

"Naw," said High-Wheeled Mike. He grinned a wretched, tortured grin. "Dammit," he said, "I never could get ahead of that scissorbill Wilkins. Jes' now he had th' gall to up an' die first!"

Johnny Griswold regarded his pipe intently. He lit a match very deliberately, puffed carefully.

"I never could get very sentimental over them two rough-necks gettin' bumped off, kid," he finally said. "Th' railroads in them days, you see, was man-killers. If you didn't want to take th' chances, you didn't have no right bein' in th' game." He puffed and puffed. "Some of them old-timers was tough," he concluded lamely.

We ripped past the tall tower at Bottle Neck, an eastbound avalanche of food. Through the open door at the end of the swaying caboose shone the dazzling, blue-white eye of a locomotive.

Slowly she overhauled us, came alongside on the parallel track. Her rods were blurred, her crosshead a streak of reflected light. Up she came, an inch at a time; I felt my scalp tingle, and there was a feeling like to bursting under my ribs. She was a sight to see.

"Who?" I shouted to Johnny.

"Oranges," from Johnny. "Oranges and melons."

We stood in the side door of the caboose, a few feet below the level of her cab deck. The roar of her passage was like a bombardment. The engineer was grinning, the fireman was standing in the gangway, watching us. We could have shaken hands by leaning out and stretching.

"Howdy, Mike!" shouted Johnny.

"Howdy, John!" I could read the engineer's lips.

Inch by inch the high-wheeled engine forged past us, then the tank, then the cars tagged Red Ball. A foot at a time, a car at a time. Johnny and I went back and sat on the locker.

"He may pass us," said Johnny, "an' again, he may not. Tom Wilkins' boy is pullin' us. That was Mike Cassidy's son that just went by. They're old men. Believe it or not," said Johnny flatly.

He smoked enthusiastically.

"Didja ever stop to think, kid," he spoke abruptly, "that it cost sixteen million bucks to put these four tracks down? Sixteen million iron men. An' all th' good it does is to save about thirty minutes' time on, f'rinstance, an orange from California. Sixteen million dollars, kid, to save thirty lousy minutes on an orange travelin' three thousand miles! Watcha think about that?"

"What are you talking about?" I demanded.

"Watcha think I'm talkin' about?" came back the skipper belligerently.

"You were talking about Oil-Can and High-Wheeled," I reminded him.

"I still am," announced Johnny loudly.

"What?" I inquiried incredulously.

"Aw, hell!" exploded the skipper, rising angrily. "You couldn't see in front of the end of your nose!"

COUNTERBALANCE

By A. W. Somerville

COUNTERBALANCE

By A. W. Somerville

T. P. PATCHBOLT was the division master mechanic. Fat as a filled balloon, short as a sawed-off shotgun, small blue eyes that held an edge like high-speed steel, a silk shirt that would have put a bird of paradise into hysterics, pants that bagged at the knees and sagged at the seat—T. P. Patchbolt, as tough as Tobin bronze, as ingenious as Archimedes.

T. P. had been down to the main shops personally to work over the general foreman, a certain Mr. Deekman, very recently promoted. T. P. went to the main shops for the very simple and excellent reason that Mr. Deekman had refused —with suitable comments and embellishments—to make various changes on certain motive power unless authority was issued from the drafting room, and unless blueprints accompanied this authority showing that these changes were not the idle whims of a fat master mechanic, but approved and intelligent innovations.

When T. P. was informed that such was the case, that words had been spoken and no changes made, that fat gent hitched a cubic yard of sag out of his breeches, cocked a beady blue eye at an imaginary horizon, adjusted a trailing sock and marched on the enemy with much muttering, more indignation and a determination to have done what a fat man wanted done, or else— He arrived. The attack was magnificent, a mighty frontal thrust, the battle was a windmill of gestures and a cloud-burst of words—and the defeat of the master mechanic was no less decisive than the battle was reverberatory. The Retreat from Moscow had nothing on the return of Mr. Patchbolt; he was utterly routed.

The general foreman had not taken the proper attitude, decided the fat man, as he thought the matter over from his seat on the hotel steps. Mr. Deekman had best watch how he drove his rivets and fitted his bolts, for a fat little man was going to ride him. Did the master mechanic of the division have to get permission from a bunch of scissorbills in the drafting room before he could change a six-inch to a seven-inch nozzle on a passenger engine—his own passenger engine? Did the master mechanic of the division have to get authority from a gang of cheap clerks before he could put brass crosshead shoes on a freight engine—his own freight engine? What the hell? Were these his engines, or did this guy Deekman think he bought them? Who did this guy Deekman think he was—Jay Gould? Every time a dumb-bell got promoted the railroad went to hell! The best thing to do with a flathead like Deekman would be to fire him or strangle him; a guy of his type was nothing more or less than a loose brick in the firebox.

T. P. conceived various schemes for putting the skids under the flat-headed Deekman. He rejected them one by one because the results attained would not reach total annihilation. T. P. had long since had the milk of human kindness drained from him by mechanical means; he had as little love for his fellow men in the abstract as has a Moslem fanatic filled with hop. He was in the middle of a very appealing little plan when he was interrupted.

It was a panhandler. He was dirty to the point of filth; he was crippled. He held out his hand and asked impudently, whiningly, for money to buy food. T. P. thrust his hand in his pocket; after much fishing he finally produced several crumpled dollar bills. Another careful search failed to produce any change. The beggar got a dollar!

"I knew you was a white man," he whined, and went on.

T. P. mentally patted himself on the back for his generosity.

"I'll bet," he declared aloud, "that that damned Deekman would have asked him for change!"

He resumed his mental obliteration of Mr. Deekman. He became as full of strategy as a military-science instructor, but he could hit upon no practical scheme to rid the suffering railroad of the obstructor of progress—who had made a bum out of the thinker a few short hours before. He had the worthy general foreman soaked in kerosene and was wiping off engines with him when the northbound hot shot came in. The hotel was a railroad men's hang-out; it was only twenty feet from the tracks.

The master mechanic eyed the massive Mountain type locomotive as she rolled by. It was his business to know engines, and T. P. knew his business. There was a slight blue haze that seemed to come from under one of the drivers. The man on the steps sniffed the air suspiciously and waddled down to where the engine had stopped. He had on a gray suit bought new the day before—in spite of its newness it bagged at the knees and sagged at the seat—a shiny silk shirt with alternate half-inch stripes of white and green and red, and glossy new Oxfords that were as near sunset as male vanity will permit. He carried his coat on his arm and he had the forerunner of all headgear stuck on the back of his skull.

The engineer was on the ground flat on his back, half under the engine, poking about very mysteriously and very profanely.

"Got a hot one?" asked T. P.

The engineer stuck his head around the flange of the big wheel and admitted in unmistakable language that he certainly did have a hot one.

"Grease all run out?" questioned the brains of the mechanical department.

The engineer acknowledged with embellishments that such was the case.

"Lemme see," ordered Mr. Patchbolt. He threw his coat down and began to roll up the sleeves of his dazzling raiment.

"You'll get all dirty," objected the hoghead. "Better let me do it."

"Outta my way!" commanded the fat man. "You'd be all day, an' you don't know a damn thing about packing a box anyways. Lemme get in there!"

"Suit yourself!" retorted the engineer, and crawled out from under.

Quite a little crowd had collected. You'll always find this true, for railroad men have a faculty for hanging around an engine in trouble in order to convince themselves that the job could be done much better if they were doing it, using their own methods. They often have to pitch in and help the other fellow do it his way, and afterward they will tell you that it was an agony to the soul to piddle away so much time when anyone with any sense could have seen that they would have saved five minutes and done a better job if someone had only used his head. But they do the job as they are told, and while doing it they keep their mouths shut, and they get the job done. Compare that with a traffic jam, with everyone blowing his own particular horn and wanting the other guy to get out of the way.

T. P. crawled under the engine in all his glory. It was a pressed fit, but he made it. It was hot as a furnace; he lay just forward of the firebox and it was greasy as an oil vat. Hot water and melted grease dropped eagerly on his brilliant plumage.

"Throw water on the outside of that box!" he shouted to the engineman.

"You'll get all wet," protested the man.

"Hell's bells, is it a tea we're having?" demanded the fat man. "Shut up and get some water!"

The fireman began passing big hunks of prepared grease to him; T. P. shoved the grease up against the axle with the aid of a stick. The axle was so hot that the grease would melt and run like butter; liquid grease dropped plentifully upon the recently laundered shirt and the brand-new pants. The owner of the shirt and pants shoved more grease into place and scowled. The first bucket of water cascaded, sizzling, over the crown brass and 50 per cent of it made a bull's-eye on the face of Mr. Patchbolt.

"Little more to the left!" shouted T. P., when he got the water out of his mouth.

Ten minutes, twenty pounds of grease and numberless buckets of water later—T. P. emerged from the firing line looking like a cross between a fat mermaid and a thousand-barrel gusher.

"Get her out of town," he told the engineer. "Keep your eye on her. Gimme some waste, my hands are dirty."

"Yes, sir," said the engineer respectfully.

"Ready to ride," declared the fat one, wiping his hands carefully.

"Board!" shouted the conductor.

T. P. looked her over as the rail joints clicked her out of town. As she passed from view to the north, he shoved his watch and a handful of waste into his hip pocket. He took his coat from the man who had been thoughtful enough to pick it up out of the dirt. He observed to no one in particular, "She lost four minutes on her leaving time. It was a damn good thing I was here; they never would have got that box packed. Who ever heard of a hoghead that could pack a box?" He waddled off with his coat hugged close to the ruined glory of his shirt.

He had a room at the hotel and he went there to change clothes. So far as he was personally concerned, he would have worn them for the rest of the day, but he'd heard that the general manager was coming in on the noon train—and he knew only too well that the boss was cranky about clothes. So he changed. He concluded that he didn't really need a bath—just tidy up a bit. It was nearly noon.

T. P. had been asked out to dinner by the chief electrician; he descended to the lobby to meet the man. The master mechanic was a hearty eater—not an epicurean but an eater; he ate early and often and he did it with gusto. He once remarked that he never pampered his stomach—just ate anything. The statement would have been complete if he had said everything. He could feed his face with the consistency of an automatic stoker for more than an hour; he could keep two waiters breathless from actual effort; he could destroy ten million calories at a single gulp. And two hours after demolishing ten or twelve courses, he could repeat the performance, including all the side dishes at hand. T. P. always lost money on his expense account; he never had the courage to put down the preposterous amounts that he paid for food.

The chief electrician found him shortly after the pangs of hunger and the closeness of the lunch counter had proved too strong a combination. The fat man was just polishing off a quarter of an apple pie and a cup of coffee.

"I thought you were coming home to eat with me?" questioned the electrician with some indignation.

T. P. declared with fervor that he intended to; that the only thing that would prevent his presence would be to have the door locked in his face. He told the electrician not to worry, that he would do full justice to the meal; he was only sort of warming up on the coffee and the pie, he explained.

The two left the restaurant and proceeded up the street. When two railroad men meet they argue—invariably. They can always find a subject. T. P. and the electrician argued about a derailment.

"What do you know about it?" demanded T. P. heatedly. "I helped pick her up after she side-swiped that nice new diner and turned handsprings. There was two dead guys, and there ain't nobody explained yet how that diner got foul of the main line. Last week she ditched herself and killed Ed Golden, goin' fifty miles an hour on straight track. They ain't said yet what caused that!"

"That 359 is a killer," expounded the chief electrician. "That's all there is to it, brother, she's just a killer."

T. P. said some unkind things relative to the spoken words of his prospective host. He added: "She ain't my engine, son, but if she was I'd cure her of these track-humpin' exercises. I'd make her lay down an' roll over when I sneezed, see?"

The electrician said some unkind things relative to the spoken words of his prospective guest: "Some engines is unlucky, see? An' the 359 is unlucky an' she's a killer, too. She'll get another hoghead an' it won't be long!"

"Not that I give a damn," said the fat man unpleasantly, "but you talk like you were full of boiler compound. Now she ain't on my division an' she can do tricks on a trapeze an' it's no business of mine, but I bet she wouldn't do that on my railroad!"

They arrived at the house without coming to blows and were met by the young wife of the chief electrician. She had only recently married, and because her husband read a few papers outside of the trade journals, she thought that all railroad men were normal people. T. P. said yes, he thought the weather hot. Yes, he wished it would rain. And these were the last words that the mistress of the house got with the master mechanic, for rain suggested water to T. P., and water was what T. P. had waded in when he picked up the 359 after she had side-swiped the diner. Which started the argument all over again and developed some rather interesting details.

Said T. P.: "An' the diner had her hand brakes set up so

that when she got smacked the wheels slid, they didn't turn.
So she couldn't have rolled down and fouled herself. Now
from where she first started to slide, see, to the main line,
figurin' in the length of her vestibule, she was in the clear.
Not more than a foot in the clear, but she was clear. I put
my own tape on her. Now I wasn't runnin' the investigation,
see—all I was doin' was helpin' pick her up an' get the main
line clear, an' so I kep' my yap shut. But I know just as well
as I'm sittin' here that the diner wasn't foul of the main line.
When that engine come up even with the diner she hopped
off and hit the diner.

"All this blah-blah about her bein' a killer don't go down.
'Course, if any of the big guys was to ask me what I thought
was wrong, I wouldn't blame it on the engine—I'd blame it
on the track; but after that spill last week, when she just
took to the trees—brother, if she was mine I'd stick her in the
back shop an' I'd pull her apart an' I'd see what makes her
act so funny. You can blame the track once and make it stick,
and sometimes you can make it stick twice, but if it happens
again we'll see a lot of new faces."

The young wife had gone inside to see how the dinner
stacked up. She returned to the porch and sat in on the argument. T. P. declared that it was a mistake to put the 359
back in service, the electrician declared that it was the proper
thing to do. The mistress of the house eventually got more
than her fill of the 359 and shooed them in to eat. They went
in arguing and they sat down arguing.

The hostess had gone to considerable pains to have a good
dinner, for she was new to the railroad family and she wished
to make friends with her husband's associates. She was possessed of sense and had no wish to put on airs.

She said to T. P. immediately after they were seated: "Mr.
Patchbolt, we want you to feel at home here; we want you to
enjoy your dinner. If you want anything, don't hesitate to
ask for it."

T. P. came out of a fog of exhaust steam and thanked her. He looked around the table—food was always of interest to him.

"We want you to consider yourself just as though you were a member of the family," continued the hostess. She thought desperately for some subject that would interest this man with the locomotive complex. She said, "Usually we have only one chicken, Mr. Patchbolt; but Edward told me how you enjoyed your food, so I got an extra one. So we'll have plenty. They are really very fine chickens. I have never seen any so well fattened."

All the good was on the table, and in the center was a large platter containing two juicy, well-browned chickens. The legs stuck ceilingward as the legs of all properly baked chickens should. T. P. focused his blue eyes on them.

"Now, Mr. Patchbolt, don't wait on ceremony," went on the lady. "If you see anything you want, just take it if you can reach it. We aren't a bit ceremonious."

"Have some chicken, T. P.?" said the host, picking up the carving knife.

"Don't care if I do," said T. P. calmly, and reaching out with his fork he transfixed an entire chicken and planted it before him! "Never saw a fatter pullet," he declared gratefully to his hostess just before he sank his teeth into a dismembered second joint.

After he had eaten, T. P. thanked his hostess very gratefully and very nicely, and she told him that next Sunday they would have two more chickens and that he must come and eat one of them. The master mechanic promised faithfully that he would, and it may be here added that the invitation was genuine and that T. P. did get another chicken at the home of the chief electrician—and a good many more after that. People liked T. P.

The host walked down to the hotel with his guest and on the way they wrecked the 359 at least fifteen times, condemned all the track that the engine had ever rolled over, utterly damned all engines of her type and class, and as a climax, as they arrived at the hotel, T. P. declared that the responsible party was the new general foreman of the back shops, a certain Mr. Deekman. Wasn't the 359 the first engine that came out of that shop after he got promoted, said T. P. Wasn't he trying to show up the other shops on highballed classified repairs, demanded T. P.

"If we ever get to the bottom of all this," quoth the fat man, "I'll bet we'll find it all goes back to a rotten job of classified repairs. This guy Deekman thinks he knows one hell of a lot, and whenever a guy thinks that, is just the time when everybody else comes to the conclusion that he don't know a damn thing. The 359 was one of his first engines. I think Mr. Deekman is in for a run of tough luck. If they'll give me one good long look at that engine I'll guarantee him some hard luck!"

The chief electrician said some harsh words—words not used in parlors and at dinner tables.

"All right," retorted the fat man. "You know so much you could pretty near tell me what makes a headlight burn, I guess!"

At the hotel they found that the general manager had left word for T. P. to come and see him, and from the wording of the message Mr. Patchbolt judged it only proper to get there as fast as his legs would carry him.

"Even on Sunday," declared the fat man to his companion, "they can't get along without me."

T. P. went down in the yard until he came to a car that looked like an observation car but wasn't, and he mounted the steps and opened the screen door and passed within. The general manager was inside, dictating profanity and hard words to a tough-looking private secretary.

"Where you been?" demanded the general manager.

"Eating," said T. P. calmly.

"Well, I haven't had time to eat yet," growled the boss as though it were the fault of the master mechanic. He turned to the secretary. "Harry, you see that Wallace puts a place for Mr. Patchbolt at the table." He turned to T. P. again. "You can eat with me," he snapped. "I'm not going to eat by myself just because you've already eaten."

"All right," said T. P. agreeably. The secretary departed grinning.

"What's the matter with you guys in the mechanical department?" demanded the boss. "Can't you even keep engines on the track any more?"

T. P. wrinkled his heavy forehead.

"Don't go scowling at me!" shouted the boss. "Look at that!" He shoved a file of papers under the nose of Mr. Patchbolt. "This is the third time in less than two months that this engine hops off the track, and she's just out of the back shop with Class 2 repairs hung on her! I wanta know what's wrong with that engine!" He pounded on the desk before him. "Three men killed already, equipment all smashed! What kind of a playhouse do you guys think this is—huh?"

The Negro waiter came in while T. P. was reading the report of the derailment and announced dinner. The general manager bit large hunks out of him for not appearing sooner. The general manager, T. P. and the secretary went in to eat.

"Glad to see nobody got hurt bad," observed T. P., trying to look on the brightest side.

"Save your joy," sneered the boss. "What I wanta know is what's wrong with that engine!"

He glared savagely at the master mechanic and started carving the meat. T. P. watched him attentively.

He finally said, "Musta been a bad rail. . . . Little more meat, please."

"Rail!" exploded the boss. "Rail! Can't you read? Third time in sixty days! Took to the woods with five cars! Hell of a mess! Rail!"

The waiter handed T. P. a dish overflowing with meat and potatoes.

"Bad rail," said T. P., in the act of filling his mouth.

"Listen," gurgled the boss, "don't say rail to me again! You nor any other nutcracker don't blame this on some poor section foreman, see? There's something wrong with that engine and I want to know who's responsible! You get your bag and go down there on 23 and you find out what's wrong with that engine! Don't show your fat face around here till you find out!"

"It's out of my territory," objected T. P. meekly.

"I don't give a damn if it's in Honolulu!" yelled the boss. "You go down there and find out what's wrong!" He paused a moment, glaring at the secretary and the master mechanic. He went on in a lower voice, "Harry, you give Mr. Patchbolt a letter—state that he's my representative, give him authority to investigate derailments of Engine 359, particularly as to possible mechanical defect of engine. Understand?"

"Yes, sir," said Harry promptly.

"Make it good for thirty days," said the boss. "That long enough?" he shot at T. P.

"Too long," said T. P. through a mouthful of meat and potatoes.

"I asked you whether it was long enough," said the boss coldly.

"It is," said T. P. between gulps.

"It's an outrage!" declared the man at the head of the table, swallowing hastily. "Engine goes crazy!"

"I'll find out," said T. P. calmly. "Then I'll tell you who to fire."

The secretary nearly fainted.

T. P. arrived at his destination at four A.M. the following day. He had managed to catch a nap by using two seats, but he had spent most of his time reflecting on the gross stupidity and inability of a certain general foreman. The master mechanic vowed that such-and-such had no right on any railroad, least of all on his front doorstep. Something should be done about it; in fact, something was going to be done about it or hunches were certainly not what they used to be.

He went directly to the roundhouse and showed the night foreman his authority for prompt and efficient action. He said he wanted a fire put in her, as he wanted to move her and see how she acted. The two men went out in the house to look her over. Her pilot was smashed, her headlight and bell were gone, she had mud all over one side where she had rolled. She was a mess.

"Know what's wrong with her?" demanded T. P.

"Hit a bad rail," said the foreman positively.

"Generally it," agreed the master mechanic. "Check her up?"

The roundhouse man told him what they had done. She trammed to within a sixty-fourth of an inch; there was no reason why she should not track in a straight line. She worked free on her engine truck; that couldn't have thrown her off. Not a single flange showed wear; she was as good as the day she left the builders. Nothing wrong with the engine; the trouble must have been that the track was out of gauge.

"Try to have her ready by ten o'clock," said T. P. "I'll have a call put on her then; might as well go through all the motions. They're raising more hell about this than they did about the eight-hour law. I'll take her out light and see how she behaves. Want you to do something for me. Let me have an apprentice to help me check her up, and see if you can find the engineer—Tom Hartman, he was—that was on her when she derailed. They say he wasn't hurt."

"Nobody hurt," said the foreman. "She run straight out in the woods about a hundred yards before she turned over. They had plenty of time to join the birdie gang. If he's here I'll get hold of him right after breakfast. Say, Mr. Patchbolt, I don't know whether we can have her ready by ten or not. We can't put a fire in her till we fix those steam pipes, an' she's got a couple bad leaks. An' she's got some bent motion work and half her brake riggin' is all busted up. We'll get in behind her, but if we get her ready by noon we'll have to throw our feet out."

"What's a few leaks?" said T. P. "Fix the pipes and cork up the worst leaks—we'll get by. Put a couple of the best men you got on her spring riggin'; I don't give a hoot about her brake riggin'. But I want her springs up to snuff, see? Straighten up her motion work so she'll get by; I don't care if she sounds lame. You put the men on the job. I'll see that they get her out. Let's get started!"

T. P. took an apprentice boy under his wing and did many mysterious things with trams and calipers and a squared scale and a prickpunch. He spent much of his time under the engine in the pit, measuring and cogitating. He inspected the engine truck, the four-wheeled truck that carries the cylinders and front end and leads the engine, as carefully as a jeweler looks for a flaw in a diamond. They strung white cord on each side of the engine parallel with the frames, and T. P. made symbols and mystic figures on one of the driving wheels with chalk.

By eight o'clock the apprentice boy was starving, but he had begun to believe that all knowledge was his. The coming of the engineer released him for the day—and, more important, to breakfast, but T. P. ignored the craving for food.

T. P. talked to the engineer for more than an hour. The man said the jack seemed to be all right, seemed to track good; they were going along at forty-two miles an hour and all of a sudden she headed out through a cornfield.

"I didn't even know we were on the ground," said the hoghead, "till I heard Fred yell. We both unloaded—joined the birds. She turned over right after we left."

"Did she ride hard?" asked the master mechanic.

"She always was kinda rough," answered the engineer.

T. P. told the engineer that they were going to take her out and that he'd like to have him go along. The engineer agreed—always glad to help out, he said. T. P. got another apprentice boy and stayed with the 359 until she was ready to go.

"Only way to get anything done in a roundhouse, bub," he confided to his assistant, "is to stay with it yourself."

They backed her out a little after one o'clock; they hadn't tried to make her beautiful. There was a big white place on her boiler shell where the jacket had been torn and the asbestos showed through, she was still muddy, and the engineer assigned by the dispatcher kicked like a steer because of the steam leaks. She had a lame exhaust on account of the valve motion being rather battered, there wasn't a great deal left of her cab—the engineer was sore about this also—and she was still minus bell and headlight and pilot. T. P. said they would use the whistle instead of the bell; that they didn't need the headlight, because they weren't looking for anybody, and that the pilot was a nuisance and he was glad they didn't have one. The fat man was hungry enough to eat a set of flues. They probably wouldn't get back before six or seven o'clock and there was no place to get food out on the road. They took an engineer, a fireman—the engineer that had been on her when she disgraced herself—and the apprentice boy. She had white rags stuck in her marker brackets to show she was an extra.

"I'll run her," said T. P. to the assigned engineer. "You get some place where you can jump if you have to. We might hit a bad rail." He grinned.

They went along about twenty miles an hour for five or

six miles. **T. P.** turned to the engineer he had talked to in the roundhouse.

"Was she always this rough?" he asked.

"She never was no Pullman," retorted the hoghead.

"Hell of a passenger engine!" said **T. P.**

T. P. opened her up a little and they swung along at thirty-five miles an hour. "Were you going much faster than this when you spilled?" he shouted.

There was no speedometer on the 359; she'd lost that along with the rest of her accouterments.

"About seven miles faster," retorted the engineer coldly.

They slapped along until they came to a passing track. **T. P.** said they would pull up here and he would look her over for a minute. He really didn't know what he was going to look for, but he got down and looked for it. The apprentice boy thought he had found a gold mine, and an apprentice boy is a skeptic who can make a newsboy look like a babe in the woods. As a matter of fact, the fat man was puzzled; he knew that there must be something wrong with the engine, for passenger jacks don't leap fences and plow up cornfields three times in two months for no reason at all, but for the life of him he couldn't put his finger on the ailment. He put up an excellent bluff, however. From his bedside manner two hogheads, one tallow pot and an apprentice boy would have gone on oath that he already knew what the disease was and that he was merely making certain investigations in the interests of science. As to what the exact ailment was, they presumed that presently he would put a name to it; in the meantime they chewed tobacco and guessed. The apprentice boy, being the youngest, had the most chews and the most guesses.

They let a freight train go by and they moved out on the main line. **T. P.** boosted the speed to forty miles an hour and set her to hold that gait. The engineer said it was only thirty-eight miles an hour, but **T. P.** was running the engine, so

the official rate of speed was forty miles an hour. The fat man
had a studious look on his face, if such was possible. At any
rate, he was studying. He held her at forty miles by a judi-
cious use of the air. When he permitted her to pick up over
that speed she seemed to ride a little differently; at least,
T. P. thought she did. He asked both engineers if they didn't
think so. No, neither one thought that it was possible for her
to ride any worse. T. P. released the air and let her go up to
fifty miles an hour; she found all the holes in the track and
bounced along with the customary multitude of crashes and
smashes. T. P. eased off on her and they dropped back to
forty miles an hour. He called the assigned engineer over to
him.

"Keep her right where she is," he ordered. "I wanta see
somethin'."

The engineer took the vacant post and T. P. clambered
over the coal bunker and proceeded to the back end of the
tank. The extra engineer and the apprentice boy followed
him to the end of the bunker and watched him from there.
He didn't seem to be doing much. All he did was hold to a
grab iron and watch the track behind him.

"Maybe he's going nutty," said the engineer.

T. P. came back in the cab and everybody asked him how
the view was.

"You boys have a lot to learn," replied the fat man.

He took the throttle again and held her at about forty-
five miles an hour. A little later he told the engineer to hold
her there, and he went down the right-hand gangway until
he was on the bottom step. He hung there, apparently doing
nothing but watching the wheels go round. He then repeated
the process on the left-hand side. He hung so far out that the
fireman was afraid he would fall and wanted to tie a rope
around him. He finally came back in the cab, his fat face
wrinkled with smiles.

"She'll never hop another ditch," he prophesied to the engineer named Hartman. He told the other engineer to cut the speed down to twenty miles an hour. "We'll phone in from Kildare," he added, "and back up."

"What was the matter with her?" asked Hartman.

T. P. told him to ride the left-hand gangway and then ride the right-hand gangway, and then see if he couldn't tell the difference. The engineer did as directed and came back and told T. P. that one of them was crazy. The apprentice boy performed some gymnastics on both gangways, not to mention the running boards, and came back and reported that the problem was beyond his powers.

They got to Kildare and T. P. bought a box of ginger-snaps with a nickel he had borrowed from the fireman. He'd left all his money at the other end of the division. At the hotel, when he had changed clothes, he'd forgotten to take the money out of his pocket. He'd also forgotten his watch. T. P. had been known to forget to go to sleep, for his head was a constant buzz of mechanical problems; but so far as was ever known he had never forgotten anything about an engine. It was also most unusual when he forgot to eat.

They got back to the roundhouse about 5:30 P.M. T. P. told the men on the engine that he would give them a dope sheet on the 359 in the morning; that they wouldn't do anything before morning, so there would be no use in their hanging around. As soon as they were gone he hunted up the roundhouse foreman.

"Put her over a pit," he ordered. "I wanta take a tire off."

The day foreman was just going off duty, the night foreman had not yet come on. The day man suggested that T. P. wait until the night force came on; it would only be a matter of an hour and a half.

T. P. wouldn't hear of it. He demanded a machinist and a helper to get the rods down on the left side so that the tire would come off, and he demanded that someone else, preferably the day roundhouse foreman, get the tire heater set up so there would be no delay. So the day foreman had to rout out a machinist and a helper and chase around trying to find parts for the tire heater—and incidentally miss his supper. The day foreman was hungry and profane. T. P. was much hungrier, very dirty and as calm as the foreman was flustered.

Now, for the information of those who have never played hide and seek in and about engine stalls, it is here stated that a tire heater is the greatest mental and physical hazard ever conceived by man. It is really a portable furnace constructed of small pipe punched full of holes, made of joints and dojiggers and snarled-up sections, and it has the faculty of winding itself into more knots than an octopus with cramps ever dreamed of. When you have no earthly use for it, you will stumble over it and skin up your shins or go sprawling into an engine pit; but when you do want it, and have to have it, you might as well look for a clean face on a coal passer. It is made so as to encircle the tire of a driving wheel and the heat is thrown against the tire, expanding it and allowing it to be sledged off the wheel center.

You've heard how the country blacksmith—maybe you've seen him do it—puts a tire on a buggy or a cart wheel—a steel tire? The principle is the same with a locomotive driving tire. The tire is smaller than the wheel center and you heat it and expand it so that you can slip it on or slip it off. Because it is so big and so heavy, it has to be sledged. When it cools it shrinks and binds, metal to metal, and the only way to get it off is to heat it and expand it again. The fuel used for a tire heater is either natural gas or gasoline, plus compressed air, and this remark is made with much unction: The only job more painful than getting a tire off is the task of putting one on.

At seven P.M. the day foreman was still hunting for parts to that numerously named tire heater. T. P. had been in behind the machinist and the helper, working with them, and

they were scattering side rods about as a farmer pitches hay.
The night foreman came in.

"Know where the parts to this tire heater are?" asked T. P.

"Wanta take a tire off?" asked the night man brightly.

"Oh, hell!" exclaimed the day foreman, and went home.

The night foreman knew where the parts were and sent a
man off after them.

"Who thought of this?" demanded the new arrival unpleasantly.

"I did!" retorted T. P.

"Well, we're the boys to take off tires," declared the night
man agreeably.

They rigged up the heater to fit the particular sized tire
that the 359 used, and after so long a time finally got ready
to turn on the fire. They got the contraption made of pipe to
take fuel after a fashion, and eventually the tire got hot.
Everybody within a fifty-yard radius had come to a boil long
before. A tire heater in action at night is to be classed among
those things which strike the eye—an overgrown, motionless
pin wheel. They make them as large as eight or more feet in
diameter, and when lit, the wheel becomes a solid circle of
blue flame. A very beautiful object at night, from a distance,
but when you happen to be nursing one you fail to see the
aesthetic points. Machinists have been known to address
them in terms that no beautiful object should be called by.

The tire heater at times is willful to the extreme; some
of them have actually been known to fall off the tire. Which,
of course, necessitates putting the device back on again; and
no machinist, apprentice or helper ever put a hot tire heater
back on a tire without burning at least four fingers. It is just
one of those things that you get accustomed to if you work
around engines. The first time you put one of the unreasonable things back on you generally burn eight fingers and
two thumbs; and also your foot, if you are weak-minded
enough to kick at it. With constant care and practice you

can reduce the burned members to four; after you take the first kick you never burn another foot on a tire heater.

T. P. nearly lost his nose looking to see if the tire had expanded enough to come off. He took a twelve-pound sledge and a Negro helper took another, and the two crawled down in the pit and sledged away at the tire. They flailed a tattoo on the metal, but never budged it. All they succeeded in doing was knocking the tire heater off.

"I figured it was goin' to be tough," observed the night foreman. "The new tires is hell."

They finally got the heater back around the tire; they practically cursed it back on. They knew that the wheel center had expanded with the tire and was binding it, but they hoped to get it off anyway. The second time they sledged it, about thirty minutes later, they drove it half off before it stuck on them. The heater, of course, fell off. T. P. said that if it was the last act of his life he would see that this roundhouse got a tire heater that would stay on. They finally got it back in place, and the third time they swung their heavy mauls the big ring of tough steel flew off eagerly and promptly, fell to the ground in a galaxy of sparks and broke three pipes off the heater.

"The thing's off, anyways," said T. P.

They got the hose and cooled off the wheel center, and when it was only hot enough to bubble water, T. P. investigated. He didn't investigate long.

"I bet they didn't leave enough lead in her to hold down a sparrow!" he declared. "Come here an' look!" he commanded.

"There's some in her," declared the foreman, after he had burned his nose and annexed some blisters on his hands. "Nobody can tell from lookin' whether she's light or not."

They scraped the lead that was in the top pockets of the wheel center into a box, and they reverently took this lead to the scales and weighed it carefully. This lead is known as driving-wheel counterbalance; it offsets the weight of the rods and the pins that are suspended from the driving wheels, and it neutralizes the motion of the reciprocating parts. If it were not for this lead, no locomotive would stay on the track at other than a very slow rate of speed, and even at slow speeds the engine would roll as though the wheels were egg-shaped, and would nose from side to side. You counterbalance an engine as to revolving parts—rods, pins, back end of main rod—and also as to reciprocating parts—the parts that move back and forth, the crosshead, the piston, the piston rod, certain parts of the valve motion. It is easy to understand. You have certain heavy pieces of machinery in motion. They set up forces that interfere with the proper function of the engine. You neutralize these forces by counterweights. A mechanic calls it counterbalance. On a locomotive the counterbalance in the driving wheels must be correct to the pound, particularly for high-speed passenger engines; you weigh the parts to be counterbalanced and you take half this weight and distribute it according to formula in the pockets of the various drive wheels. This weight is checked at regular intervals to insure safety of operation.

The foreman produced a book bulging with blueprints and formulas. They consulted it with anxious faces. T. P. finally scribbled some figures on the flyleaf and announced triumphantly, "Short over twenty pounds—twenty pounds and four ounces! I knew it!"

The foreman said soberly, "They'll run them out of the back shop like flies for this!"

"Well," snarled T. P., "what d'ya want 'em to do with the murderers, kiss 'em?"

The foreman waved his arms helplessly.

"Tell you what we'll do," said T. P. briskly. "I got to turn in a report on this—pronto. That one wheel bein' short on lead was enough to ditch her, but chances are a couple more are out, too. Tomorrow you line up the day crew for me and tell them to get the rest of the tires off and report to me what they find. You tell the foreman to weigh everything except the pins and check his figures against this dope sheet, and I want a statement as to the actual weights of every part on every wheel and I want it signed by the day foreman before a notary public. And I want that statement mailed in to the Old Man by day after tomorrow. And if I ain't here to see that nobody pulls any funny business, there'll be someone else, see?"

The foreman saw very clearly. He would do this, he promised; he would be more than glad to help in any way that he could. In fact, he would have his crew strip the engine so that there would be no delay. T. P. vetoed this flatly. Only one crew would have the job and that would be the day crew.

The night foreman agreed that this would no doubt be the best way to handle it. How, he asked T. P., did he know what was wrong with the engine?

"Easy," said the fat man in his best bedside manner. "She rode different on the left than she did on the right, at about forty miles an hour and better. When a jack is out of weight on drivers she'll sometimes mark the rail. If you don't believe this, take the rods off an engine and run her deadhead on a fast freight. They'll either break the rail or mark them, see?—if they stay on the track long enough. This one never marked no rail, but if she was goin' to mark one I figured it would be the left. Every time she took to the woods she went off on the fireman's side. She felt funny on that side this afternoon."

"How come you picked that tire to come off?" asked the foreman.

"Hell!" said T. P. "You can ask more questions! Listen! There are three drive wheels on the left side. That gives me

three good guesses, and the best guess was the first one I come
to. The only luck there was to it was that we only had to take
off one tire—we might have had to take off three!"

The master mechanic borrowed a sheet out of the foreman's notebook and made up a statement showing the weight
of the lead taken from the wheel as compared with what it
should have been according to the formula.

He made the foreman witness it, and because the machinist was there, he made him witness it, too.

"I'm goin' in on 24," he told the foreman. "You be sure
that the day man understands exactly what he is to do, for if
it isn't done I'll see that you get your share of what he gets.
Don't take no chances—weigh everything. Now lemme have
some paper to write the Old Man on, an' lemme have some
money to get something to eat on. I'm near starved."

They went to the office and the foreman let him have some
paper and pen and ink. T. P. had never been able to do anything with a typewriter. The only money that the foreman
had was a five-dollar bill, and he was far from enthusiastic
about parting with it.

T. P. talked him out of it, explaining that he hadn't eaten
for practically a day and a half—the gingersnaps didn't count
—and that he wouldn't have the slightest difficulty in eating
five dollars' worth of food, not the slightest. The foreman
finally broke down and let him have the bill. T. P. sat down
and wrote the general manager:

July 22, 1924.
Dakotah Roundhouse.

Dear Sir: I inspected Engine 359 this date. Had her fired
up and rode her to Kildare and back. Knew something was
wrong. Had her put in the house. We knocked the tire off
the left front driver and found her short on counterbalance.
Inclosed is statement signed and witnessed as to weight
found in pockets left front driver. Am having moving parts,
rods, and so on, taken down and weighed so that can check

exactly; also all tires removed and weight checked in other drivers. Recommend that wheel centers be sent to back shop and pins pressed out and weighed so that there can be no question as to what proper counterbalance should be.

Wrong counterbalance caused engine to jump track. Engine had been out of back shop 53 days, and she was O.K. when she went in back shop. They are awful careless in back shop. This is not what I ought to say, but the back shop is rotten careless. This is a swell example of the carelessness we been getting for the last sixty days.

Respectfully,

T. P. PATCHBOLT.

"If that don't knock the props out from under that lousy general foreman," murmured the fat man as he licked the envelope, "I don't know the number of threads on a one-inch nut!"

He marked the letter personal and "train telegram" and waddled up to the dispatcher's office to get it off. He then went to the telegraph office next door and wrote out the following wire:

A. R. KINGSLEY,
GENERAL MANAGER.

ENGINE 359 COUNTERBALANCED WRONG. HAVE WRITTEN LETTER GIVING FULL DETAILS.

T. P. PATCHBOLT.

"Got a place to wash up?" he asked the telegraph operator.

The operator showed him where the washroom was. T. P. got rid of some of the dirt and grease on his hands and face. He surveyed himself from all angles, and from every angle grease and dirt showed in abundance. T. P. decided that steam cleaning was about the only cure. Why waste time with soap and water? He certainly was hungry; he couldn't remember having ever been quite so hungry; he would make short work of five dollars' worth of fodder.

He left the telegraph station and walked up the street toward town, with visions of tables loaded with tiers of ham and eggs floating before dizzy eyes. He seemed to get hungrier with every step. Another vision came to him—a steak as long as a locomotive tank, with great onions running along its sides as big as hand cars, and over all a covering of tomato ketchup like a flooded field. He was passing a high board fence set back a few yards from the sidewalk. A few hundred yards ahead he saw the bright electric lights of a restaurant. He was at the corner now; he had but to cross the street and food in all abundance was his for the asking.

On the corner, with his back against the fence, sat a crippled beggar. When he saw T. P. the light of recognition came into his eyes. He whined impudently and loudly.

"Hoh!" he cried. "Here comes my fat friend. He won't forget me!"

The lights of the restaurant whirled before T. P.'s eyes. There was only one thing to do.

T. P. shoved a five-dollar bill into the outstretched paw and fled back toward the station.

SMART BOOMER

By Harry Bedwell

Harry Bedwell

HARRY BEDWELL, author of *The Boomer,* might almost claim to be the personification of his own title. Like his creation "Eddie Sand," he has pounded brass pretty well over the West. At the ripe age of sixteen, he became a station agent on a Burlington branch line. That was more than thirty years ago. Since then, vertically, his range of action has gone from tending one-man stations high in the Rocky Mountains on the Denver & Rio Grande Western to other stations as much as 100 feet below sea level on the desert line of the Southern Pacific. In between, he has been an operator on the Colorado and Utah, the Santa Fe and the old San Pedro, Los Angeles & Salt Lake line of the Union Pacific.

His short stories and articles have appeared in the old *Railroad Man's Magazine* and its successors, in *Harper's Weekly,* the *American Magazine,* the *Saturday Evening Post,* and a line of other publications, from the pulps to the slicks. His novel, *The Boomer,* published in 1942, also went into a pocket-size overseas edition for the armed forces.

As an SP operator at Alhambra, California, and more lately at Camarillo, on the busy and crowded line between Los Angeles and San Francisco, he has had the finest possible chance to see the war trains go by—every kind of train, carrying soldiers, sailors and marines and all the multitude of gear and supplies which go with them. He not only has seen the trains roll by but as an operator handling train orders and messages has had his part in seeing the job done. One result has been a story, *Priority Special*—the most recent story in this collection, both in time of writing and in the time of which it treats.

The story was first "published" as a radio broadcast on June 6, 1945. It tells how the men of the railroads—all sorts of men on the trains and on the ground—manage to move a hospital train up and over the mountains into the high desert country, with never a stop or a jar—and the reason why they did it. It is the sort of story which could not have been possible until now, for the situation which it depicts could never have existed before.

The other Bedwell selection, *Smart Boomer,* deals with an older day of railroading, when "Eddie Sand" knew both every rule in the book and how to make the telegraph keys talk—and needed both kinds of knowledge. It depicts extraordinarily well the curious mixture of group loyalties and loyalty to the job which runs through the whole business of keeping the trains moving. The story first appeared in the *Saturday Evening Post.*

SMART BOOMER

By Harry Bedwell

EDDIE SAND, slightly battered, came into the chief dispatcher's office at Little Grande, moving like a cat in a strange back yard, on the prowl, cautiously belligerent. Passenger conductors on the west end of the Anaconda Short Line hadn't been obliging with free rides on the cushions, and freight skippers and their enginemen had threatened him with violence when asked for a lift in cab or caboose. This lack of tact was a rare and humiliating experience to a young veteran of the iron highway on tour. A rambler was entitled to the courtesies of the rail when a crew was all hitched up and going his way. He had covertly ridden anyhow, but it hadn't been clean or comfortable. He was therefore resentful and punitive, and he had paused to retaliate.

Updike, the chief, looked at him once, a quick sardonic flick of shrewd eyes. There was considerable slim length to Eddie, and the glint of red in his hair might mean something. Updike placed him at once as a boomer telegraph operator, that restless breed of railroaders that is always going some place else. Lately, the drifters hadn't strayed to the High Desert Division. The crews had discouraged that emphatically. They hadn't succeeded with this one, but his disheveled appearance showed that he'd come the hard way.

Updike considered craftily. He needed another operator of just the right sort, but it wasn't likely this boomer would do. The West End was at the time involved in too much grief to add to it an equivocal, benighted casual. Yet that long string bean might be the answer to his impious prayers. His nod invited Eddie to wait.

The low sun thrust bars of hard light into the long room. A dozen telegraph instruments chanted a frantic cadence. Preoccupied operators sprawled before typewriters, swiftly punching out messages with indolent indifference. The trick dispatcher brooded over his train sheet at his narrow table. Train and enginemen of a freight crew wrangled morbidly over their report of a mishap that had befallen them on the run just completed. The yard-master shambled in to verify the make-up of an impending hot shot.

Eddie Sand took a tattered book from his pocket and sat down on the bench by the railing. He started in reading with grim tranquillity.

Conover, the engineer of the freight crew, disengaged his stubborn mind from a deliberate study of their accident report, written by the conductor and contributed to by the glib observations of the other four, and scowled to himself.

"Seems to me we had only one mischance," he grumbled, "but this account of it sounds like there'd been a dozen." He breathed heavily. "I hope it sticks."

His baffled glance fell on Eddie and frosted. His large face puckered under the stress of vinegarish reflections. These produced an expression between an impending sneeze and a cordial distaste for something he'd eaten. He seized his conductor by the arm and pointed. Inarticulate sounds became plaintive words.

"Ain't that the brass pounder what caused us this grief?" he pleaded.

Conductor Allen stared, then scrutinized. "Yes," he said, and wheeled on his two brakemen. "Did you let that smart boomer ride with us, after all?" he demanded.

The two shacks denied it with hot indignation. "We left that guy at Felicity," the hind man declared. "I saw him when we pulled out."

"Yeh," stormed Allen, "but he couldn't have come in with anybody else and be here now."

"Listen, chief," Conover implored, "this is the tramp lightning slinger what caused our accident. We turned him down when he asked us for a ride. Then he sneaked aboard anyhow. But the joke was on him"—the hogger brightened—"because we set out the car he was ridin' in at Felicity, and when I saw him unload there I heaved coal at him. I left the engine drift while I was so engaged. Which is when it cornered the boxcar what hadn't cleared on the house track."

"What joke was on who?" Updike inquired acidly.

The crews were dubious and resentful of smart boomers. The brittle and hard-bitten drifters knew train-operation rules and were obstinate about applying them. During a protracted period of disorganization, these mountain men had tossed the book away. Like spirited horses given a slack line, they'd run off with this outfit if not checked and disciplined. Now that a new set of officials rode the swivel chairs, they wanted no intruder on the line who might throw in with the brass hats.

Updike knew the answer. The men should have their ears bent forward. But not knocked down. You couldn't blast that organization without destroying it. These men were rough and tough, but competent. There hadn't yet been any definite adjustments between them and Stewart, the new division superintendent sent from the East, but a decisive understanding was rapidly approaching. When it came it would be abrupt. Stewart was the kind of official who would likely dynamite. Updike, bushy and gray and wily, was trying to contrive a balance. He studied Eddie Sand covertly.

Conover muttered, "It's funny what rubble the chief allows to clutter up his office." He glared at the boomer.

The hogger bulged from his straining overalls, but Updike knew he was as hard as nails. Conover couldn't endure a day without eight meals and snacks. Usually he boiled with

energy. But he was inclined to relax heavily after a bulk of
victuals. From the way certain incidents had occurred out on
the line, Updike suspected that the engineer napped in his
cab while running. Authority had been badly shot.

Billy Lomax, the fireman, chanted, "Run him through the
wringer and see what comes out."

Updike wasn't amused. Billy waggled with delight at anything these old railbenders did. Just a dumb kid come down
out of the mountains to put on his first pair of shoes and go
to work for the railroad.

The chief gave the studious boomer a cautious glance.
Eddie was apparently absorbed in his book, oblivious of the
ribbing. But the raucous tones were meant to be overheard,
and he couldn't have missed the remarks. His lack of resentment was disappointing.

A breathless switchman thrust his head in at the doorway and his roving eye speared the yardmaster.

"Hey," he sputtered, "what do we do with that car of hogs
Seventy-six brought in?"

The yardmaster ruminated. "Hogs?" he said.

A quiet, penetrating voice interrupted his cogitations. It
slithered through the room above the chatter of the sound-
ers. "I'd say to switch 'em down to the yard office and have
somebody take the hogs' brains out," the voice remarked.
"That way they make good enginemen and fair conductors.
Better than most."

It sounded ventriloquial, coming from the boomer's impassive lips. He didn't raise his head from the book. Everybody stared about for the origin of the observation. Then
vindictive eyes began to center on Eddie. He read on placidly.

The silence thickened. A locomotive hooted derisively
down in the yard.

Updike spun in his swivel chair. "Did you want to see
me?" he asked Eddie abruptly.

Eddie marked his book with a burnt match. Updike liked the way he got his feet under him. The tinge of red in his hair seemed charged with hostile voltage. The set of his head was slightly arrogant. You got that way when you'd mastered your craft.

"Need a good telegraph operator?" Eddie inquired briefly.

Durban, the trick dispatcher, snickered. Updike quelled him with a sharp look. Durban wasn't quite certain how he might come out of the impending shake-up. Meanwhile, he was trying to throw in with the crews.

Eddie lifted an eyebrow. "Does it sound funny to you when a good operator asks to go to work for this outfit?" he asked.

The trick man turned pink.

"I've got a job for you," said the chief, "if you're used to obeying rules and orders."

"That's what they're made for," Eddie said.

Updike flicked him another glance and slid a ten-dollar bill across the counter. "Till payday," he remarked.

Eddie's eyes became bleak. "I'll get by," he said.

Conover moaned. "If he takes that ten spot, chief," he protested, "he'll spend it on a bender, and you'll never see him again."

Eddie smiled at the hogger. "Mebbe not," he decided, and picked up the money.

That didn't create any fraternal feeling for Eddie on the west end. The division was immediately assured that he was a brass hats' man, and the crews were as subtle as a sledge in showing him that they thought so. They tried ways to break him down, but they found at once that he knew the book and was intolerant of operating frauds within his jurisdiction.

Conover encountered this first at Sulphur, where Updike sent Eddie as relief night operator.

Conover was coming west that night on Extra 3814, and Eddie had an order for him, giving him more time on Nine. Just before reaching Sulphur, the engineer absorbed four thick sandwiches within a mile and an eighth, and was relaxing as he approached the station.

When the headlight showed, Eddie got out on the platform with his lantern and copies of the order clipped to hoops, ready to hand them up to the engine and the caboose as they went by. His order board was red, and as the extra approached he swung his lantern in a highball, notice to the engineer that he had an order that would clear the board.

But Conover didn't reply to this sign, and he didn't check his speed. Eddie considered he was being hardmouthed, just to show him he didn't have to go through the routine of signals the book prescribed. But the engineer should have eased up a little. It was slightly dangerous to stand close to a speeding engine and deliver an order on the fly.

When the locomotive blasted down on him, Eddie stepped in and held up the order hoop with his lantern alongside to mark it. There was a sucking breath of hot oil and steam, and cinder dust whipped into his face. The engine slammed past. But no one snatched the hoop.

Eddie glimpsed Conover leaning on the arm rest at the window, his head bobbing on his chest, oblivious of the proffered hoop. The head end had missed the order.

Boomers get about, and he knew the answer to that one. He began to swing his lantern in a washout as the tail light on the caboose swam toward him.

The brakeman was on the rear step ready to snatch the order, but Eddie didn't offer it.

The trainman yelled profanity as he whipped by. Then he darted up the steps and pulled the air on his engineer. The brakes went on with a wham, and the line of wheels sparked as the shoes grabbed.

The train stopped a half mile out of town, then backed into the station to pick up the order.

Conover and Allen conferred outside, then stormed into the office.

"Listen, smart boomer!" Conover yelled. "Don't you know enough to deliver the order to the caboose when we miss it on the head end?"

"It don't say so in my book," Eddie said softly. "Mebbe, when there's an attempt to grab it from the engine, and it's not an order full of dynamite. But when nobody even tries to get it from the cab, then something's haywire, and I pass."

"My dumb fireman didn't wake up that we was coming to the station," Conover raved, "and he wasn't out on the step to snare it. You want to get the kid in trouble?"

"If you'd whistle for the board," Eddie suggested, "and answer lantern signals, your fireman'd know where he was at."

Conover stamped back to his engine and hooted out of town.

Eddie OSed Extra 3814 to the dispatcher, in and out, and Durban shot back at him: "How come he had to stop there?"

"The head end missed the order, and he had to come back and get it," Eddie told him.

"I'll bet you were asleep and didn't get out in time to catch the head end," Durban made the sounder snap.

"You turn it any way you think you ought to," Eddie gave him cheerful permission.

Durban did report it as a possibility. And Conover raised his voice at headquarters and said more than he intended.

Neff, the new trainmaster, got a confused notion of the incident, and had them all into his office for questioning. Nobody was much concerned about Fussy Neff. Conover could talk louder and more glibly than the trainmaster. Billy Lomax, the fireman, in confusion and juvenile loyalty, got the blame and ten brownies. Eddie answered only what he was asked and got twenty brownies and ominous words of warning from Neff.

Updike, who had sat in as an observer, caught Eddie in the hall after it was over.

"I guess Neff forgot to ask you did Conover pass you any

signals as he approached your station?" The chief made it an interrogation.

Eddie considered. "He didn't ask about that, did he?" he remarked.

Updike eyed him sharply. "Durban turned you in as being asleep on duty," the chief warned.

"Yeh," said Eddie, "he told me he was going to."

Updike was slightly exasperated. He had a suspicion of what had actually occurred and he wanted the truth brought out. But he decided he'd better not crowd the boomer. "You are through at Sulphur tomorrow," he said, "and then I'm sending you to Pyramid."

"Okay," said Eddie.

He might have taken that as a rebuke and a punishment. Pyramid consisted of a station, a semaphore and a passing track, overhung on the east by lonely Pyramid Peak, and threatened by drifting sand dunes from the west. The remainder was flat and vacant desert. Not a thing else, save when a train roared by. None of them stopped, except to take siding to let an opposing schedule by. A one-man day job, with a call bell which the dispatcher could ring with selectors if he wanted the operator when off duty at night. You'd get to talking to yourself in time.

But Eddie could get along with himself. He read a good deal in the office at night, the telegraph instruments on the long table beside him babbling of the traffic on the high iron; and even as he read, the telegrapher's part of his mind absorbed from the chatter what was moving on the division.

That night, he knew that Conover was coming west on a banana special, thirty refrigerator cars, a light hot shot that would be rambling fast.

On the other side, Ninety-two was slogging up the grade, a double-header with a hundred loads. The helper engine would be cut off at Highpoint. It was mostly downhill from there, and one engine could handle her, with luck.

Then Conover ran some hot journal boxes, because he was wheeling them too fast, and he was badly delayed. Durban was raving at him and at all the other crews out on the division when Eddie blew out the lamp and went to bed.

At 10:50 he was torn from sleep by the dispatcher ringing his call bell. That mad sound clamored through the dead quiet of the desert like an alarm. Eddie fell out of bed and stumbled blindly through the kitchen and into the office. He shut off the bell and lit the lamp and answered the wire. Durban was in a tearing hurry.

"Is the banana special in sight?" He made the sounder storm.

Eddie made a sleepy "No."

"Take an order for him," Durban snapped, and began to send it.

Eddie stopped him by opening the key. This was coming too fast when you'd just been jarred out of sound sleep. You don't take chances when the trains are rambling. The close ones have made you cautious.

"Wait a minute until I listen for him," he sent back.

Durban made the sounder yell. "I've got Ninety-two at Highpoint all set to go. You're holding him up."

But Eddie went out into the crisp starlight. There wasn't even a breeze, and the silence was so clear it tingled. The thin air bit through his pajamas like acid. A faint glow spilled over a shoulder of Pyramid Peak. The sibilant far whisper of an exhaust crawled along the mountainside. You got a feeling of unleashed, thundering power from that creeping purr. He went back to his key.

"Yeh," he sent, "he's coming."

Durban rushed into the order, but Eddie checked him again.

"Wait until I get a light in my order board," he said.

Durban boiled over. "You're holding up Ninety-two," he chattered. "You railroad like an old hen. You can put up your light after you repeat the order. He's not that near."

"It don't read like that in my book," Eddie answered him.

"Smart boomer!" Durban raved. "You'll tell the chief about this delay."

But when Conover was riding the line, you had to get all set for him. Eddie put up the semaphore and lit the light. He fired his lantern and got out a fusee and two track torpedoes and laid them on the table. Then he told Durban to go ahead with the order.

The dispatcher tore it off like ripping a rag. It changed the meeting point between Ninety-two and the hotshot from Highpoint to Pyramid, and when the two operators had repeated it, Durban told Highpoint to tell Ninety-two that he'd have the special in the clear for him at Pyramid so he wouldn't have to slow for the short grade beyond the station. Then he instructed Eddie to head the hotshot into the passing track.

Eddie considered the whole setup as slightly slippery. Durban had somehow overlooked his hand in not changing the meeting point of the two trains farther down the line, when it wouldn't have delayed either of them. That had in turn caused him to go out on a limb now, telling Ninety-two that the main line through Pyramid would be clear for him. The engineer would take Durban's word for it, but a dispatcher can't always make things come to pass a hundred miles from headquarters.

Presently the concussions of Conover's blaring stack climbed high on the Pyramid. Eddie took up his lantern and fusee, dropped the two track guns into his pajama pocket and went out onto the platform.

The headlight of the banana special moved along the mountain wall beyond the last ridge. The roll of her exhaust beat against the stars. Conover had her latched out. Then the headlight moved into sight.

The hogger didn't shut off when he tipped the rise and

swung down the grade to the station. And he didn't give any
sign that he saw the red light in the semaphore against him
as he approached. He wouldn't be expecting Pyramid to be
open at this time of night, but he should be alert to everything ahead. Eddie began to swing his lantern. Conover
didn't check or answer.

Eddie got a chill in the back of his neck that didn't come
from the atmosphere. He tore off the cap of the fusee and
scratched it alight. He stuck the wire point into a tie as the
red light inflated into a misty balloon. But the engineer
didn't acknowledge it, and the exhaust didn't ease.

Then Eddie caught the low moan of the whistle to the
west, and Ninety-two's headlight flourished in a bright halo
over the dunes. He could tell by the way it swept the arc of a
curve that the engineer was pouring it on so as to make the
short grade the hotshot was now descending. The chill in the
back of his neck slid down the length of his back. This was
going to be tight.

He squinted in the stab of light from the hotshot. Conover
might have loosely thought, at sight of the board against him
and the lantern on the platform, that Eddie had an order for
him that would clear the signal. But he couldn't miss the
peremptory fusee if he had half an eye ahead. It bloomed
like a bonfire.

Ninety-two's whistle shrieked in again above the roar of
the hotshot. The yell of it ruffled the air under his ears and
made them stand out. He fumbled the track torpedoes from
his pocket as he stretched out in a long-legged gallop to meet
the plunging special. He lost a bedroom slipper at the second
jump. But that call from the freight train behind him was
like a typhoon that caught his extended ears and shoved him
forward as if they'd been sails. He didn't pause to recover his
foot gear. The other slipper slid about on his foot and ham-
pered him. He kicked it off as he ran. He dug his bare feet

into the cinders and held his breath and stepped up his speed.

You can't judge accurately the speed and distance of an approaching train when you are sprinting to meet it with the headlight in your eyes. He cut it fine. He was near to a collision with her when he stopped in a skid. He stooped and clamped one of the track torpedoes to the rail. He'd barely ducked clear of the main line when the locomotive whiffed past him. The torpedo went off with an explosion that tore across the flats and dunes like a banshee.

Time got lost somewhere in the high desert while the refrigerator cars clattered by, and Eddie, strangling on thin dust, stood and waited for the blast of the torpedo to jar Conover out of his heedlessness. Then compressed air sizzled. The brake shoes grabbed, and the line of rolling wheels was ringed with fire. The cars rocked and bucked like wild steers.

He crammed air into his lungs and watched the tail light soar at him. He ran with the convulsing cars and snatched at the rear-end grab iron when it arrived in the dark. The iron scorched his hands as they slid up the curve of the grab, and his bare feet stung as they slapped on the bottom step of the caboose. The brakeman had slammed out the rear door. He goggled at the spectacle in pajamas that was cast up from the smoking dust.

"Get your train in the clear!" Eddie yelled. "Ninety-two's coming close and expects to find you on the siding!"

The station platform swam under him and he dropped off. The special grumbled on, slowing to the stubborn clamp of shoes. The brakeman swung down at the passing-track switch, and the green light on the stand flared red as he pushed the handle over. His lantern cut streaks in the dark as he signaled his engineer to back up. He'd seen the glow of Ninety-two's headlights over the near dunes.

The hot shot grunted to a stop. The desert silence throbbed at the temples. Then the air pump hammered as it fought for pressure to release the clamped shoes. Air sneezed at last and the reluctant brakes slackened. Drawheads mumbled as the engine stamped hard in reverse. The tail lights on the caboose bobbed and crawled back toward the siding.

Ninety-two's headlight blinked into sight like a damp moon. Above the slow blasts of the hot shot's stack you could hear the churn of the long freight's exhaust. The engineer was wheeling those hundred cars to make the short grade out of the station.

With the hotshot's headlight stabbing him in the face, Ninety-two's engineer should by the rules have brought his train under control immediately. But they'd thrown the book away on the West End. Time got lost in the solitude again while Eddie waited for a sign that he'd checked. He knew why the hogger didn't, what he was considering. The dispatcher had told him the special would be in the clear. If events disproved what Durban had prophesied, that would be up to him to explain. The hot shot had for some reason come up the main line to back into the passing track instead of heading in. She was still showing her headlight so she hadn't cleared. But, on the word of Durban, she certainly would before he got to her. If he checked all those hundred trailing cars too much, he'd have to double the hump. The sound of her exhaust eased, but he didn't touch the brake-valve handle.

Conover worked his engine with a sure, hard hand. He didn't fumble. He didn't slip a driver as he picked up his short train and shoved it back through the open switch. He knew the exact ounce of power she'd take. The engine didn't falter as Ninety-two snaked at them. The bark of the stack multiplied and deepened to a savage roar.

You couldn't stop the rolling string of a hundred loads on that grade by wishing. But Eddie tried, standing on the platform shivering in pajamas and bare feet. He didn't realize exactly when Conover had begun to screech his whistle. The racket of it was just an added note to the rest of the clamor. But immediately thin spurts of fire flickered for the length of Ninety-two as the engineer at last gently touched the brake-valve handle. He had come in close before he realized it, with the hot shot's light blinding him, and now he had to fight to keep off the special's head end.

Time didn't register, but the Ninety-two had suddenly eaten up the gap between the two trains. The hundred freight cars crowded and jostled the engine, nudging her jovially, whining at the tightening restraint of brake shoes. The engineer couldn't give the lunging line a full emergency application without risk of throwing his train all over the desert. He had to juggle it, to check and check again with fingertip precision, hold them back and keep them on the rails.

The hot shot choked and stumbled once as Conover's exacting hand urged her too hard. Then the engine took up her smooth thunder again as she scrambled to avoid the lumbering avalanche at her pilot. She fought valiantly to be clear of the high iron. The beams of the two headlights dilated around the locomotives. Ninety-two inched up.

The brakeman was stooped over the switch stand, the handle in both hands, ready to flip the points over and separate the nuzzling pilots if the hot shot cleared. If she didn't, he'd be included among the resultant splinters.

The mountain men were rough and tough and headstrong, but they could handle their trains in an emergency, and they took the hazards as an item of the job. When they had to, they split the seconds to cram all the incidents into the fraction of time allowed to clear.

Eddie caught a shadowy movement at the switch stand. Ninety-two's headlight detached itself and stared at him as the engines broke apart. The engineer cracked his throttle at once. The big jack took up her deep belly laugh as the blast of the hot shot died. Drawbars grunted and strained as the hogger shook out the slack. The whistle yelled once in high derision. Ninety-two roared past the station, storming for the grade. The hot shot subsided on the passing track.

Eddie uncurled his cold toes and grinned. "A very good performance," he decided, "but they'll throw the book at you for it."

Updike realized, with Stewart's abrupt summons next morning, that the superintendent was prepared to dynamite the participants in the affair at Pyramid. The Old Man was going to hold a hearing himself, and he was at last all set for a cleanup.

The chief had to do most of the listening at that ominous interview, but he managed a crafty suggestion. "That boomer operator," he offered. "He thinks fast on his feet, and he plays them close."

Stewart growled, "If he hadn't we'd still be picking up the pieces. He's in the clear." Then he caught the allusive spark in the chief's eye, and he demanded suspiciously, "So what?"

"Smart boomers get around," the chief considered, "and they're hard to fool. He's in the clear all right, but he could enlighten us a good deal on what actually happened, if you'd ask him. He won't lie, but he won't give you any more than you ask for."

Stewart said, "Yes?"

The hearing was as frigid and as noncommittal as the crews could make it. They realized that this was at last a showdown, and they held to a blind faith that they could cover up. Stewart had to chisel fragments of evidence from them with cold and biting steel.

There was a chance that the worst hadn't been proved when Eddie was called. The men studied him sullenly. He could line up with their tactics and likely save several jobs. But they'd always said he was a brass hats' man. They hoped now that they'd been wrong about that.

But Eddie began to show at once how right they'd been.

For the first time that day Stewart got brisk and prompt replies to his volleyed questions. The operator neither hedged nor expanded. He stated. And his statements were damning to all concerned.

A thickening cloud of hopeless and resentful silence gathered among the men as the examination buzzed on endlessly.

The boomer was laying it all out there before the Old Man exactly as it had happened without mitigation. He fitted the items together into a convincing picture that condemned them all. They'd known he'd do it, but they'd hoped to the last that he wouldn't.

Stewart dismissed him at last with an abrupt "That's all."

The stunned quiet was stirred by the shifting of feet and the low mutter of sullen voices.

"Not quite."

The tranquil voice slithered through the grim murmurs. It sounded ventriloquial coming from the boomer's impassive lips. Eddie hadn't moved from his chair.

Stewart's clipped mustache bristled. "What's that?" he snapped.

"You haven't got it all yet," Eddie said. "Not like I saw it."

It didn't seem possible that silence could become more dense than it had been. It shut in like a vacuum. Stewart's metallic tone when he broke it made men flinch.

"There's something else?" he inquired ominously.

"Yeh," said Eddie. "There's a little more. I've been around, and I've seen men handle trains. Right now I'd say you'll seldom find a bunch on any man's railroad with the nerve to stick it through with sudden death and violent destruction only about six inches away. And I mean sudden death. Any one of them could have stepped back or unloaded, and there'd have been a smash. They didn't do that. They all stuck and played up to each other and pulled it out without a scratch. Mebbe you haven't been around much. Mebbe you don't think that's extraordinary. But wait till the next time with crews that don't know the mountains. If I hadn't known they'd stand by and pull it out of the fire, I'd be running yet, because I was close enough to be included in the pieces if Ninety-two had kissed the hot shot. That's all."

Eddie got down.

Stewart hesitated, and encountered Updike's bland eye. He knew now what the wily chief had been trying to show him. He had sensed hard faiths and alliances among these men that he hadn't encountered in operations on the prairies. Now he could credit their obstinate convictions and their loyalties for associates with whom they faced the daily hazards of mountain traffic. He was beginning to appreciate their mettle. He studied them briefly across his desk.

"I think," he said, "that we have now gone through the initial period of our association. From now on we are going to understand one another. Everything that has happened up to this moment is cleared from the record. It's all behind and forgotten. We start from scratch. Which is going to make it harder on anyone who so much as nicks the rules from here out. You will find I mean that literally. That's all."

The congestion at the doorway developed into a mild stampede to be out of the room.

Conover stopped Eddie in the hall by getting in his way.

"Look, boomer," he gulped. "If you think it took nerve to stick to the cab in the face of Ninety-two, I'll say it took a lot more to stand up to the Old Man the way you did just now."

Eddie grinned. "Take it easy, hogger," he advised.

Updike fell in beside him and steered him toward the dispatcher's office.

"Had enough of Pyramid?" the chief asked.

"Nearly," said Eddie.

"I've got a job for you in my office next," Updike suggested.

"I guess not," Eddie decided. "I just paused here to hand out some retribution to your crews for refusing to give me free transportation. I might come this way again, and I'd not want to sneak my rides. Pretty quick now I'll be shoving off."

"I was afraid of that," Updike sighed. "Boomers always move on or they wouldn't be boomers. But any time you have some more of that rankling spirit, bring it back to the High Desert Division."

"Okay," said Eddie.

PRIORITY SPECIAL

By Harry Bedwell

PRIORITY SPECIAL

By Harry Bedwell

HARVEY WHITE had been called to take out a hospital train. He brought his engine from the roundhouse in the early dark, and the brakeman tied her onto the line of cars, with their Red Cross markings, all made up under the flood lights in the coach yard.

Inside the forward ward car, young faces peered expectantly from the rows of bunks. Some of those faces had been scorched by tropic sun, while the color had been washed from others through long hospital days. Most of them were radiant at the thought of going home for the remainder of their convalescence, or at least to hospitals close enough for the folks to visit them. It wouldn't be long now till nearly all would be free of hospital restraints. *Bro*-ther!

But their exuberance was tempered and restrained by the presence of the three boys in the forward righthand bunks. These three lay without movement, literally like logs. In their eyes was the watchful, haunted look of men dogged by pain. They were very tired.

The other patients couldn't guess why those three had been included with the casuals. It didn't seem as if they should have been moved at all. The Major had them on his mind something special, and he'd seen them all through some pretty rugged going. But travel was sure rough on those fellows. Covertly the other patients watched them as they caught the glint of the conductor's lantern through the windows, flashing up in a quick highball.

" 'Board!"

The engine's whistle sounded faintly up forward. The tension in the eyes of the three in the righthand forward bunks tightened as drawbars grumbled. Helpless, they waited desperately for the shock of sudden movement. The mumble of the wheels took up a slow rhythm as the train glided into motion. There had been no impact, and gradually the look of dread faded. The eyes took on light. One of them sighed hopefully.

"Not so bad," he murmured.

Sergeant Ernie Wall, in a forward bunk across from the motionless figures, listened to the jostle of draft gear with intense satisfaction. He absorbed through all his senses the slow mutter of wheels at rail-joints and the far, deliberate throb of the locomotive. The yard lights through the window—switch lights and block signals, green and red and yellow, and the diamond point of a switchman's lantern making diagrams in the dark as he signaled his yard engine—all wove a pattern that dreams are made of.

To Ernie, all this had been a part of life ever since—well, it began at the beginning of memory. And now the good God had been kind and let him return to where the roadbed was set firmly in ballast and didn't crawl about in jungle mud. It would be swell to work the trains that really ran by the time card.

He glanced at the three still bundles in the bunks across the aisle. He frowned. It hadn't appeared to him that those boys should have to stand the grind of a long trip. They were drawn out as thin as wire, and it didn't look as if they could take much more. But they hadn't let out a murmur.

Then before the train had moved ten car-lengths, somebody came scampering out of the gloom, flagging it to stop. Someone attached to the staff of the hospital train was late.

Harvey White, up in the cab, heard the conductor's signal, whistling him down. A switch was just ahead of the engine's pilot. If he moved out to the fouling point, he would block other trains. Harvey put an extra pound of pressure on the brakes for a quick stop. A shudder ran down the coaches as they came to a stand in the grip of brakeshoes.

Ernie felt a stab of pity as he watched the three across the aisle take the sudden jar. Their jaws clamped on the stabbing pain, and their faces were honed out into gaunt lines. It took long seconds to drag themselves from the paroxysm. Then came the sibilant intake of breath between set teeth.

Russ Dillon, the one in the end bunk by the door, spoke faintly.

"Mister, I used to enjoy me a railroad ride on a freight train, when we shipped the steers to Kansas City, and I went along to nurse 'em."

He grinned to show he was desperately joking.

"But I guess they handle cows better."

Wes Tolover, in the next bunk, slowly unlocked his jaws.

"Bro-*ther!*" he murmured. "I felt that one make three quick round trips from my northwest tonsil to my southeast big toe, and it made all the stops along the way."

Little Johnny Lane, in the third bunk, tried to ease some of the strain from his racked body.

"And that'd be some travelin'," he remarked, "what with all that length you've got to your running gear. Now me, it was all over and done, just like that."

"Sure," Wes Tolover chided. "You ain't big enough for a collision to register in. But you was the guy last night complainin' about a tom cat stomping about the ward."

The train began to move. The slight vibration of the ward car crossing switch points caused the faces to contract again. The boys were spent. Yet when the rear door opened and closed, they tried to clear their expressions of the ravages of suffering and to make them serene.

"Here comes the Major," little Johnny hissed.

"Now, set yourse'ves."

Major Laughlin, commanding officer of the hospital train, came in quietly. He looked down on the faces they had tried to ready and shine for his inspection.

He asked quietly, "How does it ride?"

"Ho-kay, up to now," they chorused with emphatic cheerfulness.

But the Major wasn't deceived by the blithe voices or the fraudulent enthusiasm. The smiles were too thin, and he traced the tension in the depths of the eyes that met his so firmly. They couldn't conceal their memories of suffering endured and their dread of recurring shocks. They were worn to a brittle edge.

Back there in the general hospital, he had watched them drift out of the shadows and make their bid for sound life again—three young fellows who had come down out of the high desert together at the first call, trained and gone into action together, to be finally caught in a foxhole by a mortar shell. They came of a lean and stubborn breed, as the monkeymen had found, and they began their recovery well.

Then reviving life seemed to hesitate. The spark began to flicker and fade. Their spirits wilted. They drooped.

Searching for cause, the Major examined their background, their past that was so brief and recent, and he came to realize that these boys from the tall, open country put down deeper roots than urban men. He had once been stationed in the brisk uplands that had bred them, and now he noted the hungry look that smoldered up when he talked to them of their homeland. Remembering the sparkle of those empty spaces, and the air that kindled the spirits, he had made certain that lying motionless in the hospital, hour after dreary hour, with all horizons shut in by the fogs of the coast, had put a blight on the stricken boys who were used to limitless sunlight. They faced nothing but blind, gray windows, when their eyes were accustomed to infinite bright distances. You couldn't lure the spark to glow in that damp gloom.

Yet they couldn't, in their broken, helpless condition, endure the journey. They didn't have enough endurance remaining to withstand the torment that must accompany any sudden movement.

Nevertheless, as the dull days drifted by, and the life in them pulsed slowly, the Major had to balance the effects of suffering and fatigue the journey would cause against the certainty that in their sunny highlands they would quickly mend. He mentioned casually the possibility of their going home, and found that he was committed to get them there at once, when he saw the fierce, wild delight that flared in their faces.

But now, with the journey but half over, the Major had the discouraged feeling that their chances of ever reaching the high desert were remote. They were too close to the uttermost limit. And it was at that instant that some one drove his automobile out of the darkness and crossed directly in front of the hospital train. Harvey White had to check quickly to avoid hitting the car. His sharp blast on the whistle seemed to lift the machine clear of the crossing. But the rhythm of the wheels had been broken. The Major heard the muffled grind of brakeshoes taking hold, and the ward car shivered.

The three tried to fight off any expression or hint of the torture they endured. They put all their grit into taking it without flinching. But they couldn't keep back the quick grimace, and their faces grew stark. It took an unreasonable length of time to erase the effects of the shock, after Harvey released the brakes and the train picked up its smooth pace.

The Major's expression then was pretty grim. He couldn't chance taking them farther. He turned to the orderly and said with a rare touch of brusqueness,

"Tell the conductor we will have to stop at the next station and remove three stretcher patients."

The eyes of the three boys turned on him in a kind of blinding look that hit him like a club. He felt that with all his science and skill, he had let them down. The searching looks seemed to charge him with treachery.

Then their old habit of moving in as a team asserted itself, and they set themselves doggedly to overcome the Major's decision to turn them back. Down and helpless, they began a shrewd maneuver to gain them a chance to return to the places and the people that had begat them, where the spirit could thrive. The eyes that had learned to read the signs of weather and the sly movements of the wild life of the uplands became quiet and alert.

Russ Dillon's drawl slid into the clean snip of running wheels.

"It's all right, sir." He grinned a little starkly. "That wasn't near as bad as havin' the wind kicked out of you by a hoss. And that's been done to me often."

He watched the Major like something trapped.

Wes Tolover took over then, but he had to strain a little to make his remarks whimsical.

"Wasn't even as bad as havin' a ol' cow step on your foot," he declared. "Ever have that happen to you, sir? It hurts all the way up into your eyeballs, and it makes you so blind mad you want to cut the ol' cow's head off."

Little Johnny Lane sniffed his disdain.

"That little old pink-eyed bronc of mine has tossed me so high and wide, it shook the ground so when I lit, the neighbors over there on the other side of the ridge thought another meteor had hit Arizona. Mister, I was raised by gettin' myself all busted up. So a little old wiggle in a train-car don't bother me."

That crafty assault was harder for the Major to withstand than machine guns. It took all his training in clear diagnosis to subdue his impulse to give in to them. He had to remind himself firmly that they couldn't longer bear this punishment of sudden disturbances. They were his professional responsibility, and his calm judgment must decide. He shook his head reluctantly.

It was almost intolerable to watch hope ebb from the three faces. They had caught a glimpse of their keen uplands, and then it had been blotted out. The hurt was more marked than physical pain.

The Major turned with impatience on the waiting orderly.

Ernie Wall, on an elbow at the edge of his bunk across the aisle, knew now why these three were making the trip. Burned into his mind were the days when fever surged through him in furnace blasts, and in his delirium he had tried to struggle through endless, smoking distance to reach the Sacramento River, high in the Sierras, on the other side of the world. One plunge into that cool, laughing stream would extinguish the conflagration that was searing him to a cinder. You wanted to go home when you were sick.

Ernie moved blandly into the crisis.

"That don't have to happen again, sir," he said genially.

He met with cordial assurance the impact of four startled glances turned on him suddenly.

Ernie's voice was cultivated at a trade in which instructions must be clear and concise, and usually given above the racket of rolling wheels. His remarks had a high muzzle velocity. The Major's glance was abrupt, and he was prepared to be terse in return.

The three considered Ernie with a cautious scrutiny that checked him over in detail. They were stout fellows, hard to discourage. This might amount to something. They gathered instantly, and pounced.

"Is that a fact?" Russ inquired. "Then we've got mighty little to worry about." He made it genial and hospitable, but he was watchful.

The Major had to check the rising tide of hope before it went over the dam. He interjected a shade gruffly.

"What do you mean by that, Sergeant?"

"Something got on the track, close enough ahead to make the hogger pinch her down," Ernie explained. "It won't happen again, after we get out of this blamed city traffic."

A stray missile from that fusillade struck the Major a glancing blow. He inquired severely, "Hogger? How does a hogger pinch down?"

That was a tactical error. It left a hole that little Johnny Lane went through like a shot.

"Yeah, what do you mean—hogger?" he piped. "Us, we come from cattle country."

Ernie brooded over Johnny with compassion. That boy's education sure had blank spots in it.

"The hogger is the eagle-eye," he signified patiently. "The engineer. The man up front there who pulls the train."

"Ah-h-h!"

The sigh came from the three with gusty relief, as if the rejoinder had solved a nagging puzzle. None of them knew where this was leading, but they felt in their reviving, hopeful hearts that Ernie was their kind of folks, a friend and fellow confederate to help them out of a hole. They moved in on him with all their fine guile.

"This engineer seems kind of sudden in places." Russ nudged proceedings with a sly shot in the dark.

"If they wouldn't bother him," Ernie sizzled, "like flagging him down for a quick stop just when he gets under way, and bust out onto the main iron right in his face, you wouldn't get any rough stops. That's a good eagle-eye. If you could get the old delayer to keep his hands off him, that hogger could take us through without a jolt."

They had Ernie hooked. Wes prodded him gently.

"Delayer? That don't sound so good. Now, what's a old delayer?"

But Wes had his retreat all prepared in case the delayer turned out better than he seemed.

Ernie was slightly pained at such unenlightenment.

"He's the DS—the dispatcher. The man who handles the trains!"

"Bro-*ther!*" Wes retreated. "That fella has himself a job! Handles trains! I guess he's a mighty uppety man."

"He gets 'em over the road," Ernie explained. "Meets and passes 'em. Puts 'em through the siding, or down the main iron." He bent a severe glance on the upturned faces. "He does it all from an office building, and he don't see the trains he manages."

"No-o-o-o!" they murmured, and Wes gave him another nudge.

"Then why do they call him the old delayer?"

"Aw," Ernie deprecated, "it's just the crews he puts in the hole who call him that."

The Major started to interrupt, and then he didn't. He had seen the sharp lines ease out of the three faces, and the dogged look was gone from their eyes. They were watching Ernie like terriers at a rat hole. His abrupt jargon and confident air had taken hold. As a fact, the Major nearly joined in the unanimous query the three thrust at Ernie.

"Then who the dickens are you?" they demanded.

Now, Ernie is a forthright person. But that interrogation, slammed at him in three keys, had him stopped. How do you explain who you are, when it has taken years to come to your present state of being? Nevertheless, Ernie never backs off from a tough assignment. He tried to be reasonably reserved, but the high pride in his trade would creep up around the edges.

"As a kid," he said, "I was a call boy for the Southern Pacific."

He paused, and for a few sharp seconds he seemed to have slipped from the ward car. But those three knew where he had gone. Back home to boyhood. Pictures flickered behind Ernie's eyes as he looked beyond the rows of bunks, with their olive drab blankets and the dim faces against white posters. The smells of drugs and antiseptics blurred as he sniffed snow water and pine trees. Time slowed and turned back to the days—

He'd sure been a proud kid. Call boy for the Southern Pacific! He could feel the exultant leap of his bicycle under him as he vaulted into the saddle and sped down the street. That was at Dunsmuir, up there where the Sacramento River chuckles all day in the sun, as if slyly amused at the mighty efforts of the locomotives blasting at the mountain grades.

Calling crews to cover the schedules.

"Wantcha for a drag west at two forty-five P.M. Kick the covers and rise and shine."

Blinds drawn and edged with sunlight, and trainmen and enginemen, groggy with sleep, sitting bolt upright in bed, fumbling to sign his call book.

He'd learned to make himself handy about the place, useful in doing little chores for the other fellow. He'd helped the trainmaster's clerk keep the runboard straight so there'd always be crews on tap and called on time. They all knew Ernie would do it if they asked him.

"Ernie-e-e! Tell my husband when he gets in—"

"Ernie-e-e! Tell my groceryman—"

"Ernie-e-e! Tell your mother—"

And the crews got so they'd leave it up to him to get them their days off.

"Hi, Ernie-e-e! They say the quail up on the flats are so vicious they'll run out and bite you. Can you let me off for a round trip while I go up there and battle those birds?"

An engineer, bringing his big Mallet down the siding headed for the roundhouse, in from his run, leaning from his high cab.

"Hi, Ernie-e-e! Mark me off for a couple of trips. Fellow down from the crick where I got my cabin says the trout up there are now about my size. Tell your Ma I'll bring her some fat ones."

Sure, he'd learned quick to make himself useful—and welcome. Railroad wives loading him with cookies hot from the oven. He'd dreamed of those cookies out there in the jungle. Lots of things made easy for him and his mother that you didn't know exactly how they came about. And his mother was proud of him. Gee! They didn't pay you higher in any coin.

The pictures shifted at the end of school. Ernie took a dim look at the three faces staring at him from across the aisle.

"I got to be an ashcat pretty young," he considered, "because those eagle-eyes went out to see I made a good one. They didn't let me overlook anything about those calliopes."

He thought this was explicit enough—that he'd told them he'd become a locomotive fireman.

Ernie was lost again in misty time. The grim affairs of war —all those steaming months in a railroad outfit of the Army in the China-Burma-India area, where repairs to motive power and rolling stock were made with baling wire and a pair of pliers, where elephants that really weren't dreamed up wandered onto the track to block rail traffic, and the monkeys stole your rations—all that recent past dimmed into a far, stormy background. The gorgeous Orient slunk into smoky recesses of his mind, and the bright, brisk years along the Main Line came flooding back. The myriad sounds of a locomotive's cab drummed in his ears. He could hear the stubborn, subdued roar of the firebox, the throb of the injector and the contained mutter of pressure in the big boiler. The odors of the jungle were overpowered as smells of hot oil and leaking steam swept across his face. He felt the sway of the Mallet as she stormed the grades, moving the merchandise, and he could hear again the bark of her stack and the clear call of her whistle climbing the canyon walls in bounding echoes.

He came out of the anesthetic of dreams, and gave himself an admonitory shake of the head—a young veteran railroader reproaching the youth he'd recently been. Kids sometimes got too big for their britches. Wanted to go places.

"After a couple of years," he sighed, "the smoky end didn't look so good as a carhand's job. So we moved down here, and I got me a job on the parlor end of the train. I made a pretty good stinger," he admitted.

Ernie missed the blank looks he got in reply to that. He couldn't stop those pictures flickering—the wind whipping at him as he stood on top of his mile-long freight train, a hundred and more refrigerator cars of fresh fruits and vegetables headed east to the markets, iced bunkers dripping under the blazing desert sun, and the long horizons heaving to the rock of the cars.

He could hear the wash of rain against the windows of the cupola where he sat on guard, watching the line of cars squirm out ahead, and the protecting automatic block signals flinging out their arms, dark against the gray bowl of the sky far up there beyond the thin smoke of the locomotive's stack.

Ernie shook his head again in reprimand at his own fickle past.

"Then I thought I'd like to be a snake," he grinned. "A regular old railbender."

The faces across the aisle had gone plaintive under the strain of following him. The pressure of curiosity developed in Johnny Lane to the point where it was necessary to pop.

"Does that mean you are a railroader?" he blurted.

Ernie's face clouded. He had considered that the three of them had been with him in his flights along the high iron. He was nonplused that they hadn't followed him across the years.

The Major found that he had been somewhat enthralled by that succinct sketch of life on the railroad and its bewildering vernacular, and he interrupted before Ernie went adrift again.

"Ashcat and carhand and smoky end," he enumerated, and shook his head. "A stinger sounds waspish, but I don't suppose the snake you mentioned really crawls."

"I'll say he doesn't," Ernie stated.

Then Harvey White, up in the cab, interrupted with a long blast of the whistle, which reminded the Major of the crisis in which he was engaged. The tension had somehow lifted, and the dull strain had eased from the faces. Ernie's initial assertion came back to him.

"Sergeant," he said, "you remarked a while ago that these sudden stops, which result in jolts and jars, needn't happen again."

"*If* the DS would keep his hands off us from here on, sir," Ernie amended.

"Well," the Major inquired sharply, "how do you arrange for the DS to keep his hands off?"

Ernie relaxed in his bunk and let the pulse of running wheels flow through him. He knew every curve and tangent, almost the individual sound of every rail-joint sliding under him. In a matter of seconds he knew exactly where they were on the line.

"We're coming into Alhambra now," Ernie said, "and we're going to stop. Let's see how the eagle-eye does it when he's not forced."

They had lost momentum, but the Major couldn't tell by how much. There wasn't any ominous grinding of brakes. The train drifted quietly, and then all motion was gone.

"I told you that was a good hoghead." He nodded a veteran's approval. He snared the Major with a candid eye. "The station is there on the left. There's a door marked TRAIN-MEN in the L that sticks out of the middle of it. Go in, and on the other side of the desk you'll see a fellow with a headphone harnessed to him. That's the brass pounder—the op.

You tell him what you want the dispatcher to do for you."

"The brass pounder?" the Major asked.

"He's the telegraph operator that handles the train or-ders," Ernie explained patiently. "You just ask him to tell the DS to give us a good run, and to slip it to the hogger to take it extra easy on how he puts the air under his train."

The Major realized, after he found himself under the sta-tion flood lights before the little door marked TRAINMEN, that Ernie had practically hustled him from the ward car. He pushed into a dim anteroom, and there, to reassure him, on the other side of a high-back desk, in a brightly-lit alcove, was the man with the headphone clamped on his ear. He was deftly tearing yellow tissue sheets from the piles on the desk, arranging two sets of train orders.

Then the Major had misgivings. Ernie wasn't glib, yet he had without effort talked him, the commanding officer of the hospital train, into acting dead against his considered pro-fessional judgment. With no amount of urging on Ernie's part, and without even consulting the train rider (the pas-senger department's liaison representative) or the conductor, he was doing something he didn't understand himself. Ernie was certainly persuasive. And that railroad lingo of his had been fascinating. There were more involved terms in the Major's medical vocabulary, but none so pungent. Ernie had hypnotized him with his idioms. What he had best do now was hold the hospital train here and call for ambulances to take those boys to the nearest military hospital.

He half turned away, and then the train order operator glanced up with a quick, attentive eye. Si Youngblood was on duty that night at Alhambra; a lightning slinger who had taken military leave from the Southern Pacific to fight in major engagements through France and Belgium to the bit-ter end of World War I. Si's look invited confidence; and it reminded the Major that he would have to confront those three in the ward car with his final decision. He hesitated, and then Si's friendly eye lured him to try a blind venture.

"I am in charge of this hospital train," he said, "and I have three patients who are in heavy casts. They are already greatly fatigued with travel, and any jar or abrupt movement causes them a high degree of pain."

Si Youngblood's fingers paused in sorting the yellow tissues, and his eyes darted to the Major's face.

"You said—in heavy casts?" he inquired softly.

"Yes. They can scarcely make any movement at all." The Major hesitated. This is where he moved into the unknown. "One of the other patients has been what he describes as—ah—er—a carhand and an ashcat." He searched Si's face for signs of levity. "This—this sergeant suggested that I ask you to request the DS—the dispatcher, I think it is—to give us a good run, and to keep his hands off us. Does that sound reasonable?" the Major demanded, a trace desperately.

Si's eyes didn't falter. He folded the train orders into two neat squares. He had caught a glimpse of the three boys, enveloped in casts and helpless, and he had a moment of gratitude that he was back on the Main Line where he could perhaps be of service to them. It was a payoff he was eager to make.

"It is all quite reasonable, sir," Si assured him quietly. "That sergeant is a railroad man." He smiled and nodded. "He knows how it's done."

To the Major, events seemed to move in split seconds then.

Si slipped on the headphone and spoke into the transmitter.

"This is Alhambra," he identified himself on the dispatcher's wire. "The officer in charge of the hospital train says he has some patients aboard who are all bound up in heavy casts so they can't move, and any little rough handling is mighty hard on them. He'd like the engineer to take it easy on the starts and stops, and he'd like you to give the train a good run—so those fellows won't have to take it the hard way."

Ed Farwell sat on second trick dispatcher, Los Angeles to Colton. Ed is a cool, wise veteran, as exact as a calculating machine. He handles quickly all the flooding problems a dispatcher must dispose of, but you will never rush him into a hasty decision. Despite the swarming traffic and the myriad adjustments in train movements it required of him, he caught the same picture Si had seen, and from that moment on he kept the hospital train in the top drawer of his mind where critical operations are filed for instant use.

"Okay, Alhambra," Ed Farwell decided promptly. "Tell that officer we'll give him a good ride. And when the brakeman gets the orders, tell him to ask the engineer to come to the phone. It's Harvey White, and I'd better let him know about this. We'll make a Priority Special of her, and give her the railroad. Copy three for her. Colton, make a bunch . . . Hello, Bloomington . . . Ontario, copy five. Engine 4390 run extra leaving Alhambra Thursday, October 26, as follows with right over all trains. Leave Alhambra 7:20 P.M., San Gabriel 7:27 P.M., El Monte . . ."

"Right over all trains." The special train of the President of the United States makes its run on just such an order.

The brakeman took the orders, and then Harvey White loomed in the dim anteroom and pushed into the operator's bright alcove.

"Hello, Splinters," Harvey growled into the transmitter. "Now what have I done?"

To the Major, standing alone in the dim anteroom, the one-sided conversation sounded somewhat contentious. But he caught the sly twinkle in the engineer's eye, and the confidential smile that went with it.

The fact is, that Harvey and Ed had grown up together in Southern Pacific service, to become, as time elapsed, oldtimers—that seasoned clan of dependables. It began at Indio back there when Harvey was firing the locomotive and Ed was a youthful telegrapher, doing a job of handling the trains out of that desert terminal; a good head on his way up. They'd shared a room, and their ambitions. Pooled their resources of clothing and cash, embezzled each other's girls, stood together in any crisis and to the end of the run would enjoy being indignant with each other.

Ed edged his tone in reply, just so Harvey wouldn't know how tickled he was to hear that trustworthy voice, and to know old Harvey would be up there on the smoky end of the Special as she made her run.

"Look, Harvey," he said briskly, "there are some badly hurt boys on that hospital train of yours. They can't take much knocking about without a good deal of suffering. So see if you can't subdue your rowdy instincts. Don't make any swipes at that brake valve handle. I'll keep you going without stops if I can, and I'll let you hold the main line at all meeting points. I'll pass the word to the dispatchers on the other districts, and they'll co-operate. We'll not touch you. Now, run along and be good to those fellows."

The little smile slipped from Harvey's face and his eyes became sober.

"Okay, Splinters," he said. "We'll give them a good ride."

He glanced at the Major on his way out, and then he paused.

"Are you with the hospital train?" he asked.

"I am the commanding officer." The Major nodded.

"We'll take good care of your boys," Harvey promised.

He went out and crossed the platform under the flood lights to his engine.

Si Youngblood was back in his chair, harnessed to the dispatcher's wire, slapping out orders on the typewriter. The Major watched him an instant, a train order operator at his post. He was a minute, essential part of a great system, fitting exactly into the vast scheme to move men and matériel to the fronts when needed, a pin-point on the steel web of rails which bound the nation closely together. That iron highway was restless with rolling wheels all across the continent as locomotives stormed through the dark, carrying the load, taking the war to the enemy.

It was pretty big. Time was a harsh and arbitrary element to these men. It was inexorably on the move. They had to crowd the minutes and split the seconds to make them fit all the things that must be done to keep up that swift pace, when delay might mean disaster on some beachhead on the other side of the world. The Major had been in the ante-room but a few minutes, yet he had caught a glimpse of a surging, organized effort. These men were engaged in a task almost as big as war itself, and in stride, almost lightly it seemed, they had undertaken one more responsibility: a little extra care for the wounded.

Yet with so many urgent matters to contend with, they couldn't appreciate the desperate position of his patients. There wasn't that much time available to them. Some slight flaw might develop in those complicated operations. A mere sudden check to the speeding train might be the end for those boys. He weighed the chance that blighted hope might snap the slender thread of their resistance, against their remaining strength to withstand further punishment. Reluctantly, he decided that they didn't have the vitality left to take it.

Back in the ward car, the Major braced himself against the searching looks from those three upturned faces.

"These railroad people," he said, "are pretty busy moving all this war traffic. There are so many other trains on the line—"

He tried to make it cheerful and confident, as if it were only a slight delay. But he didn't deceive them. He was turning them back from home. The hunted, trapped look deadened their faces. They were held so rigidly in the casts they couldn't even make a rebellious gesture.

The three faces grew dim. They seemed to retreat into the shadows, and to drift out of all reach. The Major was searching desperately for any means to bring them back, when Sergeant Ernie Wall's emphatic voice smacked the strained quiet.

"Did the brass pounder get word to the dispatcher, sir?" he asked.

"Yes, he told the dispatcher," the Major answered vaguely. The three faces came out of the shadows and swiveled slowly toward the opposite bunk. The eyes probed. They were down to the last chip, and they were playing it straight out as they always had—three fellows from the high sunlight, in alien country, quietly placing their final bet.

"And did the dispatcher get word to the eagle-eye, sir?" Ernie persisted.

The Major's thoughts fumbled back to the dim anteroom. "Yes," he nodded absently, "he called the engineer to the telephone and talked with him."

"He did?" Ernie sounded as if a miracle had occurred. "Well, sir," he chuckled, "when the hogger and the DS team up, you'd just as well give 'em the railroad. Because they'll take it anyhow. You've got not a thing to worry about from here out."

It may be that men bred in the highlands are all kin. The boys from the high desert read the young veteran from the high Sierra as if he were a page of bold print. He was as tenacious and unabashed, and at times almost as vociferous, as the iron horse he had so zealously followed. Added to which was a trace of swagger. But he wasn't a gold-bricker. He wore a sergeant's stripes, hard-won insignia. He was the guy who was with you when the going was toughest. And Ernie had himself just come out of the shadows.

Ernie had moved in. He had the situation in hand. He leaned over the edge of his bunk and grinned. The three relaxed. They grinned back. The Major was aware then that there were elements of the spirit that medical science could not reach. They knew better than fine professional diagnosis what was good for them. The tight air that had seemed as if it would suffocate them all eased out of the ward car.

Ernie cocked a knowing eye at the Major. He was listening to far, familiar sounds. An expression of deep satisfaction came over his countenance. He gave a complacent nod. And his next remark jolted the Major.

"Had you observed, sir, that we are on the way again?"

The Major glanced quickly out of the window. The city lights were streaming by, thinning rapidly as the Priority Special swung out into the open country at a growing speed. Yet no one, except Ernie, had felt it when Harvey White quietly put his train into gliding motion.

Harvey was thinking of the three helpless boys in the ward car behind as he eased the Priority Special out of the Alhambra station, and he brought her up to speed carefully.

The far green block signals sprang up, heralds that the way was clear. The order board at Bassett bowed the Special by. Second 825 was in the siding at Puente, and two lone engines coupled together—power moving to a critical point—were in the clear for him at Marne. He got the Main Line light at Pomona, and the lights of the town crowded in for a moment, then dropped behind.

Up in the dispatcher's office, Ed Farwell was making some close calculations in his effort to keep open a hole in the flooding traffic through which the Priority Special could make her run unchecked.

The yardmaster at Colton came on the wire, talking fast.

"Look, Ed," he pleaded. "I've got more trains coming in here than I've got railroad to fit 'em. You'll have to take Second and Third 371 and Third 825 out of my yard so I can bring Fourth 825 down from Loma Linda, let Third 824 come in so I can shove her in the clear in time to let that Priority Special around her."

Second and Third 371 were troop trains. Fourth 825, close

behind them, a solid hot shot of war stuff. None of the three would stand much delay. Ed would have to use all his ingenuity to keep these trains out of a tangle. He brooded an instant. Put Second 371 in the siding at South Fontana; Third 371 in the hole at Ailsa and Third 825 in at Bloomington, to meet Third 824 and the Special. Double the hot shot coming down from Loma Linda through the pass at Colton, and keep the Special up the Main Line. They could do it if everybody railroaded smartly. He gave the picture to the yardmaster, and added, "I'd like you to take the Special right through your yard without stopping her, and let her out onto the CTC. She's a hospital train that I don't want touched. Okay by you?"

"Yeah, we can give it a darned good try," the YM agreed. "I hope nobody stubs his toe and ties us up. You say that's a hospital train?"

"It is," said Farwell. "And there are boys aboard who've taken too much already. Don't let anybody in your yard get in her way."

"OK, Ed," the YM said briskly. "I'll see to it myself."

It would take a number of close-fitting orders to arrange those schedules into the frame of fleeting seconds. Trainmen, enginemen, switchmen and the train order operators would have to work together like a high-geared machine.

The lights of Ontario twinkled beyond the wedge of the Priority Special's headlight and closed in. The red eye in the order board at the station winked twice. The train order operator crossed the platform and set himself beside the main line, holding an order hoop. Mac McNaughton, Harvey's fireman, came down from his seatbox.

Harvey had a wavering moment when he wanted to caution his ashcat that this was one time he must not fail to catch the orders. If McNaughton missed the hoop, they'd have to stop and back up and recover the orders.

Harvey took a slow breath—and didn't warn his ashcat.

The kid would handle it. Mac had come up the proper way, through the roundhouse. Wiper, engine watchman and then fireman. Next, and it wouldn't be long now, he'd be taking his examinations to move over to the righthand side of the cab. He didn't need to be cautioned.

Harvey watched the instant picture that snapped in sharp details under the headlight, and then flashed behind. The fireman gripped an iron rung with one hand and leaned out and down from the gangway. The operator, standing in the racing beam of the headlight, held the hoop high and steady, while the locomotive closed in on him. Young McNaughton adjusted himself in his crouching position as he gaged the hoop. Then mind and eye and the fine, easy flow of muscles fused into split-second co-ordination. His right arm hooked out in a swift gesture. His hands slipped through the loop of the hoop as the operator flitted by below him. He turned and handed the flimsies to Harvey. The big engine seemed to chuckle approval as she flung the town behind her.

The orders gave Harvey the pattern of meeting points. And there was an added message from Ed Farwell: "If you can make the west end of Colton yard by 8:45, will send you through Colton without stop. Third 824 is ahead of you, but should be out of your way by that time."

Harvey grinned. Old Splinters was sure trying to give him the railroad. He checked his watch. If nothing held him up, he'd whistle the Colton tower by 8:41.

Second 371 whistled her meet from the west end of the passing track at South Fontana. Third 371 was tucked in at Ailsa. Then a yellow block light showed up there beyond Bloomington. Third 825 had her hundred cars in the siding there, but she had slowed Third 824 going in to Colton. Harvey had an anxious moment when it seemed he might miss that 8:45 appointment at the tower. Then the block lights blurred and flickered up again in merry green splotches against the backdrop of the night. Old Splinters could sure figure them close!

Harvey slowed through the yard. Then the target lights of the CTC invited him to run again, and the Special picked up her road speed.

Sergeant Ernie Wall leaned on the edge of his bunk and looked down with cheerful complacence upon the three upturned faces.

"The Major sure must have laid it out for the dispatcher," he declared. "The old DS takes us right through the Colton yard like it was just a mile post, and turns us over to the CTC without a bump in the whole trip. It'll be easy now to Indio, riding the CTC."

The three eyed Ernie in return with a mixture of doubt, respect and suspicion. They acknowledged that so far his prophecies had been fulfilled. But it didn't seem quite likely that this could go on forever. Ernie had been enthralling them with tall tales of the iron horse, and he'd reached pretty high. These three from the high desert, who knew all there was to know about the other kind of horse, were just a little suspicious that Ernie had been ribbing them in a broad way. They had some brisk stories about sure-enough hosses they'd work off on him at the proper time. CTC sounded as if it might be a gag, but they were troubled by cautious curiosity, and little Johnny Lane couldn't restrain himself.

"Just what is this CTC, mister?" he piped.

Ernie's brow puckered as he concentrated on that cunning and intricate device—Centralized Traffic Control. For one thing, he said, it had whipped wartime congestion on the hill. He grew intent as he considered the big control machine with its levers and switches which shows in button lights the exact position of every train on the district at all times.

"The dispatcher," Ernie brooded, "maneuvers the trains

from his swivel chair with a series of levers right there within reach of his hand. Slows 'em and stops 'em, then sends them on again. He opens a siding switch forty miles away and puts a train through the pass and out at the other end, while at the same time he brings another train up the Main—without stopping either of them."

They put their minds to that one. Ernie was a great guy. And anyhow, it was a good story.

"Can the DS man tell from his machine," Russ Dillon asked slyly, "when the engineer's got a stomach ache?"

But Ernie's ear was tuned in to the sharp crack of the engine's exhaust as the grade increased. The exultant bark bounced high into the starlight from the walls of San Gorgonio Pass. The air had a clean lift. The lights of Beaumont swam in through the windows as the Special topped the hill.

Then Ernie became aware of a stir in the opposite bunks. The current of life had suddenly quickened. The eyes of the three burned with an expectant glow. They seemed transfixed as if they had come upon a miracle.

"Be doggoned!" Russ Dillon broke the quiet reverently.

"Yes, sir," Wes agreed. "And so will I!"

Little Johnny Lane's nose was feeling the air like a setter dog. He bubbled over.

"The desert!" Johnny whispered. "Mister, don't that smell good!"

Through the odors of drugs and medicines, germ-proof cleanliness and the scent of engine smoke, they had caught the first faint smell of their homeland.

It was nearing midnight when the Special drifted through the Indio yard and then picked up her running speed as the desert opened up under the long beam of the headlight. Sleeping towns showed a twinkle of light against the dark loom of the mountains, and their names lilted in Engineer Harvey White's thoughts: Coachella and Thermal. And

Mecca where the solemn date palm trees from the deserts of Africa stood stiffly in the starlight. The arch of the sky swung overhead as the long, empty flats flowed by.

Harvey loved the desert run. He averred that men who worked their predetermined hours, chained to a routine, never really lived. From the frame of his cab window he had a running, everchanging view that made each trip a new adventure. This lonely land had a perpetual fascination. There was sun and silence, and the moonlight covering the floor of the empty spaces, reaching to the shadowed horizon where the mountains lay. Storms that fell from the black night, and the hush of three o'clock in the morning. Before it came, you could feel the new day rolling up over the bulge of the world. Then the dawn flung up its streaming banners, and in the crisp quiet you could have your untroubled dreams in the rocking cab, with your engine running free and the clear block lights flashing up against the daybreak to beckon you on. It seemed then that you were at the edge of a world of enchantment that lay somewhere just beyond those low, dying stars. Your thoughts eased out of the cramps and strains of worry, and you remembered the faces of the good comrades who had come down the long iron trail with you—boisterous kids who'd seasoned into quiet-eyed, slow-spoken men, taking their responsibilities square. It took reliable men to follow the high iron. That was a satisfaction, to know that you were one of the dependables.

The Special drummed her steady pace across the straight-away that stretches along the gray sand dunes. Glamis flickered by. Ogilby winked once and was left behind. River smells softened the sharp air, and then a hollow rumble came up from below as the train swung across the Colorado River bridge. The Priority Special nosed into the Yuma yard.

McNaughton crossed the deck.

"Think we did all right by those fellows back there in the hospital cars?" Mac asked soberly.

"We did our best, son," Harvey assured him.

"Must be some railroaders among them," Mac figured, "and they'd sure think small of us if we didn't."

The Major was tired and dully depressed when he slipped quietly into the forward ward car as the Special rolled up to the river. It was the dead end of night, when life is at its slack and resolution is infirm. His training in the science of medicine warned him that he might have been too hopeful for his three patients. The strain and misery of the long trip might have worn them down too far. In a weak and crowded moment he had allowed that sanguine sergeant to confound his best judgment, and now he was afraid that somewhere along the way the glimmer of white light they lived by had flickered very low. There was only a hair-line to mark their way, and the Major glanced sharply at them in the dim light to catch a hint of where it had led them.

Maybe something had entered the ward car from out of the solemn spaces of the desert. Miracles do not happen, but a tincture of the tall country that had bred them seemed to have permeated the other odors, and for an instant the Major was conscious of elements from beyond our horizons, something from the other side of the low stars. For he recognized the look on the three upturned faces, and it stood him still and thoughtful. The boys weren't asleep—but they were dreaming.

The Major was a little dazed in his elation. And then, as he turned away, he was again confronted by that other figure in the opposite bunk. He caught the glint of a grin in the dusk, unabashed and slightly indulgent, like a cat with cream on its whiskers.

And that reminded the Major of all that inexplicable nomenclature of the rails. A hogger was the engineer who pulled the train. The ashcat was the fireman, and a brakeman was a carhand. Then he came onto one that he had hesitated to probe. It had a pernicious sound. Who was a *snake*? He put the question cautiously now, prepared to withdraw it if Ernie showed resentment.

That dim look came over his face. Ernie had gone back for a moment to a packed railroad yard. He was hanging to the side of a cut of cars and hearing again the little switchers chuff and clang and the sullen rumble of drawbars. He came out of it slowly.

"A snake," said Ernie, "is a switchman. They're properly proud of the name, but you've got to avoid a certain tone of voice when you address them as such. They're a lusty outfit. There are three in a crew—the pinner, the fielder and the engine foreman."

This apparently could go on forever. But the Major decided to forego the lexicon of railroad epithets as he became curious as to how the Priority Special had been able to make its unchecked run.

"With all the people involved," the Major said, "how did you know they could be marshaled and co-ordinated at a moment's notice, all across the miles we came, to do the numberless things that must have been done?"

How did he know? Ernie drifted again. That boy, too, could dream. They'd said he'd done a good job in the Army. He'd nearly shot the works out there in the sultry jungles. An honorable discharge awaited him after they'd tinkered with him some more in the hospital. Then he'd be back following the iron horse again.

That keen night air of the desert had a lift, and the tinge of engine smoke made it heady to a young veteran railbender. Ernie went off the deep end in something of the brazen speech of the high-rolling wheels and the vernacular of the iron highway, with the pride in his craft creeping up around the edges.

"Why," Ernie decided, "that's just how it had to be done."

He reflected on the people who had connived together so deftly to give the Priority Special a good run. They were the associates he'd worked with and jawed with in stove-pipe conferences in roundhouse and switch shanty, and at the lonely little train order stations along the way when they'd gone in the siding for a meet, and they'd argued the fate of nations, and how to run a railroad.

"I've worked the locals and the hot shots with this outfit," he nodded. "I've likewise followed the calliopes, and caught cages in the garden when they heaved the cuts at me like baseballs. Besides which, smoked the big jacks over the Hill, and called the crews. Yeah, when traffic was light and the going easy, and highballed the perishables when they stepped on each other's block as we moved the green stuff out of Imperial Valley. And I've never seen that gang fall down on a job yet. It's men and women with the know-how, hitting it off together. They get along. They fit."

He looked down upon the glowing faces across the aisle.

"Such a bunch would just naturally handle an occasion like this without a stumble," he pointed out with candid conviction.

The Major said, "Good night, sergeant," and slightly dazed went gratefully back to bed.